manifesto

Roy Jones
Reminiscences of a
worker correspondent

Published by Manifesto Press Cooperative 2025

© Roy Jones 2025

ISBN 978-1-907464-65-2

Typeset in Bodoni and Gill

PREFACE

Roy Jones is a journalist of an unusual kind, a real *worker cor* *ondent*. He became an reporter on the *Morning Star* after a hard apprenticeship as an itiner industrial worker, as a militant trade unionist working as a pipefitter on industrial sites throug out Britain where the weather was as challenging as the bosses (and bosses' placemen) who made a guaranteed weekly wage an uncertain prospect.

Proud of both his traditional manual skills and his newly acquired craft he was respected by trade union leaders as much as he was trusted by workers on picket lines not least because he brought to his reporting a sharp intelligence combined with a real insight into the daily problems workers face.

These *reminiscences* arrived at Manifesto Press as a series of witty, entertaining, insightful and politically perceptive political accounts of his unusual life and work. Some recalled in conversation and recorded by friends and family, some culled from his decades of clippings, some the product of discussion with his colleagues and comrades.

The finished text bears the marks of its transcription from oral and written accounts and we are indebted to Manifesto Press volunteer Alan Tucker who carried through the first and most rigorous edit. Alan is a former engineer, systems analyst and project manager, and technical author and the text is the result of his discipline and energy.

We owe a debt of gratitude to Roy's family, his late wife Gladys, a presence thoughout these pages, and to their daughter Christine Lewis Jones for their help.

Nick Wright

MINERS STRIKE
Read the truth

MORNING STAR

BEGINNINGS

MY FATHER, Sidney Charles Jones, was born in 1902 in Neath, South Wales. His father, my grandad, Charles William Jones, was a steelworker, born in 1874 in Manchester. He went to war in France in 1914 aged forty. He was gassed there, and died as a result in October 1921 without any recognition that he died for his country. Those not actually killed in action were ignored. His father, Edward Lemuel, had moved from Ruthin, Denbighshire to work in Manchester, so my roots lie in Welsh-speaking towns and villages.

My mother, Doris Burling, was born on 19 April 1906. She and her father, George Henry Burling, were both born in Birkenhead, he in 1874, after his parents had moved from Oldham to Merseyside. Both father and son were boilermakers in the Camel Laird shipyard.

George Henry's wife, Elizabeth Harriet Burling, nee Manning, was born in 1879 on Inishmore in the Arran Isles, Ireland. She was the daughter of Chatham, born Edward Wallace, subsequently a coastguard in Galway, who in turn was the son of Alexander Wallace born in Peterhead in Scotland. Thus my ancestry includes natives of England, Ireland, Scotland and Wales. Sydney Charles Jones and Doris Burling were married on 26 December 1929 at Mother Church, Hawarden, Flintshire.

My father's working life was shaped by the steel industry. He moved from Summers of Shotton, Deeside to work at the Burnells Iron Works in Ellesmere Port. This was a small family-owned sheet mill, one of the last heavy industrial works, and among the most antiquated. The hard work of fabricating sheets of metal was carried out by hand, with not a switch or a button used in the process. Imagine an artist's impression of hell; fire spewing out when the doors of the furnaces opened, while singleted workers, shod in steel clogs fed the heavy iron bars, now red hot, to a pair of huge rollers through which they were repeatedly transformed into sheets of different gauge, then to be cut and corrugated. The team was made up of furnace-man, bar-dragger, heaver-over and roller. The latter was the leader. My dad was qualified for this job, but in those days the Steel Workers Union chose who should be roller, and he refused to join because of that.

This highly dangerous working environment led to burns and mutilations for careless workers. It was a common sight around town to see men with fingers, hands and arms missing. As a child I watched a neighbour, Bob Finney, with both his arms off to his elbows clean his own shoes and even more skilfully down a pint of bitter using a fitted forearm and hand extensions. Another, Charley, lost one arm and became a barber to earn a living!

The steel workers' hard graft risked dehydration so that at the end of a shift it was straight to the Railway Inn, with the bar counter covered by pints of mild or bitter for the avalanche of custom.

My father drank his fill with the others. An abiding memory is looking down the road to see a solitary distant figure riding a bike that veered from one side of the road to the other, as I shouted 'Here he is now Mam', keen for my dinner, which never started without him. His was a well paid job during the 1930s, and this is one of the reasons that we were able to afford the house into which we moved, leaving cheaper houses for those less well off.

In 1939 Sid went to work back in Deeside, travelling the twenty-miles round trip by bike. When returning home one night he was hit and dragged along by a lorry, leaving him with a fractured skull. He recovered enough to go back to work during the war, but continued to suffer until his death in 1949.

My mother was the eldest daughter of six and was just fifteen when her mother died. She lived with relatives until my grandad moved to Queensferry, North Wales to open a grocery store. Doris was a woman formed in the 'Roaring Twenties'. Her family was well enough off for her to enjoy the theatre, films and dancing, the latter she talked of frequently as being their favourite pastime,

Photographs showed her in high heels, silk stockings and the smart shortish dresses of the time. She smoked from an early age, and recounted that her dad would shout out 'that bloody Doris is upstairs smoking again'. She insisted that if Sid went to the pub, then she would go too. This was in the days when, if women went into pubs they were put in the best room or the parlour, where swearing was not tolerated, while the men went into the bar where it was. As a child I would go with them, and with a packet of crisps and a bottle of pop, I would wait in the Red Lion's covered doorway in summer, when it was warm, and winter, when it wasn't.

Doris's biggest influence was that she read a lot. There were always library books about the house, written by a wide variety of authors, and I joined her before I was five. One night after dad's death she revealed something the significance of which I did not realise until much later. Their courtship during the 1920s lasted longer than she wanted, with Grandma Jones being reluctant to let her only son get married.

My mother told me of her determination to get her man, and without saying what the method was, it was clear that she did so by a sort of subterfuge. It was only when I was about 40 that I cottoned on to the fact that I was conceived out of wedlock and born on Boxing Day 1929, and after their marriage, my birth was registered on April 27 1930.

When my father died aged forty-seven, in 1949, and as a consequence I was discharged from the RAF, I was soon courting. My Mam, in turn, looked askance at losing me, an added factor being a brother, Leslie, just three, resulting in nearly three years' courtship before our marriage in 1955 .There was no subterfuge considered as I remember.

Both my parents voted Tory, reasoning that people with money must be cleverer than the rest of the populace, but I never discussed politics with my father or mother in my youth. My parents never urged on me the schooling needed for a good trade or profession. I shared the newspapers they read and the wireless, and thus too their attitude to the news. The daily newspapers from the 1920s to post war were on the side of the establishment, but compared with today, aided by first rate journalism, at their heart they were with a mixture of news, features and sport. There was hardly a hint of the disturbingly dumb fare put before the people during recent decades. The ownership of newspapers and politics were more diverse, with the *Daily Herald*, the *News Chronicle* and the Co-op's *Reynolds News* firmly on the left.

My Dad took the *Daily Express* and *Sunday Express*, which were nothing like today's titles, although owned by the Tory-supporting, Canadian millionaire Lord Beaverbrook. I mostly read their sports pages. The wireless was constantly on, controlled by my parents, with the news, drama, music, comedy and sport, and especially the popular music of the day, ranging from dance bands to ballads and musicals. From Children's Hour, with stories and songs, to the Brains Trust, featuring social and ethical problems of the day, the radio was on constantly. During the war radio produced some of the great journalism, featuring on-the-spot reports of journalists under fire with the armed forces in the field, with spectacular reporting from aircraft during combat, from convoys and from the battlefields.

We took in lodgers and one, Joe, a bricklayer from Burnley was a lefty. While he lodged with us, George Orwell's *Animal Farm*, was a BBC Book at Bedtime and stimulated a conversation.

For a year, until 1934, we lived in rooms in Ellesmere Port, until we moved into a new three-bedroom council semi, with gardens back and front. This was on Rossmore Road on the Overpool estate, and was virtually in the country, with farmland stretching out from our front door. In 1934 these were revolutionary dwellings for working people, and contained an indoor, upstairs toilet, a bath and a sink. The kitchen was where we ate, rested, read or listened to the radio. Coal in its black leaded grate was our only source of heat, with some members of the family burning their legs, which left scars.

I remember life as longer, colder and more rainy, with snowy winters beginning on cold and frosty mornings. Raking out and lighting the kitchen fire was a daily chore, and when central heating came in the 1970s, it was an amenity that made life not only more comfortable, but it also became a factor in the chance for working people to live longer.

The back kitchen was the domestic engine-room, with its gas stove, where Mam cooked the meat and potato pies, Sunday roasts and on Sunday, prepared cream teas. Clothes journied through mothers' hands from dolly tub, to mangle, and then to be hung out to dry, their whiteness the pride and joy of housewives.

The front room or parlour was used on occasional Sundays, Christmas or when we had visitors. My Dad was laid out there before being taken to Hawarden, to be buried near his mother and father. I went from that parlour to the church on my wedding day. It was home in all its senses.

Ellesmere Port's Station Road was the hub where its populace was provided with its wants from cradle to the grave. It was a town fit for purpose. If this is a too rosy account covering the Depression, the Second World War and its austere aftermath, I aged between five and twenty-five; years when we are at our most robust and resilient, and I was and lucky to be so. Its society embodied closely-knit families, friends and neighbours. There were Boy Scouts, Girls Guides, knitting circles, coffee mornings, night life in the pubs, and two cinemas and dancing to records in church halls.

Churches were well-attended, with the clergy a social presence beyond baptisms, weddings and funerals. Mr Ron Walton, funeral director – 'top grade coffins only' – was across the road from the Sportsman's Arms.

A stream of people knocked on the door, including the gas, electric, post and milk men. Mr Newmark, a little Jewish tailor, and 'tally man' clothed us for a small sum. African and Asian pedlars sold their wares door-to-door. But it was not until 1983, in London, did we meet our first Spanish bike-riding, onion seller.

For thirty years we knew the names of the forty families that were born, lived, were schooled and skilled or were married in the town. Not much disturbed the equilibrium of life; the only 'scandals' I remember was when a husband left his wife and a teenage girl was made pregnant.

Shopping, mostly done by women, was the a social glue that kept each local enterprises in place, and the eclectic mix of the wares on sale made each shop individual.

Most shops hired delivery lads, and while I was still at school and aged 13 I worked briefly for the Co-op butchers, doing general duties in the shop and deliveries. This involved using a basket-laden butcher's bike with meat parcels for delivery to the posh homes in Whitby. Being more skinny than strapping I found it difficult to get on the heavily-laden bike. If I got to the top of a steep hill, even by walking, it was likely that the front-heavy machine would wrestle me to the ground, spilling the parcels on the ground with meat bursting through its wrappings.

Tired out by the effort to rewrap and replace the parcels in the basket while holding the bike in position with my knees, especially if it was raining, I was easily exhausted, and the customers were not best pleased by the state of their meat. I gave it three weeks.

Ellesmere Port was transformed as part of a second, 20th century, industrial revolution. The population grew from 30,000 in 1950 to 44,000 in 1972. The 1930s Great Depression had given way to preparations for war. There was 'an army of happiness' because, as depicted in *The Ragged Trousered Philanthropists*, the workers had 'plenty of work'.

The town possessed a 19th century infrastructure with a railway, road, and water transport system, including the mighty Manchester Ship Canal, which was kick-started when the Wolverhampton Corrugated Iron Works was built in 1905. Industry grew quickly with the production of cement, flour, paper, bitumen, oil and chemicals, plant, metal containers and carbon black. The 'Shell Road' grew to be the biggest oil and chemical complex in Britain. In the early 1960s the US motor giant General Motors built the Vauxhall car plant, which initially employed 5,000 workers rising eventually to 12,000. In 1968 a fertiliser plant was built.

This investment engendered smaller scale engineering business and services. Skills were gained locally and skilled workers imported from north west England, Ireland, Scotland, and Wales drawing in families who sank new roots in the town. New housing schemes extended Ellesmere Port on all sides with the 'incomers' and the 'Porties' initially in an uneasy relationship. The tension should not be exaggerated, but when a large number of people, 'foreigners', even if from just ten miles away, encounter locals in a short space of time the strain was manifest.

Later on, when I stood as a Communist candidate in Ellesmere Port town council elections, I was frequently told I would get a vote if I could stop the influx of the Scousers, who were 'taking our houses and our jobs'. If I had taken this up I reckon I could have won.

The industrial enterprises increased the town's social amenities by opening their own sports clubs and complexes, where families and guests played football, cricket, rugby, tennis and table tennis. These became the backbone of local competitive leagues.

Works clubs staged dances and cabarets with top acts; Ken Dodd made his debut at the Shell Club, rhythm and blues, folk, rock and roll and jazz bands entertained. Attendances were at their height in the 60s and 70s club scene when members tucked into chicken in a basket, with beer and spirits cheaper than the pubs.

These were undoubtedly paternalist, but not in the manner of the 'Firm's Days Out' as depicted in *The Ragged Trousered Philanthropists*. The provisions made for staff away from work recognised the part firms played in the communities and commitment to the social conditions of the towns.

The fight for better wages and conditions and health and safety was fought as fiercely then as in any other time in industrial history, with great strides being made by the trades unions and their members. There was a sense that industrial enterprises saw value in this different dimension.

Then companies changed their philosophy by shedding unprofitable functions, which actions were visible on the balance sheet. In the 1980s the employers began to sell off their clubs and abandon activities that had only intrinsic and not a book value.

This extended to nearly every aspect of training, even where it benefited employers to improve the skills of their workforces. Margaret Thatcher, who famously proclaimed that there was no such thing as society provided the theory; Ellesmere Port employers provided the practice.

Our estate, the Overpool, was truly rural. It was a burgeoning estate of late-1920s vintage, with tree-lined roads and avenues. The shops, including the chippie were built to purpose.

In the 1930s and 1940s we were as likely to see a horse and cart as a car. It was still a rural area, with Charlie Dodd's and Bill Jones' farms 400 yards down Rivacre Road. Their farms encompassed both arable and livestock, with the cows milked by hand, after which came 'mucking out.' Cow muck in your boots doesn't make you grow! I mucked out sheds and stables that were smelly in the summer and bitterly cold in the winter. There was a chance of not-too-hard labour at harvest time, with jobs ranging from cutting, bailing and loading hay in the 40-acre field, or stacking stooks of corn and loading carts. Our reward was the lunch-time jam butties, cakes and jugs of tea brought by the farmer's wife for us and the real farm workers. The days ended when we climbed on the hay cart drawn by the two giant shire horses that needed no guidance. How is that when you were ten-years-old, the summer sun never stopped shining? There were orchards that provided an opportunity for the boys (and some girls) to 'scrump' apples as a late evening activity, with the chance of being chased by the owners adding to the thrill.

Early education and the war From 1934 to 1944, for me there was no debate about education. It was universal, but fixed from a time when the ruling class was educated to rule, the professional class educated to assist it, and the working class to work! Those at school mostly neither aspired to reach upwards nor were inspired to do so. We knew our place. The war changed all that, when the working class and its progressive, middle-class allies sought something better.

The depression and the pre-war struggle against fascism passed me by, and I had but a superficial knowledge of Britain outside of my own environment. At five I went to the John Street Junior School, and at eleven to the John Street Senior School, leaving when I was14. The school was organised in a fairly simple way, with the senior school classification streams being Standard year 1 A, B and C; year 2 A, B and C and so on. I started in standard 1 B and made it to 5 A in the final year. The headmaster Mr Stirk, Mr (Taffy) Hughes and Mr Davies made up the all-male staff. When I got to the 'Big School' in 1941 all the male teachers had gone to war. There were no men in the junior school.

The system's intentions were clear. Reading, writing (under the heading of English) and arithmetic were its base. History included little about countries and peoples outside the British Empire, and thus focussed on the British capturing lands from the people who lived there or fighting with other nations to capture lands that they had colonised. This was supplemented in films featuring actors, such as Errol Flyn, extending and defending the empire in India, Africa and the Orient, with many scripts taken from authors like Rudyard Kipling.

In hindsight Geography was also basic and eccentric, with exotic peoples like the Eskimos of the North Pole dominating, and 'heroes' such as Robert Falcon Scott, who in the race for the South Pole perished with his comrades. What we saw through newsreels were cheery white-toothed and black-faced children handing a royal princess some flowers. English was simple, with little grammar, but was redeemed by a Miss Davies, who read to us, and encouraged us to read, and extolled the virtues of G.K. Chesterton and the Father Brown stories.

Punishment was by way of 'the stick' or cane on the outstretched hands of those guilty of indiscipline. I was punished for talking in class. On Fridays those to be punished lined up outside Mr Stirk's door with the agony prolonged by the long wait before the ritual 'six of the best' was administered. Stirky simply said 'Hold out your hand' and wielded the stick, which stung a lot.Those having suffered the punishment would emerge either saying it didn't hurt, while others told the truth. Hurt it did.

To those who advocate bringing back the cane, I can say that I reckon it a very ineffective deterrent. In the same way that prison is full of long-term offenders, there were more regulars than newcomers to Stirky's room. Mr Stirk taught me a lesson I never forgot. At an interview at the end of my school days, for an office job at the Bowaters Paper Mill, I had expressed a doubt (to the interviewer) as to my ability to do the job on offer.

Back at school Mr Stirk called me in and told me I hadn't got the job, and that he had been told of my doubts. He proffered the view that you should never tell anyone this. His rough advice was 'say nothing and let them find out for themselves' ; advice which I have followed to this day.

Our cultural background was broadened every Saturday morning as hundreds of screaming kids went to the Kings picture house in Little Sutton to the Two Penny Crush, where, after spending our pennies on gobstoppers, sherbet and liquorice, we feasted on cowboy heroes like the Lone Ranger and Tonto.The white-hatted heroes were cheered and told to "look out behind you!" The black-hatted villains booed. A roughly-fashioned science-fiction movie, or a monster-from-the-deep, chilled us. When a film broke down 'put a shilling in the meter' was chorused and the staff shone torches to quieten the raucous, and threatened to chuck us out if we didn't behave.

With our heroes' lives left hanging by a thread, we raced home across the golf links with the cowboys chasing the Indians, unmercifully lashing our imaginary horses. These activities were all consuming, full and of reasonable contentment, we were not asked to grow up too soon, and for me childhood was enjoyable.

I was at school for most of the war being nine in April 1939 and leaving in 1944. I don't remember it greatly affecting what we did, nor that it helped us to understand what was going on. I don't think we lost a day's schooling throughout, but many in big cities did. The only other way in which the war was brought to our attention by teachers was when we moved the flags onto large maps, signifying our soldiers' advances, and later those of the Russians. I don't remember many backward moves. The end of the war in Europe coincided with my leaving school aged 14 of which my most vivid memory was running down the road whooping and cheering. We had left school for good on an appropriately bright sunshiny day.

For the sports of our childhood and youth we were simply equipped with bats and balls and the ability to turn any terrain into a suitable surface. Football was where boyhood ambition to be a professional lay. The football field was behind a little wood. Written into childhood football folk-lore was the rule that whoever brought the ball, if he was sinned against, would threaten 'to take my ball home'. We played without referees, and any goal disputes were difficult to settle, as we had only coats for goals posts. Offsides were generally ignored. Our skills and stamina honed, we gravitated into the Ellesmere Port and District (Wirral) Leagues then graduating to the Cheshire League or even higher.

One such player was David (Dave) Hickson. On his death in 2016, I wrote for the *Ellesmere Port Pioneer*: 'In Overpool in the 1930s and 1940s we local lads played our football ploughing the same furrow with the same ambitions as local heroes and internationals like Joe Mercer of Everton and Stan Cullis of Wolves, both who captained England. Dave Hickson, an Everton, Aston Villa and Liverpool centre forward in the old fashioned mould was one of us'.

During the 1938/39 season I made the journey into the Goodison Park ground of Everton FC following a tradition established years before – in the Port. It was a Derby game against Liverpool. In 1951, I took this same journey with Dave Hickson. We knew each other from the age of six, and our Mam's were friends for over sixty years. We went through school together and remained friends throughout the years.

In the 1950s most fans had the opportunity to rub shoulders with their heroes who travelled on public transport to the Saturday match. The status of footballers was not then matched by fat salaries. I went to home games with Dave, by bus to Birkenhead and onto the Mersey ferry, there to be joined by a couple of the Everton players, John Willie Parker and Ted Buckle, then on the tram where the conductor would refuse Dave's proffered fare!

Dave was worshipped by many, as stepping almost straight from the tram to the field, played in front of fifty, sixty or seventy thousand adoring fans.

I dreamed along with the rest, and after finding myself as goalkeeper for local team, Springfield, I was picked for a Port and District representative side to play against Sheffield FC, Britain's oldest football club. I was fixed up with a trial for Wrexham and did well enough to get signed on, but through injury progressed little.

Later, working at the Shell refinery, I played for firm's teams and then, sitting on its committee as its press agent I worked closely with our two local papers. In summer we played cricket from early to late, it seemed in never-ending sunshine. When by common consent someone was adjudged out, then out they went. At times we played in the road, stopping only to the shout of 'car coming'. Among the vehicles that disturbed our play was the fleet of coal-burning, steam-powered lorries from Frost Flour Mills. In fact these were really railway engines travelling on the road with solid tyres.

The Rivacre Valley's outdoor door swimming pool attracted thousands of bathers. It had one, five and ten metre diving boards for our finest divers, and for the young and fearless to claim their colours by jumping off the top board. Because only the sun's rays heated the water it was always cold. Nevertheless, I climbed the railings on some early mornings to feel just like a millionaire swimming in a private pool.

The earliest ideological influence on me when young was at Sunday schools, three of which I attended. In the 1930s most children went to Sunday schools, which had started in the 1780s as an education for the working classes by organised religion. What's the use of bibles if they couldn't be read.

There were also organised Christmas parties and summer trips to New Brighton and Rhyl, rather than worship, although something of that nature must have taken place. St Francis Overpool Church won my final allegiance, and I was confirmed into the Church of England but with no great spiritual vocation. When I finally became a communist the least of my considerations was religion's place.

St Francis Church housed a Boy Scout troop. The Scouts were founded in Britain by Lord Robert Baden Powell, a hero of the 1907 Mafeking siege, and the movement has spread throughout the world, maintaining a substantial world presence. The motives of Baden Powell have been argued over for a hundred years. In critical opinion he reinforced ruling class dominance with rituals, promises and laws that strengthened the status quo, pledging to love God and be loyal to the Queen.

From my experience, I doubt that many of his adherents ended as paragons of virtue. Nevertheless, being truthful, loyal to parents and obeying the injunction to be helpful, courteous and kind, and seek no reward for protecting the weak, defending the helpless, being a friend to all 'no matter what country, class or creed', is to be welcomed and is not completely at odds with socialist virtues.

As a Boy Scout I met the Rev E.M.B. Southwell, the Vicar of Ellesmere Port and District Commissioner for Scouts, and Dave Williamson, the scoutmaster of the 7th Troop. He was an electrical engineer from a working class background who had lost a leg in a motorcycling accident. At 'their knee' (in the Vicarage) I listened to talk of words and music. Dave could recite huge chunks of Shakespeare or Gilbert and Sullivan, and they would both quote lines of hymns pointing to illogicalities. Dave, noting my skinniness, quoted Julius Caesar: 'Yon Cassius hath a lean and hungry look". I found out later that the quote continued "He thinks too much. Such men are dangerous, Give me a man as sleeps at night etc.'. I'll have some of that I thought.

At Scout camps, after a rainy night, we had to dig trenches around the tents to keep the insides dry. We would sing of a God who 'sends the snow in winter the sun to warm the grain, the breezes and the sunshine and soft, refreshing rain.'

In 1945, E.M.B. introduced our public to the Boy Scout Gang Show. Our show was called the High Spots and was staged in the Church Hall. The show was professional enough, and gave pleasure to our audience. composed mainly of proud family members. In the first one I was 'the star' of the show; well, kind of, with six appearances in songs and sketches. The following year I was just in the finale, dressed in a kilt as Scottish singer Harry Lauder singing 'Keep Right on to the End of the Road.

The Second World War was not the drama for us in Ellesmere Port as for those citizens in other towns and cities across Britain. There was still rationing of food, fuel and clothes. When I was sent shopping, I would often forget some item, returning home, only to be chased down the front garden path by my Mam, who cuffed me across the head in time to the admonition 'Go back again, and don't come back without it'. When we ran short of coupons, I would have to plead with Mrs Shaw of the Corner Shop for an advance on the following week's allowance.

Most precious was coal, which in the long winter months was used so sparingly that you never felt really warm. Coke was made from burning coal to make gas, but it didn't burn easily, and yielded poor heat. Delivered in sacks from the local gas works, about three miles from home, on all kinds of contraptions from bikes, prams and sledges, it arrived to a Dickensian scene devised for film, peopled by the most shabby of characters. Standing in long queues outside the gasworks wall, we kept warm, clad in old coats, gloves, mittens and balaclavas. In the worst spells of winter the biting cold and fog was made worse by people burning rubbish. The journey home was night-marish if like me, you had lost the mittens and failed to secure the badly-tied sacks of coke.

Liverpool, Bootle and the Wirral were the most heavily bombed areas, with a death toll second only to that of London. Merseyside provided anchorage for naval ships with its ports, and dockers handling over 90% of all the war material, food and fuel brought into Britain from abroad. The first major air raid on Liverpool took place in August 1940, when 160 bombers attacked on the night of 28 August. This assault continued over the next three nights, then for the rest of the year.

In December 1940, referred to as the Christmas blitz, 365 people were killed. The last German air raid on Liverpool took place on 10 January 1942, when the bombs killed 2716 people in Liver-pool, 442 people in Birkenhead, 409 people in Bootle and 332 people in Wallasey. This shows how lucky I and my family were despite the proximity of the Manchester ship canal and docks. Just three bombs, I think, landed in the port's confines.

June's clear blue skies became filled with German bombers flying in close formation, with the droning engines clearly heard. Around them white puffs of smoke denoted anti-aircraft shells ex-ploding, but which did nothing to deter their flight.

Ten miles from their targets the skies darkened, with the flames stretching miles across the horizon. In the shelter people heard the hum of the German bombers returning from Merseyside and were able to leave the shelters and go to bed for a short time before getting up for work.

We saw for ourselves the devastation of Liverpool's flattened buildings and shops as we had visited them often and they were no longer there. The scars left by these ferocious attacks were on view for years afterwards.

One day my mother and I visited Aunt May in Birkenhead, and were on a bus at the very be-ginning of an air raid. The bus stopped and we were running for the rail station shelter when a bomb fell near with its warning whistling sound.

I remember diving to the ground with passengers and bus crew while the conductor stumbled, with loose change from his bag jingling all over the street. After a short time in the bomb shelter we were soon on the way home, unharmed.

We did once see a 'dog fight'. At about 100 foot a German bomber was then accompanied by two Hurricane fighters which, it seemed, guided it to Hooton Aerodrome, just two miles away.

On 6 June 1945 we celebrated Victory in Europe in front of the shopping parade on Overpool Road. I vaguely recall the singing and dancing and goodies to eat. For others who suffered more than we did it would have been a much more memorable occasion. The threat of injury and death was over. What a pity that not a single lesson was learnt from the carnage.

I was by then fourteen years old and working for a living. On leaving school I started work with no qualifications, as the charms of the snooker hall had ended my night school career after just one year. Instead I went to work as an office boy at Burnell's Iron Works where my dad worked. I earned £1 five shillings a week, and gave £1 to my Mam. I paid for my own clothes and was having a good time. I was able to buy my first second-hand bike, which was 'done-up' by Dad. This was a great event in the lives of young boys. Later I bought my own drop-handle-barred racer for £5 to be paid off at five shilling a week. On this I travelled the sixteen miles to New Brighton and Hoylake on the Wirral, and then to Southport and the North Wales Coast.

The Welsh mountains and valleys are a challenge to young limbs, but stopping in small towns for huge mugs of tea and great big sandwiches, scouting the rivers such as at Llangollen, staying at youth hostels with their cheap board and cleaning duties at morning and night, was a real adventure.

The bike played a part in my lack of success in my first job when, unable to get to work on time, I blamed my late arrival on (too) frequent punctures and broken chains. A year after my start the excuses were wearing thin. I made my excuses and left.

Bikes made me a criminal. Riding home without lights I was twice tracked by policemen on their bikes and failing to outspeed them meant an appearance in court and the shame of a punishing fine.

At Burnell's were men who had worked there before the war and who, when they came home, some from prisoner-of-war camps and made their first visits to family and friends, rarely mentioned their time in the conflict. As with the men from the trenches in World War 1, they rarely talked of their experiences. Gladys' father, Albert, briefly told something of the war to his wife, but never again. A neighbour and workmate, Jimmy Homer, recounted being captured, and spending three years working in the Polish salt mines, and when he was freed by the Soviet army, he was transported in an open carriage, cheered all the way by the Russian people, and given presents of cigarettes and licorice, before embarking at a Russian seaport and being shipped home. But I don't remember any great celebrations when the men who had fought the war came home and settled back into family life and work as best they could.

Things were different to conditions with the end of the First World War, with its hollow claim to be the war to end wars, followed by the desolate days of the Depression.

The War ends At the end of World War II there was a determination to seize the moment to bring change. Few predicted the drastic change in the political climate, when in 1945, the Conservative Party led by its war hero Winston Churchill, suffered a massive defeat and Labour was returned to power.

These historical events impinged little on me and my friends. I paid no heed to them. In our teenage years we took up work and filled our leisure time easily enough, and climbed into our £5 made-to-measure suits. My circle of friends had opportunities for varied, interesting and (eventually) relatively well-paid work. They were welders, brickies, plumbers, refinery operators and shop and office workers. Close to full employment continued for about twenty-five years, with the foundations for our futures that would include marriage and children.

Local district councils, which post-war, were Independent or Conservative-dominated, gave way to Labour administrations, which naturally included many trades unionists.

The trades unionists were mostly tough pragmatists, driving council house building for millions, while the private sector met the demands of those who could afford to buy. The pace of change in post-war Britain, in contrast to the 1930s depression and even with the cost of the war, was astonishing. The British working class applied itself to the task of rebuilding Britain from the rubble, both material and spiritual, that had been left by the war and the bombing.

With my office job gone I became a tea boy at a dockside company, then worked in a garage, and at sixteen moved to the weighbridge of the Lobitos Oil Company, until I was called up to join the Royal Air Force.

The Royal Air Force National Service was for healthy males aged seventeen to twenty-one years old, who under the National Service Act 1948 were expected to serve for eighteen months. This was extended later to two years.

In February of 1948 I received my papers and underwent a medical. I passed what seemed a simple test for what I imagined such a serious responsibility. Then I tore open a finger, thus delaying my call up until August. My Mam said she had never seen me move so fast before I took a train to Padgate, Warrington, where I became a raw RAF recruit.

I joined 8 Flight made up mainly of Midlanders. Although it was peace time, there was a chance that you would end up in a real war. Many were sent to Egypt, Malaysia or Korea, with some being killed for their troubles.

Off the parade ground we lived in billets, from where we were woken by a (very) early morning

'Wakey! Wakey!' Eighteen of us lived cheek-by-jowl, with the coke-fired stove shined up, as everything is according to the armed forces creed, 'If it moves salute it and if it doesn't paint it white'.

We were inspected for uncreased uniforms, buttons and brasses brushed a burnished gold, and boots classically treated with spit and polish.

Our short-back-and-sides haircuts allowed the 'Am I hurting you' treatment from the inspecting Flight Sergeant, inevitably accompanied by the hoariest of old service jokes 'I could be, I'm standing on your hair.' We were supervised from dawn to dusk by a squad of non-commissioned officers, strict disciplinarians, with the constant shout of 'Airman!' heard across the parade ground, alerting you to something wrong. The constant drilling eventually got us to a standard that we never thought we could reach.

Off-duty time was spent mostly in the NAAFI, with its age-old canteens, and fitted out with table tennis, snooker and darts, where we would drink away some of the wages of four shillings and ten pence a day. One night a Scotsman, Jimmy Deuchar, produced a trumpet on which he superbly played a couple of pop songs. Jimmy turned out to be one of the finest (modern) jazz trumpeters and arrangers. Working with Britain's best bands his work took him to Germany and the United States.

Quickly a remarkable sense of comradeship developed between complete strangers away from home. With the resilience of young men of eighteen, nothing was taken seriously for too long.

That it 'made a man of me', I doubt. I know it took me a step further along the road to drinking and smoking. It is hard to see what National Service achieves to foster self discipline. We were told what to do and did it. I enjoyed it, but being eighteen years old, the odds were that I would.

RAF Police The eight weeks came to an end with a passing-out parade, where, with a band we marched in step before the senior officers, our parents and friends. In 1949 I was a Royal Air Force policeman stationed in Llandwrog on the North Wales coast. This was a working station where, it was said, surplus poison gas bombs were coated in lanolin and thrown into the Irish Sea.

After twelve-weeks basic training, the selection process meant choosing from groups A aircrew, B skilled mechanic or C catering or the RAF Regiment or Police. One choice had to be from group C, and of these I chose the RAF Police. The twelve week training was mostly square-bashing with physical training in a gym and in the wintry countryside around Pershore not at its most inviting.

Police training encompassed common and criminal law as well as the military's King's Rules and Regulations by which service men and women had to abide. Our own tutor decided from day one that I was particularly dense and made this clear to the rest of the class. This situation didn't resolve itself even when we had our final exam results that put me top with 94%. "It is possible, of course, that some must have been looking over their mate's shoulder. Isn't it Jones?"

We had to know how to record, charge and present evidence pertinent to a case. Most cases were dealt with by the camp commander with serious cases going higher. Punishment would be 'Jankers', involving turning out on parade in full uniform for inspection followed by other duties. I also managed to take part in a boxing tournament between our unit and an army camp. This entailed an elimination contest between 'volunteers' (you, you and you!). In a 'box off' I beat an opponent who was even worse than I was, by picking him off with left leads. On the night the ring was surrounded by our and the army's cheering supporters.

My opponent never let me get a look in – coming at me with arms flailing windmill fashion in a move I could not counter. At the end of the second round the sergeant in my corner said "For fuck's sake do something. They are all laughing at you". Such as what, I wondered. I was glad to hear the bell, because after three two-minute rounds of boxing I could hardly lift up my arms. It was the most gruelling physical contest I have ever been involved in. I enjoyed a special after-fight dinner and treasured for years a bronze loser's medal, which I eventually lost.

Following this came another memorable moment, when on the first Saturday night out we visited the local pub to be greeted warmly by the locals, who I was sure had never met such a raw recruit as me before. Neither I nor any of the other recruits were aware of the most potent (legal) alcoholic drink in Britain, and I drank three and a half pints of the local scrumpy cider and fell violently sick over a hedge and into a ditch. Unable to regain my feet I managed, just, to stave off being sick. I must have lay there for an hour before regaining my composure enough to stagger back to camp for a bad night. I have never drunk scrumpy since!

After passing the necessary tests, and now being a corporal unpaid, I arrived at RAF Llandwrog one black February night in 1949. RAF Llandwrog was a working camp where the main duties for the twelve police were to maintain a 24-hour guard at the gate of the airfield (where four large hangars housed the station's operations), main gate duty and the Saturday night town patrol in Caernarfon.

The sergeant in charge was easy-going as long as we kept the two Nissan huts we lived in tidy, did our duties and dressed smartly. We mixed with everyone else on the camp, although we had use of a corporals' mess. I was one of eight servicemen named Jones known by their numbers. I was Jones 240! Life changed dramatically with the arrival of a new sergeant, a red-faced, big-nosed Welshman who was immediately christened Cherokee. He was an RAF regular who had decided on change. To our horror he immediately decided that we would parade every morning, whether we had worked all night or not. Our beds, kits, huts and ourselves were to be inspected, although nothing like this had happened before. After a couple of days we were up in arms over our treatment and Cherokee's attitude.

Fuelled on Sunday night by the NAAFI's Corporals Club's ale, complaints of 'unnecessary bullshit' developed into a call for action. We decided we would no longer put up with unnecessary bullshit, and we assembled outside the Commanding Officer's office first thing on Monday morning to make our demands. If we had any knowledge of things military we would have known that we risked being charged with mutiny!

Monday morning dawned, I dressed and made my way to the CO's office to find I was the first there. An Irish lad joined me – but that was it – we had notified our desire to see the CO so there was no turning back. We discussed tactics and decided to change tack and to tell the CO one at a time – that we wanted an overseas posting. After asking the obvious question – have you got a girl into trouble – the CO granted our requests. In the event my Irish comrade received a posting to the Middle East and I to the Far East. Our goose was cooked. The moral of this story helped me for the rest of my working life – if you are up for a fight and only two of you turn up, make sure you have a plan B.

Life in Wales February 1949 I arrived at RAF Llandwrog in February 1949 by train to Caernarfon on a night as black as pitch with the rain sheeting down. The bus took me three miles to the gates of an uninviting land of my fathers.

Daylight revealed a large airfield close to five miles of sandy beaches with Dinas Dinlle westwards and Caernarfon to the east. There were living quarters, a cookhouse, canteen and NAAFI Club. Eight RAF police were housed in a Nissan hut next door to the gatehouse, from which we checked the movements in and out of airmen and goods.

The police contingent included two dog handlers with Alsatians. One of the dogs we had was a savage beast whose handler, a cockney lad, just about managed to keep it from devouring an airman or two. We guarded the airfield gates in eight hour shifts with 24 hours off. The tedium of the shifts were leavened by riding with an officer on a station truck in order to transfix rabbits with our headlights and shoot them.

I was posted too with Corporal John Moore, an art school graduate from Blackpool, a heavily-built, soft-spoken, gentle giant, who the moment he gained the rank of an RAF policeman became a tyrant. John enjoyed himself on Saturday patrol in Caernarfon catching airmen in an act contrary to the rules, sneaking up behind them and bawling down their ear. But I just couldn't do it. I never charged a single person. I was tempted, I admit to accept bribes, like five Woodies (Woodbine cigarettes) offered by an airman eager to get away on leave.

A foul winter was followed by an early spring and glorious summer. Walking the sunny sandy shores under clear blue skies with some good mates and attentive girls with all the innocence of a nineteen-year old. It was enough of an idyll for me to sign up for twelve years more service.

I was still then on standby for the Far East when my father Sid fell ill and died from a tumour on the brain. With the help of our family doctor I was given a compassionate discharge to help at home with my widowed mother and brother Les aged three. My father died in Walton hospital in Liverpool. I saw him just before he died and can't remember what I felt as he sadly lay there. My mother mentioned that he felt he missed out on being a granddad to our children. He worked hard all his life, that, and a few pints is what I remember of him. He owed the world nowt. At the age of nineteen I had to see to all the arrangements for his funeral in Hawarden cemetery which was ten miles away. This kept me busy, then Auntie Kate came to stay with us.

I wonder what would have happened to me and how life would have turned out if I had entered twelve years of service life? It is certain that I would have turned out a vastly different person.

Return to Civvy Street I was demobbed from the RAF in March 1950. At four in the morning, on Sunday, 25 June 1950, the Korean war broke out, one of several conflicts in the Far East involving Britain. Was I lucky or what?

I went back to shift work at Lobitos as a plant operator working for a decent wage. We had a Labour government, trade union strength growing and unemployment was low. I had to find more money to maintain our household than most sons but there was no hardship involved. In 1950 I first joined the Transport and General Workers Union, I paid my dues at ten pence a week in pre-decimal coinage (four pence in new money). On 27 April 1951 I celebrated my 21st birthday working from four a.m. until 12 o'clock midnight.

August 1951 was marked by a holiday to remember, when six of us sailed from Liverpool to Douglas in the Isle of Man to stay in Mrs Smith's Irewell Hotel. The sun shone all week and we swam, danced in giant ballrooms to big bands and chased (and caught) girls and could take a drink in the island bars, which were open 12 hours a day.

The day always ended with a sing-song. George Millington, Louis Ruffer, Don Piggott, Jimmy Harris, Robin Hooker and I never fell out. I name check these for the record, but there were many other friends equally deserving of mention.

We spent our Saturday nights in local halls with exotic names like the Majestic, dancing to five-piece bands, with the boys on one side of the hall cracking hackneyed lines like 'I don't fancy yours', and the girls on the other side demanding of their mates to 'quick dance with me – he's coming here'. With the quickstep, slow foxtrot and the waltz the evening eventually ended dancing cheek to cheek with your (latest) favourite partner. We carried on singing as we walked six to eight miles home after missing the last bus.

Until the age of eighteen, you just didn't drink beer. But there was a ritual in some families that on a boy's eighteenth birthday his dad took him for a pint. On special occasions coach trips took us to Blackpool to dance to big bands that featured great musical skills and individual virtuosity. We massed in front of the stage facing a wall of sound, and on the bus home try to get hold of a girl's hand.

Singing was a big thing, which for me included the St Francis' church choir, but mostly it was every Friday or Saturday, and at Christmas and weddings in the pubs and clubs. Later, at union conferences every one would sing or pay a forfeit. Some of the singing was to the highest standard and often with a revolutionary bent. A favourite song, Joe Hill, the ballad of the American trade union martyr, was popular but particularly hard to sing and often ended in excruciating failure.

Roy, you ask, did you sing? Once I performed at Towyn in the Sandy Bay pub. When I indicated to the MC that I would sing, our three daughters beseeched: "Mum! Mum! don't let him". At Ellesmere Port's Labour Hall one charity night the club secretary, Charlie, asked me to perform. Payment was in kind with a couple of tickets for the club's Christmas do. I was to do two spots, for which I prepared with a tape of Al Jolson songs.

On the night, as nervous as hell, I couldn't find a note. Charlie came in the interval and suggested, kindly that I might leave it there. Pride would not let me, and the second time it was OK.

In November 1951 there was a change in our regular circle. I was with Jimmy Jones, a mate from work, at a not very well attended dance in the Labour Hall, and there were two girls sitting opposite. I fancied the tallish and pretty one, with sparkling eyes and bouncy brown hair. I can't remember her dress and how it looked but the odds are it was immaculate.

A couple of dances later and I escorted Gladys Ledsham home, and she became part of our gang. As well as sharing lots of things together and having the same tastes in music and musicals and laughing at the same comedies, it became a long courtship. This was due to the situation in our house, with Les still being young, and before my Mam went back to work. Gladys also worked at Lobitos. At Christmas we all put on our glad rags for the work's dance in Chester Town Hall.

Gladys, as with all the girls in their long evening gowns, was swept to the dance floor to dance to an 'orchestra', while I queued for the refreshments and sank a few beers while the girls took a Babycham or two.

The relationships with our two families went smoothly; I got on well with her Mam and Dad and Gladys got on well with my Mam. We were able to survive a long courtship. Gladys had four major distinctions, being fiercely loyal, she's against injustice, is the most unselfish person on earth but has enough stubbornness to fight her corner when necessary.

Awareness of social injustice In 1952 Gladys and I saw the US western, *High Noon*. This featured a lawman, who on the day he is to get married, hangs up his badge and is due to leave town. Marshal Kane is told that Frank Miller, a man he sent to prison years before, is returning on the noon train to meet up with a gang of deadly killers and exact revenge. When the marshal seeks the help of the townspeople he has protected, each turns his back on him. In the drama of facing up to Miller and his gang, he triumphs and rides off into the sunset with his bride.

The screenplay was written by Carl Foreman, who, when he was a student was an advocate of socialism and joined the US Communist Party. In 1951 Foreman was witchhunted and blacklisted before moving to England. In my trade union and political life I encountered blacklisting later, and although not as dramatic as Carl Foreman's travails, I experienced a few bad turns.

In 1952 I was dealt a blow to my rights and pride, when a job, with its substantial pay rise, which I considered on service alone should have been mine, went to someone else. Angered by this injustice and being on night shift I waited until nine o'clock and confronted the refinery's managing director Abe Cluer, railed at him for the injustice and told him I was finished with Lobitos for good! I found out later that my Achilles heel was the six till two shift, which with my inability to get out of bed, was a factor. As I cycled home I was enraged. Was this the first hint of the militancy with which I would face up to employers in the years to come?

The left wing historian, Eric Hobsbawm, described the years 1947 – 1990 as the 'Age of Extremes', and argued that a temporary and bizarre alliance of liberal capitalism and communism against the challenge of fascism in the Second World War saved democracy. The confrontation between socialism and capitalism was the main driving feature of this Golden Age. For my generation, relative to what went before and what came afterwards, the post war period was a Golden Age, or about the best there has been for Britain's working people. We took advantage of conditions favourable to the working class organisations in a situation that happens very rarely. In the ebb and flow of the struggle between the rulers and the ruled we made mistakes, but on balance made the best of our chances, which brought great advances to the working class. What became ordinary to most working people, following the deep Depression and six years of war, was in fact extraordinary.

The construction of housing, both private and council, increased year on year. Council houses were built to legal minimum standards of light and space, with a preponderance of three-bedroomed, semi-detached homes. Life outside the home also changed, and almost anything would attract record crowds, while many more people played organised games than had done pre war. The entertainment industry changed. The Bingo craze stayed hugely popular, while cinemas, variety and drama theatres played to packed houses. A greater interest in politics was manifest, with high election turn-outs and political party memberships healthy and growing. Labour was boosted by trade union affiliation, and shop floor activists. Political parties were predominant in local politics at the expense of so-called independents, showing a highly level of understanding. Women, who in the war had taken the place of men in production, mostly lost their jobs in industry, but gained employment from the rise in economic activity in retail, catering and office work.

The birth of the National Health Service, soon to be the world's biggest employer of labour, along with a vast extension of hospitals and other services created many new jobs. Such was the need for labour that all governments of the day recruited men and women from the colonies to come to our aid. Gas and electricity power generation and their supply industries were under public ownership, and they fueled the economy. Private capital had failed, and public ownership underpinned the post-war recovery.

To 'The Shell' – September 1952 Soon after leaving the Lobitos Oil Company, I was back to work at the Shell oil refinery, cycling to join its five thousand workers along the 'Shell Road'. I filled drums and road and rail petrol tankers, and worked shifts at the Bitumen plant. During the night shift at the Bitumen plant, I 'penned' a piece entitled 'When in Doubt Form a Committee, which was printed by the *Ellesmere Port Advertiser*, as were two other articles, for which I was paid ten shillings and sixpence per piece; (fifty-two pence in today's money). I tried my luck with the *Advertiser's* editor for a reporter's job there; my offer was declined. My journalistic career went into its gestation stage! They don't know what they lost.

I remember giving my first political opinion on anything. On 30 July 1956, Britain, France and Israel invaded Egypt, then recently freed from British rule, and bombed Cairo in response to the Egyptian president Colonel Nasser's nationalisation of the Suez Canal. The British prime minister, Anthony Eden, made the case for Britain but there was little support from other nations, including from the US president Eisenhower. I was working the night-shift, and I clearly remember backing Britain and the invasion, and condemning Nasser and Egypt. I suppose I remember this so clearly because in a couple of years time I changed my views completely!

At home, Les was too young to be left on his own. When Mam found work, and with me on shift, Gladys looked after Les, travelling from her house to mine and back again on her bike. This meant going far beyond any obligations called for in a relationship. In the summer of 1954, three years after our first meeting, Gladys and I celebrated our engagement; buying the ring on holiday in the Isle of Man, while staying again with Mrs Smith in Douglas.

The wedding took place on August 27 1955 at the Ellesmere Port parish church, where on a glorious summer's day we made our vows, accompanied by a good showing of friends and relatives gathered at Frost Flour Mills Club. The ham salad cost seven shillings and sixpence per person, about forty pence in 'new' money. Gladys' Dad bought a twenty-five-gallon barrel of bitter; two hundred pints for a fiver!

Gladys and I stayed for the meal and a bit longer, then when we had changed, we were driven to Liverpool airport to catch a plane to the Isle of Man. We were told later of the great afternoon our guests had. In those days we were good at parties. For a £4 hire the four piece band of piano, drums, bass and alto saxophone led the way through the evening. On arrival at the airport Gladys nipped to the toilet, and this became a feature of our married life! The most exotic ones found were in the Rome Coliseum and St Mark's Square in Venice. The worst place for the lack of any was in France, from Paris to Lourdes to Biarittz, where all were in a poor state.

Gladys was in the Liverpool Airport ladies, busy ridding herself of the vast amount of left-over confetti and was unaware of the loudspeaker plea for Mr and Mrs Jones to please take their place on the plane for the Isle of Man, which was on the runway waiting to take off. Like movie stars we ran across the tarmac and up the steps into a propeller-driven aircraft and into the air across the Irish Sea to our honeymoon island, where on the following day, the glorious sunshine gave way to clouds, which shrouded the island for the rest of the week. Did we care?

Our married life started, as it did with many others then, in 'rooms'; in our case the front parlour and back bedroom of Fred and Mrs Jennings in Straker Avenue. There was no better place to be. They were always helpful and we were still with them on 4 July 1956, when we had our first child, Christine Ann, just ten months after our wedding. In 1956 we were allocated a semi-detached council house at Gawsworth Road, on yet another new council estate being built just a little way from where we were living. We stayed with social housing, choosing to rent in what were decent properties, rather than buying a house on one of the large, privately-owned housing estates, which were priced then at about £4,000.

Footie, writing, pipefitting and writing again I played football as goalkeeper for Shell, and once again working shifts, joined the club's committee and became its press officer, reporting games for the local newspapers. It wasn't until much later, at a National Union of Journalists' annual delegate meeting, when a Halifax reporter complained of the local greengrocer reporting semi-professional games, that I understood how journalists, rightly, frowned upon amateurs doing their paid work for free.

I learned my first lesson in diplomacy, when as a selector I was questioned by the first-team goalie after he was dropped in favour of the second-team goalie. I explained that we thought the second-team goalie the better choice on form. At this my inquisitor went off furious at such poor judgment. Later I met him in a far better mood, the team's coach had explained that it was a chance to give the other lad a go against a weaker team. Lesson; when faced with a question of judgment, tell lies.

By 1946 the need to rebuild the nation's public services and industrial base meant training and retraining workers in skills previously guarded by craft trade unions through the tradition of 'serving your time.' The pipe-fitting trade was a newish one, dealing in large and small pipework needed in power stations and oil refineries. Shell Stanlow ran its own pipe-fitting training courses that were six weeks in length We were thus christened "six week wonders". I took a fancy to the job and with Eddie Abel of Shell's engineering department being chairman of the Shell FC, his help landed me the job. In October 1956 I joined Shell's training scheme and by March 1957 I assumed the title of pipe fitter. A case of 'not what you know but who you know.'

Pipefitting at Shell The work involved plant maintenance, and offered the opportunity to be on a plant 'shut down', which entailed overtime. The prize was the 'Cracker Shut Down', the closure of the refinery's biggest plant that 'cracked' the crude oil into other petroleum base products.

It lasted six weeks with two twelve-hour shifts night and day. The plant's importance meant a strict deadline, a opportunity for power-mad foreman to never allow a minute more than was stipulated for starting, finishing times and breaks. Working a winter night shift sixty feet up in the air, in a howling gale and wielding a ten pound hammer on a three inch nut was a chastening experience, but it paid well for a chosen few.

There was a construction section with welders and riggers working from drawings, where what you learned was a big help in finding well paid work, for the contracting industry was undergoing a boom. Shell adopted a paternalistic role, which included discussions with the trades unions, with both the Transport and General Workers Union and the craft unions and looked to mutual agreement rather than dispute.

On wages Shell stayed in front of the game. It could well afford to, given the profitability of the oil and chemical industry in the thirty years after the Second World War, and since. Their policy was never give up on negotiations. This tactic worked well in the 1970s when they were one of the first companies to introduce multi-skilled craftsmen into their maintenance sector; the unions accepting the consequent loss of jobs

Shell Stanlow provided the best of health and safety conditions, and supplied overalls and clothing. Every plant had changing and eating rooms, lockers, toilets and wash basins. The canteen food was at reduced prices.

The trade union organisation was firmly established with the plant operators and labourers in the TGWU, with its own convener and shop stewards committee and the craft sector with the same. Those joining the company were encouraged to join the appropriate trade union. Management and staff were housed in a multi-storey building nick-named 'the Kremlin.' The 'staff' employees were not trade-union organised until the 1970s, when Clive Jenkins of the Association of Scientific Technical and Managerials Staffs and Ken Gill's TASS won union recognition and a hike in salaries. By recruitment and merger Clive Jenkins union expanded from 65,000 members to a figure approaching half a million. Staff who had previously seen themselves as above union membership joined in droves. Gladys was on the staff of Burmah Castrol at Stanlow and her wages rose by about a third. She was briefly the minutes secretary at the consequent ASTMS branch, formed in Ellesmere Port, but quickly saw it as a chore too far.

The 350 pipe fitters organised by the Transport and General Workers Union were classed as unskilled and paid sixpence an hour less than the 'craft' sector staff. During 1957 the anomaly of the pipe fitters pay was tackled with a transfer of engagements from the T&G to the Heating and Domestic Union (H&D) being sought. A number of pipe fitters, not including me, found this out and started recruiting the pipe fitters into the craft union. It took three years for the H&D to secure a majority of the 350 of them and recognition of that union and craft status.

The TGWU, accepting the justice of our case, put no obstacle in our way and so Shell recognised the H&D and immediately our officials put the case and won craft status at 6p an hour extra.

The weekly meetings of the Ellesmere Port branch of the Heating and Domestic and Coppersmiths union were for members to pay their union subscriptions and deal with unemployment, sickness and funeral benefits. It now included 350 Shell members after everybody joined.

At this time, on most of the construction industry's major sites there were 'closed shops', where to have a 'paid up' union card meant the difference between a job and unemployment. In many industries this meant you had to be a union member to get a start. The branch had the authority to allow or deny membership to applicants. The qualifications for membership were rigorously examined for both pipe fitters and mates (or labourers). The union branch was a forum for debate for many ordinary working people.

The trades union movement's origins were in the Middle Ages, with the founding of merchant and craft guilds. Guilds would make sure that anything made by a member was up to standard and was sold for a fair price. Guild membership was an honour and proof of a skilled craftsman. This tradition existed into the 19th century.

Stonemasons and carpenters obliged to travel to work away from home, for example on castles, churches or cathedrals and the homes of the great, were paid travel benefits by their guild in order to find work. The guilds also limited or allowed new entrants during times of full employment or when unemployment increased.

This protection of standards and restrictions on employment became in modern parlance 're-strictive practices' and translated as 'resistance to change'. These terms were hung about the necks of trades unions by employers, governments and other opponents of trades unions, which were blamed when Britain's under-invested and outmoded post-war industries lost out to modernised continental and far Eastern industries.

There was more about trade unions then than just work. In the 1960s, the branch developed a social side – financed by football tickets – with a Christmas party for kids aged twelve and under, with sandwiches, cakes, jelly and pop. There were sing-songs, led by who else but me, and games with over a hundred children, which verged on mayhem. Father Christmas, aka our Manchester union official Harry Evans, gave each child a present. At night we held a dance with the branch members and their wives.

Christmas in 1957 had ended dramatically, when at 5 a.m. on Christmas Eve, Gladys woke me to say she was in labour and I should go to the phone box and call the ambulance. At near midnight Alison Marie Jones was born at Clatterbridge hospital.

With Christine now at 18 months, we made an arrangement to place her with Gladys's mother. For me this meant a three mile walk with the pram, while on a very cold early morning, Christine just cried and cried as we made the journey there. By January 1958 we had two children, a decent house and I was 'was part of the union' and due to earn a decent wage.

In July 1957 Harold McMillan became prime minister. A 'One Nation' Tory, he championed a mixed economy and the Keynesian strategy of public investment to maintain demand, winning a second term in 1959 with an increased majority over Labour, which was then led by the right winger, Hugh Gaitskill.

Benefiting from favourable international conditions and low unemployment, and high, if uneven growth, Macmillan told the nation they had 'never had it so good.'

Taking into account Britain's early industrial revolution, our own wealth in minerals, including coal and the super exploitation of the colonies of the British Empire, that was not saying much. After centuries of exploitation and abject poverty suffered by millions of its citizens Britain's ruling class had little to boast about.

Post-war social reforms included the Clean Air, Housing, Noise Abatement and Factories Acts, the introduction of a graduated pension scheme as additional income to retirees and a re-duction in the standard work week from 48 to 42 hours.

Allen Hutt, in his book *British Trade Unionism*, tells of a 'Tory decade' from 1951 to 1961, in which the organised working class sharply confronted wage restraint, increased prices and rents, cuts and a squeeze on social and health services. At the same time the concentration of ownership and capital was proceeding at a pace and to an extent never before seen in this country.

Workers' job security, Hutt concluded, was threatened by increased productivity allied to the growing threat of redundancy owing to automation. He warned of a lengthened working week through chronic overtime.

Harold Wilson's claim that white hot technology would bring wealth and security proved unfounded. British trade unions grew stronger reaching 9.8 million members in 1957 and then to 10 million before peaking at 13.1 million in 1979.

Unemployment at no more than two percent in 1946 held steady at the 500,000 mark until 1967, grew to over a million in 1976 and has never fallen below 1 million since.

Political Awakening One branch night in 1959 we heard the results of the union's election in which turnout had been low. I said to the man next to me that 'this is the way that the Communists get control of the union.'

The man was Joe McCullough, a fitter and a member of the Communist Party of Great Britain (CPGB). 'Have a pint after and I'll explain some things to you' he said. The ensuing discussion set me on a pathway to political conviction, strengthened by my experiences as a trade union militant and the political argument that shop floor militancy on its own is not enough.

On the morning of 20 November 1959, and with Gladys pregnant again, I was about to go to work. Her call that she thought the baby was due revealed me at my most cowardly. I shouted 'I've got go tell our next door neighbour and scuttled off. The baby, Elaine Carol was born that evening.

This then heralded the tumultuous 1960s, with changing life expectancies from the very young to the old. Popular music changed from being largely based on US music, to Britain's own musicians – most especially the Beatles – taking the world by storm. We had three girls and by the end of the decade they were growing up into teenagers.

Entry to the Construction Industry 1960s At the beginning of 1960 the stories of huge construction sites attracted me, and the industry's "good money" more so. The petro chemical site at Shell Carrington in Manchester was one. I couldn't wait to pack in the Shell job, but before being certain of a job at Mattys I made the mistake of putting myself out of work without another job. The Port H&D branch secretary Bert Draper, had the ear of the bosses at Matthew Hall the construction company involved in the recruitment of pipefitters. However, I was soon in work with William Press Ltd., a contractor at the Associated Octel's site at Stanlow,

The agent, Fred Smith, ran a tight ship manned by trade unionists with a shop steward but Fred and his foreman Fred Parker had no messing about with trade union interference in the job. Fred and Fred were minor tyrants, tight on timekeeping and finishing with their men being long time employed and loyalist. They kept in with the client to get further contracts and enjoy a continuity of work. The Octel job helped me learn to use the cutting torch.

Scouting In 1958 I returned to Scouting after a visit from my brother Les and his mate Bob – both members of the 7th Overpool scout troop. Their scoutmaster had left them and unless they could find a replacement twenty-five boys would lose out. The first hurdle was to get into shorts again having not worn them since 14 years of age. I donned the shorts and, readying the bike and with Gladys holding the door open, I peddled up the road hoping not to be seen!

It was thoroughly taxing trying single handedly to keep twenty-five young boys interested in the weekly troop night. They being a considerable mix of humanity in demon form made it so with their frenetic physical natures. The highlight of the year was the rigorous summer camp, which took place without anything of today's safeguards. Why we didn't lose one, with all of them making it home safely remains a mystery!

We camped in North Wales, Devon and Derbyshire. In the latter place it rained every day, and at night I ministered to the sick. By the end of each week I had lost weight, but the experience was rewarding and may have added something to these young lives.

I was by then at the beginning of my conversion to left politics and contend that the 7th Ellesmere Port Scout troop became the only local socialist boy scout group.

The two contractor Freds lived on the same estate as me and later, when I stood in the local elections for the Communist Party, they were canvassed for their vote. I don't think I got it and talking to foremen Fred in the pub one night his view was that I should have stuck with the Scouts.

Shell Carrington Petrochemicals In October 1960 I at last got a start at the new Shell Carrington Petrochemicals site, which employed about six hundred workers. The workers were made up of 'locals' defined as Manchester, Merseyside, and Ellesmere Port, who were bussed in.

It was the first petro-chemical plant in the world outside the United States to produce primary plastics, which were then praised for durability, but are now condemned for the same reason.

A site agreement was in place, with the basic wages, fares and conditions payments agreed. Matthew Hall, the main mechanical contractor on site had a shop stewards' committee, a senior and deputy for the six trades, with each led by a convenor and deputy convenor. The committee met weekly in a local hostelry.

The agreement "encouraged" employees to be members of the appropriate trade union, and shop stewards checked that they were. No paid-up union card meant no start. This then was a "closed shop" on an "organised" site. The site organisation's rules, though unwritten, were soundly progressive, and based on combating the effects of heavy physical work carried out in inclement weather. To this end, at Carrington and other big construction sites, working out in the rain; a practice that British workers had endured for centuries, finally ended.

Working in such conditions for long periods was a major factor causing rheumatism and arthritis, which leaves most building workers in pain in their older years and often long before retirement. This is the norm for construction workers, pain in old age is expected and tolerated.

At Carrington there were cabins for all, with lockers and changing room. Wet weather gear was provided despite working in the rain being banned. There were proper washing facilities and cabins where we took our breaks, each cabin with a "Peggy" (tea boy) of its own. There was a canteen for meal breaks. A new set of hand tools, two pair of overalls, gloves and a pair of steel-capped safety boots were allotted to each worker and regarded as handy for a bit of gardening.

Whenever a first drop of rain was detected and a rush to the cabins looked premature, management and steward debated. Cheers rang out when the stewards won the argument and the men settled into card games. When the management won a chorus of boos greeted the foremen as they called us out.

Snow was a different case, maybe with a ground covering for safety. But we stayed out in the coldest of winter days and sometimes at nights, with only oil-drum fires, around which we huddled, with the time relieved by some great "crack". The conditions brought out the best in the many workplace raconteurs,with their unique working class philosophy and take on the world and the ways of human beings.

The forty-hour working week had just been won and we went to great lengths to curb overtime, arguing that it was not unreasonable to say that a forty-hours working week was enough for anyone working in the construction industry. If the management said it needed overtime to cover an operation that could not be done during normal time, it had to make the case to the stewards. If they agreed, it had to be explained to a "paid for" mass meeting for the workers approval. This may seem foreign to some but why should it be the bosses to decide.

The disciplinary code erred on the side of the employee, with enough warnings to make the sack likely only for the most outrageous of offences. The shop stewards were assigned to a working group or gang, but on a site the size of Carringtons there were enough issues to keep them busy on union duties.

The influence of the Communist Party members in the leadership of these site committees brought a kind of democratic centralism to the shop steward and site organisation. The stewards' committee would debate an issue on what to recommend to the workers. It was then expected that every steward world fight for that decision. Proposals would be put to the site membership and after debate and a majority vote a position was adopted by all, giving the strategy adopted the best chance of a victory. This did not mean victory was certain but it made solidarity the centre of the struggle. On a big site like Carrington there was a time in the middle bit of the construction cycle when the initiative lay in the hands of the workers and this gave an opportunity to make big advances in wages and conditions.

Trade unions were becoming a force for change in Britain, and because of its nature the industry was fertile ground for industrial militancy and for left-wing politics. At present, conditions in the construction industry have reverted to the period when the bosses had the advantage. The Communist Party was a force in the workplace battle of ideas, and despite losing membership in the wake of 1956 remained influential in industry. In 1959, when some Communist Party members in the leadership of the Electrical Trades Union were accused of fraudulent conspiracy during the 1959 union elections, this was used against the Communist Party to some effect by the right in the trades union movement.

For my part I looked to the portrayal of socialism in the visionary manner, as described by William Morris, and remained focused on the battles conducted by the left, both in industry and in the broader political context. Drawing on my industrial experience at the1966 Party Congress, and speaking for the first time in a debate, I challenged the *Marxism Today* faction which dismissed the role of the working class as the leaders of its revolutionary struggle. My experiences at the Carrington site convinced me that advances for the workers and the trade union movement were inextricably linked to politics. Through these experiences I became convinced that the Communist Party, with all its limitations and faults was important in advancing the causes of the workers and their families in Britain.

Party members were heavily involved in union organisation. The party did indeed, "plot" the lines taken to lead the site's battles on wages and conditions. We shared the genuine aims of the workers and comrades in the party apparatus, and in the unions we worked collectively to get the line right. We never thought that our actions were at that time and place aimed at an immediate collapse of capitalism. It was more about the working class fighting for its own interests and gaining organisational strength and confidence. On the site there was a small group, the ultra-left Trotskyists from the Workers Revolutionary Party, which had something of a base in Liverpool, who brought their own particular brand of militancy, usually linked to unachievable objectives.

Sales of the *Daily Worker* were well-organised on site and the paper daily addressed the issues of the day in a way that the workers understood. With the daily sales went weekly collections for the paper's fighting fund. The party and its allies on site organised collections and support for fellow workers in the struggle, with guest speakers from these disputes addressing the cabins, or on special occasions, mass meetings offsite.

There were half-day strikes, usually on a Friday, in support of specific calls for action, such as against wage restraint. One mass meeting featured a Communist speaker whose demand that people should "control the means whereby we live" has stayed with me ever since. The fact of hundreds of workers taking time off the job to go to a political meeting was not uncommon at workplaces of all kinds throughout the post-war period. It was a situation that worried the nation's rulers.

At this time New Years Day was not yet a bank holiday, except in Scotland! The New Year's Eve festivities nevertheless took a toll, and many failed to turn up for work, ensuring that any kind of productive output was unlikely. When the numbers turning up to work on the sites on a cold January day were few, the bosses tried to shut sites, without holiday pay, Stewards insisted that any "of the lads" who wanted to work should be paid. The site would open, not many turned up, and those who were there were sent home at lunchtime; on pay. This scenario was played out around Britain, so that in the end bosses' organisations with the trade unions in support, decided to sue for common sense and on 1988 New Years Day was made a public holiday.

CPGB recovery and revival The formation of the CPGB's Ellesmere Port Branch in 1963 marked a recovery in CPGB membership after the 1956 Hungarian uprising and Krushchev's denunciation of Stalin. Deep divisions in the party had led to a loss of twenty per cent of the membership. Questions around the Soviet Union's action in Hungary had led to a widespread debate, and steps to more open discussions at meetings and in print, including in the *Daily Worker*, and the setting up of the discussion journal *Marxism Today*. At the heart of the debate was the party's adherence to Democratic Centralism, which was scrutinised in a debate and special party congress on "Inner Party Democracy".

The Ellesmere Port branch's formation came after the election of the Harold Wilson government, with Barbara Castle as minister of labour, and the introduction of productivity agreements in industry. We had a stimulating mix of branch members with Alan Abrahams, a UCATT building workers' convenor on large building sites, Ronnie and Joyce White, he being a tanker driver, along with a teacher, a postman, a car worker and council workers, plus barber Maurice Jones.

About thirty members spread the word and put the case for socialism, without hiding our communist credentials, leafleting on the topical subjects of the day, explaining, as we saw it, the answer to the problems of the town and its people. We held open meetings under our communist banner at the Grosvenor pub, and included friends and willing 'fellow travellers' who shared our political beliefs. This continued until the landlord acted on customers' murmurings and said that, sorry, we would have to go. We transferred to the Grace Arms where the landlord welcomed us. We ended our nights by singing a song (On a clear day you can see for ever) before he heaved us out.

The Liverpool folk artist Pete McGovern featured frequently. I organised a folk concert in 1967 at the Liverpool Philharmonic Hall which seats 2,200. The audience was thin, with Pete inviting all the audience to move to the front! The bill was topped by Ewan MacColl and Peggy Seeger, the most famous folk singers at the time, with Willie Russell, the now famous playwright of Blood Brothers etc. On the night over a thousand people were marshalled by McGovern who created a decent atmosphere. We covered the cost of the hall and little else. For the record Willie Russell was paid £8. McColl and Seeger (after realising our plight) chose to forego their fee. The night ended for me in a last-minute dash across to the front of the stage to thank everyone, and was highlighted by me knocking over a glass of water and spraying the front row.

Communist candidate at local elections In 1965 I stood for the Communist Party in the Ellesmere Port council elections being the first communist ever to do so. This news appeared, and was greeted on the front and inner pages – with a picture – in the local *Pioneer and Advertiser* newspapers. The *Pioneer* front page carried my picture proclaiming a councillor's duty "to protect the services of the people without burdening them with ruinous debts". Inside was "the Communist View" and "the case for socialism". These are not often seen in print these days and certainly not in regional or local newspaper form aimed at ordinary citizens.

I proposed "a real Socialist policy," to solve the issues of the day and outlined practical and progressive policies. "In seeking election as a Communist candidate I am trying to show that there is a real alternative to Conservative and Labour policies. It is a real Socialist policy, I make no apologies for the politics involved. Local government is more and more tied up with what happens nationally. The days of the country squires are long gone.

I pointed out that the main obstacle to getting improved amenities was the vast sum – £377,000 – which was 80% of the money taken in rents paid by the people of the town. My solution to this problem – as per Communist Party policy was to borrow from the public loans board at %. This was something the government would have had to sanction. To find the money from elsewhere I suggested cutting defence spending.

"Given the resources, the town could be developed in a different way with much better facilities on the estates, the town centre, places for entertainment and for relaxation. These then are some of the problems we face and I have tried to show some of the answers as I see them". A handsome election address front page had my details and the Party's aims. On the back we revealed the amount of money Shell made per employee in a year. Given Shell's influence locally, I'm not sure if this helped me much in the employment stakes!

The Stanlow ward's 2,600 electorate lived in 1,500 council and private houses but working-class homes. The branch fielded about ten of its members and stood in the ward where I lived. The Port's Labour Party was not happy. At that time, the TUC rules allowed individual Trades Councils to ban communists, a "disruptive force" from their ranks. The Port's Trades Council had no such ban. The Labour Party members on the Trades Council succeeded in forcing a vote to re-introduce the ban so as to exclude me! And they did. It was nine years before the ban was lifted. Communist Party members and branches worked assiduously on local issues, kept standing in local elections but with very few council seats won and none to parliament.

On Merseyside, one person stood in council and parliamentary constituencies (Roger O'Hara in Toxteth). One seat was won in Birkenhead after thirteen years of campaigning. Unfortunately, in the pressure of the Council Chamber, and dealing with a case of travelling people, his socialist principles deserted him and he voted for eviction.

I was active locally through the Trades Council and our estate's Wolverhan Welfare Committee, which staged dances at the Port's Civic Hall, featuring local Merseybeat bands. One band, called The Beatles, played for a fiver a gig.

While I was on the election trail I upped the 'ante', dealing with complaints from the tenants and residents with some success. My biggest success was the creation of a footpath through houses on our estate, which lessened the journey to town by a mile!

In canvassing my opening gambit was simply: "I am Roy Jones, the Communist candidate for the Stanlow", to which most people responded quite civilly. While the subject of discussion was initially local, the Cold War mentality meant that the subject of Russia was never far away. But now and then someone would show an interest in communism.

Illusions grew when a vote was promised and was followed by another in the same street. Any such illusions disappeared as the vote was counted in the Civic Hall. A comrade joined me at the count, where we knew quickly we had not done well. The result revealed that Roy Jones, the Communist candidate's vote was 33! Now I can reveal for the first time that in the high excitement I had spoiled my own ballot paper or it could have been 34. The Labour vote was 1,800.

This demanded all the bravado I could summon, so head held high, I engaged in chat with my opponents. Some Labour Party people thought our campaign might have jeopardised their vote, but when the reverse was proven, they were magnanimous in their victory. The majority of our comrades were deflated by our poor vote. Just two months later, when the sitting counsellor died, a bye-election was called. Even with our finances and morale at a low ebb we went to it again to improve our vote to 41.

By 1966 the branch had recovered its revolutionary zeal enough to decide to stand in two seats, with our comrade Joyce White standing in her own Great Sutton Ward. This for Ellesmere Port was fairly posh. This time we were helped by a number of enthusiastic students, but our vote tally was less than fifty. In 1966 Joyce and I stood again with pretty much the same result. In the election of May 1967 we were on the campaign trail again. This time we had the use of a party van, flying a multitude of red flags and on its roof the latest in amplification systems. It was the centre piece of our campaign and in one day's mighty push for votes we drove round the town giving forth and selling the *Morning Star* as we went. In the popular Rivacre Valley beauty spot one of our crew, Ernie Nutbrown did a great job selling at what we later found to be a greatly increased price.

We mass-leafleted the area, where we were to hold an open-air meeting in the middle of the ward. We assembled, set up our gear and perusing our notes, were ready to give of our best to the crowds. On this warm summer's day we readied ourselves for the people to arrive, we waited and we waited. When the time came to open the meeting, we were without an audience, except for the figure of my father-in-law, who had taken his place on the grass a hundred yards away. It was a big park. Was it the weather that kept the people away? We did not know. What better things could the populace have to do on what was a warm sunny day other than listen to us? It remains a mystery.

As the chairwoman, Joyce decided to make a start and opened the meeting. Everyone made their speeches, four in all, with the sound reverberating around the surrounding housing estate, pinging back at us in triplicate. Our modern sound equipment did a magnificent job. If our message did strike home there was no sign of it from the houses nearby; not a door opened; not a person stirred; not a curtain twitched. When he got home, when asked by his wife how the meeting had gone, my father-in-law replied with a sly sense of humour, "It was hard to find a place in the field"

The 1968 election campaign, my last, was boosted by a crowd of workmates – electricians and plumbers from Wigan and around – who turned out to leaflet for us. In this last of my local election campaigns, five in all, I did pretty well single-handed, helped reluctantly by my children. My vote advanced from my original 33 votes to 130. That I have stood in numerous local elections and for official posts in trade unions without ever winning one has not undermined my ambitions.

I'm not sure about the political outcome of those four years on the campaign trails. My lasting memory is of posting thousands of leaflets through stiff and unyielding letter boxes, behind which savage dogs waited ready to tear them, or my fingers, to shreds.

Public meetings are a feature of local election campaigns, and although audiences are usually small, by featuring straight-forward reports highlighting political issues local newspapers play a useful role. Thus a Civic Hall meeting featuring the Communist Party's general secretary, Gordon McLennan, was well reported especially as the legendary industrial organiser Bert Ramelson spoke at the same venue. Although it clashed with the 1968 European Cup final, shown live on television and featuring Celtic, there were still about 30 people in attendance with a £30 donation from an appreciative attendee. The meeting and Bert's speech, written up by me, was fully reported. Bert illustrated the financing of Britain's nuclear deterrent as like "a family paying to smoke and drink at the expense of food and clothing". In the pub later a local complained saying "I don't think much of what that bloke said at your meeting that we should give up smoking and drinking".

Leo McGree was a famous Merseyside building workers' leader and Communist. He was renowned for his humour and a quick wit, sharpened as the socialist message was taken to street corners and when hecklers had to be dealt with. The stories were legion. A heckler shouted: "Hey Leo you know everything, how many bones on a kipper". Leo replied: "Take your shirt off and I'll count them". In 1970, while on the dole, I researched Leo's life, with the intention of writing a book and talked to many of his comrades from the hunger marches, the fight against fascism, the Spanish civil war and working-class politics in general.

Their devotion to the working class cause took them to Paris and over the Pyrenees on foot to fight for the International Brigade against Franco and afterwards to join the armed forces to fight fascism. They were truly astonishing people, engaged in momentous class battles. Many went to prison. Leo was charged after one incident and when the bench asked him what he thought of British law now, he thanked the 'Comrade Judge'.

After I had accumulated enough material for a short book, a Manchester comrade – Jack Askins – asked for a copy of the manuscript to see about its publication. Soon afterwards, when I was working away from home, Gladys asked if I knew anything about the McGree book. In the *Morning* Star that day a Leo McGree book written by Jimmy Arnison – the paper's Northern Correspondent was reviewed.

When questioned, Jimmy said he had been given my material, and tidied it up for publication. His name went on it, with thanks to Roy Jones for his contribution. I don't know what was explained to Jimmy by Jack as to the source, or whether Jimmy was just unthinking or wilfully taking the credit. At all events it was just too late to do anything, and nobody did.

Paid-off On July 4 1962 after being paid off at Carrington, four of us left our home town in a car driven by big Dave White. We were headed to Swansea's then industrially-blighted valley, to take up a job with Stone and Webster at a plant for Monsanto Chemicals.

On site, doing the preparation work were about twenty of the mechanical trades. Lenny Stevenson and I found digs in Sketty in Swansea where we joined a local young Spanish engineer.

Lenny and I shared a double bed, and with this and dinner, breakfast and an enormous lunch box served up by the landlady, we were charged £3 10 shillings a week. With £5 a week "digs" money we travelled daily in a chartered bus to and from the site ten miles away. It took a couple of days sorting out our gangs' fitters to mates, and I was asked by an oldish Pakistani, who said "I think you a very good man" and he asked if he could be my "mate". Who could refuse an offer like that?

The rates and expenses for the job had been negotiated by local union officials, and included a paid fare home every six weeks. The Americans running the job hoped to save these outgoing costs by avoiding disputes. In this they failed. As we settled in, with no weekend work, we organised shop stewards for each trade. I was steward for the H&D and inevitably asked for more. A paid meeting with the trade union officials was arranged for 2 p.m. in the Port Talbot Labour Club. By the time the meeting started drink had been taken in vast amounts. After about thirty minutes of super-heated debate the officials gave up and beat a hasty retreat. Nothing had been resolved and when in October I received news of a job in Sheffield with better prospects of earning more I left the job. The better earnings proved illusory.

I hitchhiked from Swansea to Sheffield to work on the new Tinsley Park sheet mill. Universal Engineering was a Merseyside firm that employed mostly Merseyside lads the majority of whom I knew. In my first digs at Wath-on-Dearne, I shared a room with a black mining student from Ghana, and the land-lady asked me if I didn't mind sharing. By coincidence that country had declared its independence, and its president Kwame Nkrumah was often on television. Each time that happened my room-mate would jump to attention wearing an enormous grin.

I moved to Sheffield where a large influx of Pakistani families had been hired to work in the cotton industry. They were largely shunned by our own kind, and were subjected to racist jokes. There being no proper housing provision meant that there was exploitation by Pakistani landlords, who housed their fellow migrants in great numbers in the large, old Victorian terraced housing. This inevitably led to jokes about over crowding where "a bed collapses and seventeen Pakistanis in it were injured". About twenty of the lodgers were in digs next door where we had to queue for the bathroom and wash while somebody was on the lavatory. We were exploited by white landlords.

The Tinsley Park site had an agreement on wages and conditions that had been signed before the job started. The agreement was for too little money or overtime for men working away from home, and we were keen on an improved agreement! This was likely to lead to conflict, and I was soon made H&D steward and became a kind of shop stewards' convenor.

Tinsley Park, between Sheffield and Rotherham, had once been a coalfield, and was a wide open space with no hiding place from the ice, snow and bitter winds. On Boxing Day 1962 the weather went from bad to worse when snow was followed by a big freeze that lasted until March 1963. Four of us were in digs in Winkobank, a Sheffield Estate on the highest local hill. At night we threw everything on the bed to keep ourselves warm. Our landlord strengthened the case for labelling Yorkshire folk as "tight", when after dinner we gathered in the living room with its three-bar electric fire. He would enter, complain about the heat and turn two bars off.

On site there was again a war of attrition as we sought an improved pay rate and condition money. This led to two one-day strikes that were remarkable in that half the workforce had worked before for UK Engineering and its general foreman, Big Andy Green, and were kind of his "loyalists" The situation was a bit anarchical, but in the end the management yielded. The dispute ended when Hugh Wilson, a Geordie, became the new site agent and agreed to a deal that included cutting absenteeism. The job settled down and we made the best of things to get some money off the job. The best negotiating situation ever I encountered was when the pump house, built on a coal mine, started to sink! This required a pipeline to be run quickly across the site. The welders thought the situation merited extra pay, so with the pumphouse sinking behind the site the agent as we spoke, it meant my plea for treble time was granted. Thus the golden guinea job.

One day, when the job had settled, I walked out of a cabin with a labourer through a sea of mud. He wondered aloud if I could do something about the quagmire. I considered this was beyond the power of a trade union official to resolve.

In 1964 I worked at the Distillers plant on the eastern side of the Humber River. We worked on columns at great height in icy cold conditions. The conditions were catered for by a good digs' dinner and breakfast, with a lunch-time "carry out" that contained enough to feed me and a mate.

In March 1964 I went to the Regent Refinery at Pembroke Dock, with digs in Milford Haven. This meant going to work in a ferry boat across "the Haven" on beautiful spring and summer mornings. In digs with a Mrs Murphy in Milford, with six Scots and Irish lads – we again had to queue to use the toilets and bathrooms. But the food was good, and in contrast to the earlier two jobs that was a summer of sunshine in an idyllic setting. On Sunday we drank in the British Legion, and afterwards in Mrs Murphy's kitchen. Later we would go to a picture house, but rushed out before the pubs closed and never saw the end of a picture. There was a paid fare weekend home every six weeks. We heard tales of mass fights between drunken protestant and catholic workers before the coaches had gone ten miles.

In 1966 I got work for the first time at Vauxhall Motors. We made six-metres long pipe drop legs, that took water, air or lubricant from the headers in the roof to the machines. The plant had a social club bar that was open during working hours, where contractors were allowed. My "mate" Tommy appeared after lunch the worse for wear. His job was to lift one end of the pipe up to where I was working astride the steel work in the roof, and screw the pipe end into the header. The six-metres-long flexible pipe took on a life of its own as he tried to find me with the other end. I was precariously balanced trying to grab the pipe as it wavered wildly hither and thither. This ended with me, at risk to life and limb, failing to grab the pipe. I told Tommy to make the f*****g tea!

Vauxhall introduced the Japanese-style 'just in time' method of work ing. This was much more intense than normal, and I wondered if it could make the work less boring. Maybe, but this was far from William Morris's vision of work as part of a fulfilled life.

Into 1967 I returned to Shell Carrington on a contract with US firm, Stone and Webster. I was briefly the site convenor to no good purpose. Wilf Charles, a veteran CPGB member explained basic Marxist theory; the "dialectical" approach to politics, with the following question. It is by asking "Is water good for you? but is answered as follows; "Yes, it is to drink, but not if you are drowning in it."

Wilf was responsible when the *Morning* Star Fighting Fund told its readers of a £100 donation from the Shell Carrington Site shop stewards committee's funds; except that it hadn't yet been agreed.

In November 1967 I was at work at the Bradford Road Gasworks, Manchester, where for a week I stayed in a bed and breakfast with the usual communal sleeping in six beds, where on each successive day, were added more beds until they were six side by side. Combined with the large dog guarding the larder, this saw me opt to hitchhike daily the forty miles back and forth to work. Manchester lived up to its reputation by raining heavily most days.

At Christmas 1967 for the first time, but not the last, the union's out-of-work benefit of £4.50 a week, paid fortnightly, was most welcome. There were times when the union money was vital and was spent right away on bread, milk and the bare necessities of life.

I have since thought that challenging wrongs can become a habit, when the best course might be to leave things alone. In this instance, when ten of us started a job at Vauxhall's, there were soon demands to do something about pay and conditions! The workers looked in my direction, I argued it was too soon to have a go as we could get the sack. My advice was ignored and we took our gripes to the agent. The following day we were all sacked! But sometimes you win.

On the Shell Stanlow site, Sulzer was a small company contracted by Shell. The firm kept strict starting, break and finishing times. Working out in the worst of weather, conditions were poor, with only buckets of hot(ish) water to wash in, and that on our own time, Most of the thirty workers at Sulzer had been with the firm for years, and suffered in silence. When I joined the firm, with a reputation of a kind, conditions became a topic and soon the H&D shop steward resigned. I was elected to the position and a majority decided it was time to challenge the bosses and their regime. It was hard going. The practice of working in the open in the rain, or under tarpaulins in wet-weather gear continued. There was payment of "condition money" when conditions met certain criteria. One that was never paid, was a penny an hour if we needed to wear "wellies".

The foremen and managers were amazed when a crew of three refused to work in the rain and demanded decent cover. The bosses, thus challenged, for the first time conceded the following; adequate rain cover, proper washing up time and facilities, and an extra penny an hour for bad conditions underfoot, to be paid throughout the winter, including to those working under cover on concrete floors. There was some satisfaction with this bit of dignity at work especially from some of the old timers, but when work became short, there were redundancies, and I was one.

Harold Wilson's Governments 1964 – 1970 With working people looking for better things, thirteen years of Tory rule ended on 6 March 1964. Harold Wilson's Labour government was elected and re-elected in September 1966. However, Labour showed little sign of solving Britain's economic problems of low productivity, lack of international competitiveness and a balance of payments deficit. Full employment meant that attacks on free collective bargaining were blunted but Labour remained committed to incomes policies. As an economist, Wilson promised a white-hot technology economy, but followed the same right-wing solutions to Britain's industrial problems, and in doing so alienated workers and their trades unions, who should have been his allies.

The Communists said of the British economy; "The roots of the problem lie in Britain's imperialist past and present; excessive export of capital instead of home investment, arms expenditure and a low growth rate of essential industries. Communists opposed all and any version of regulated wage controls".

The Communist Party said productivity bargaining posed "a threat to the workers ability to win a bigger slice of the wealth they produce". It was "asking workers to pay for their own pay rises through their own efforts and redundancy". An aim was "to convert shop stewards from being key lay trade union officials to leading the daily class struggle at the place of work on behalf of the bosses".

One productivity deal that was writ large in Labour history was a battle of wills as intense as at Marston Moor in the English Civil War and it was won by the Parliamentarians. It was over tea breaks. In the construction industry, no matter how high or out in a field workers were, at 10 a.m. and 3 p.m., tools were downed and the men repaired to their cabins for freshly-made tea and a butty. In 1946 the "National Tea Break Strike" won a place in the National Rule Book of the Building Industries agreement. This was our "bible", registering hard-won industrial rights. In 1961, the building employers sought to overturn the agreement by ditching afternoon tea breaks. This led to a rash of "Tea Break" strikes, which the trade union leaders settled by conceding breaks 'on the job' and then by selling off the breaks themselves for a penny an hour. The pattern of buying off conditions was followed throughout the industries where tea breaks had been taken. Then "Tea Machines" spread through plants and factories at the expense of the "Tea Ladies" jobs.

Wage rises had to be matched against concessions that raised productivity (or as workers understood it 'the rate of exploitation'). As Lewis Carroll's Humpty Dumpty said: "a word will mean whatever I want it to mean", and so with productivity.

In 1969 employment secretary Barbara Castle and Wilson went for the jugular with a White Paper, 'In Place of Strife', which proposed greater state intervention through anti-trade union laws, one being to make collective agreements legally binding, and another instituting an Industrial Relations Court, with the right to apply penal sanctions to force unions to comply. This was too much even for the Trade Union Congress, and it urged Wilson and Castle to have it scrapped, promising to put its own house in order, but the damage was done and the thin of the wedge was weaponised by Thatcher in her 1979 government. In the end the bosses got almost all they wanted, and Thatcher was able to carry through a massive de-industrialisation of Britain.

Victimisation and black-listing In July 1985 I wrote in the *Morning Star* of victimisation in the building industry and described my personal experiences of black-listing over twenty years. I wrote that black-listing is the classic way of removing militants from the class struggle. The first sign was a list in a foremen's cabin, with the initial letters 'NTBT' not to be trusted by your name. By 1985, the date of the article, such crudities had given way to "a sophisticated means of central surveillance". The best, but not always successful way to "get on" was by "showing your face" on the site. Obstacles included locked gates, gatemen and threats to call the police. Solutions included sneaking on site with the employed or going under the fence.

Application forms, introduced as a device to detect "troublemakers", went to extreme lengths, wanting to discover the routine information, where you had worked in the last five years, but also what organisations you belonged to and any hobbies you had! In trying to hide my record I put the names of German and French firms I'd worked for in far-off places, but to no avail.

Eventually, from being a 'cause celebre' you became a nuisance. Shop stewards, bogged down in the problems of the site and having tried and failed to get you a job, could very well do without this extra burden. Then came a time when the game was up. The first sign was being told of a job "up the road" that was taking men on. Then the steward would slip you a few quid to "go and get a pint". There were, of course, victories, when persistence, subterfuge and industrial action paid off.

To be accused of not wanting to work was common. One day in the 1970s when she quarrelling in the street with a playmate my youngest daughter was told "anyway your dad's always out of work ". Leaping loyally to my defence she replied "Your dad's always drunk". As chances of a job faded you had to put on a brave face. Problems mounted as you battled with Social Security and when bills arrived. Gladys, coping with little money and three kids, was the worst off as a victim's victim. That she did so with some fortitude said a lot about her. We were always aware also, that knowing my plight, mates would buy me a drink or a loaf of bread when that was short. It was a case of keeping in mind the old working class motto: "don't let the bastards grind you down".

At Shell Star – February 1968 In 1967 the construction had started of the Shell Star fertiliser plant, at Ince Marshes, near the Port, and I tried my luck, beating the blacklist and landing a job with the main contractor, the US construction company Chemico.

I had been on the dole for months along with the obstacles, when by coincidence, Hughie Wilson, the labour manager for the UK construction company on the Sheffield job took the line that the company had my name, and I would be considered along with the other applicants. I thought my chances were slim. The stewards were sympathetic and one day, when talking with them Billy Summers, the electricians steward and site convenor, said out of the blue: "We're not having this. We'll have a go". This started the ball rolling, and with the stewards intimating trouble if the company kept to what looked like victimisation, the Chemico bosses agreed to meet our local trade union officials. The stewards put the case to the officials and Billy Hart, of the Construction Engineering Union, a Liverpudlian and an uncompromising character, said "OK then let's go". Hart being asked "Do you think there's a case then?" replied "Listen, I can make a case out of an old boot!"

This Hart did. Wilson lost his cool and attacked me as a bad timekeeper, lazy and not much of a pipe-fitter. This opened the door to the challenge "prove it" from the union officials. This the Yankie bosses accepted and, with my pipe-fitting tasks watched over by two foremen, I passed the test. This was Chemico's first contract in Britain, and the US 'can do' style was far from the way British construction workers did things. Our customs and practices baffled them, with the different demarcations between trades completely lost on them.

There was the full complement of shop stewards to 500 men: six and their deputies. Billy Summers of the electricians union EETPU was the convenor. Brian Mehan was the H&D steward, and very soon I was his deputy, and Kenny Morley the PTU steward represented the pipefitters.

Kenny Morley from Kirby, a particular friend, came to work on one the ten buses conveying us to and from work. With management agreement it was decided that if a bus ran over an hour late, those waiting could go home on full pay. When enough of those on a bus fancied a day off, they would have a whip round for the driver who would declare himself late.

The Yanks complained of time spent on stewards' duties. When it was explained to them that this meant that any problems could be dealt with quickly, which in fact they tended to be, the bewildered American in question would go on his way shaking his head.

The Site Agreement at Shell Star Trying again to head off militant actions and failing, Chemico and the trade unions had signed a site agreement before a man was recruited to work. Good conditions were won with the provision of proper amenities. In the spring the job was fully staffed, and the aspirations of the stewards grew, urged on from the shop floor, which wanted more money. The company was vulnerable to the possibility of militant action. With the market for farm fertilisers rocketing, the Shell Star company wanted more productivity from the workers. The bosses made it clear that they needed more effort and complained: "When it's raining they all go in the cabin and when it stops they all go home". The stewards stock reply was that there would have to be an "incentive", with the Yanks insisting that the wages should be incentive enough! The calls for some action on pay grew.

A mass meeting under the huge site warehouse – where a high ceiling enhanced the acoustics and battery-powered hand-held megaphone – heard the stewards words greeted with the cheers from the massed throng of men in working gear. The platform put the case that we deserved more pay on the basis that the construction industry was making profits enough from our work while our payment at the end of the job would be the dole.

Government incomes policies meant it was nearly impossible to gain higher pay without facing demands for changes in working practices that could undermine, or abolish, conditions that had been part of British working lives for decades. The Stewards Committee had within its ranks speakers for every occasion, men able to eloquently address massed ranks of workers. Their 'agitating and educating' was a far cry from the style of middle and upper class debating societies.

As it is often claimed. the audience was easily lead, but was sharp enough to keep the speakers on their toes and was also able to sum up quickly points put to them. Our speakers could explain, arouse or calm a meeting, make the most of a less-than-satisfactory victory, and make a defeat sound like a win and make people laugh. When a steward, in despair, proclaimed; "I sometimes wonder where we are going" the reply from the back of the meeting raised a laugh: "Well Dave, you've been leading us long enough".

The response to the claim for more money was blunt; "nothing doing. A deal had been done and could not be undone. It was then "make your mind up" time for stewards and the men to show we were serious. One action was a "work to rule", and following all the rules imposed on construction site work would slow the job. A steward proposed that workers should just do what foremen and managers instructed us, in which case "the job will never get done".

A work to rule was chosen, and this increased the tension between bosses and men, but not without a laugh or two. One such came by what might be called the 'Arts and Crafts' movement on site. The plant processes involved the use of small-diameter, stainless steel pipe which – being ring-finger size and cut and polished with a soft rag – made for a good looking ring.

An inch diameter pipe at three inch long, with welds runs from end to end, produced a wooden log effect added to which was a miniature and highly polished axe to adorn any mantelpiece. A Yankee boss came upon a welder not working. His enquiries as to why elicited the reply that there was nothing to do. "Why not" the irate Yank asked: "Couldn't he be making a fucking log?"

Victory at Shell Star In May we negotiated a £4 a week award. The lads were happy and were making a few bob. We thought this until, as I told the *Morning Star* at the time, Barbara Castle found out and didn't like it. To retain the £4 there must be strings. Barbara herself had told us "£4 is a lot of money you know". This came to pass, and the officials negotiated a deal with the management and that they, the officials, would put it to the men as "the sensible thing to do," not trusting the stewards to put the case for acceptance. This usual view of a shop stewards' committee having some kind of evil influence over their members on site was shared by the Yankee bosses, who saw their troubles about to be ended. They had only just begun.

The mass meeting of Chemico employees took place in the warehouse, when senior local officials, instructed by national officials to take the official TUC/Wilson government line, said that productivity deals had to be done. Their very first words spoken, indicating that there had to be strings to any deal, raised a murmur that became a roar of opposition, with the result that the officials were visibly shaken by what they faced. To a storm of protest they walked away leaving the message behind that "right you're on your own then".

In September 1968 a *Morning* Star headline read "Construction men's far-reaching fight at Shell Star" by Roy Jones, a steward on the site". "A giant fertiliser plant is being built at Ince Marshes, Ellesmere Port" the intro said and that "It has become the centre of an industrial dispute involving marches, pickets and police". It was subtitled; "At Stake: The structure of an the industry – Where No government legislation has improved the plight of the construction worker yet".

I told of the productivity deal where "the strings were far reaching and the men felt that these would fundamentally affect the industry", and that "any productivity agreement is designed to reduce the labour force and thus increase unemployment; the construction industry's worst enemy".

The agreement reached by the officials was entitled 'Interchangeability'. The onus was on the management to have enough men of each trade to cover most eventualities. Instead they wanted to be able to interchange men from one craft to meet a shortfall in another.

Productivity at Shell Star They wanted to blur the lines of demarcation that had been drawn up to protect not only jobs, but also the safety of workers by specialisation, for example, the erection of easy-fix scaffolding by all, as opposed to that erected by one trade, scaffolders. People have died in accidents on easy fix scaffolding. They also sought the avoidance of disputes on the shop floor by involving trade union officials. But in many industries a job only lasts for a short time, and action on grievances needs to be taken quickly by stewards on the spot, because if they are allowed to drag on, the job can be over before disputes are settled.

It was argued: "If Barbara Castle wishes to intervene, it should be by taking away the casual nature of the industry, or by providing acceptable sums of money when unemployment occurs.

There was then a supplementary payment based on what they had earned while in employment, which was subsequently taken away. It was felt that she should tackle the problems of the man who is sick and gets nothing other than National Insurance benefits, unlike in most established industries: "As it stands the fight for the highest basic wage obtainable must be allowed. After a job was finished the worker wasn't left with much to carry him through the lean times that come to every construction worker."

The Strike at Shell Star The withdrawal of the officials left us to stew, but a vote was taken and the deal was unanimously rejected. The work to rule was reimposed and we continued to work as we sought further to get a settlement on our terms.

In August 1968 we were left with nowt but strike action, and without opposition just that was voted for at a mass meeting. We were joined by the other main contractors on site so that 1,200 construction workers were on strike. Thus one of the most major disputes ever seen in the mechanical engineering construction industry began.

Leaving work on a Friday lunchtime to an uncertain future brings a tingle of excitement mixed with some trepidation, a jovial outward mood is of the nervous kind heightened by a few pints before going home. The wages in hand would not last long, leaving our families with uncertainty, and with even the most understanding of wives and children livelihoods being put in jeopardy; the strains will grow if there is no quick conclusion to the dispute. This we realised.

At Shell Star we were determined that people would know about our dispute and its target. On the first Monday morning we set about picketing the site. The employees lived far away from the site but we made it clear that we needed as many as possible at 7.30 a.m. to "man the barricades". It was legitimate picketing, telling people about your plight and asking them for support. Nobody told the police what was to happen! The mere presence of our massed ranks at the crossroads entrance caused traffic chaos, not only on roads to the site and to the villages, but on Oil Sites Road nearly to the Port and the main north Wales road.

Those affected met it with good humour, though some white van and lorry drivers were upset and said so. Lorries "honouring" the picket turned round, to cheers. Men working on the site who were let in to pick up personal gear came marching out, loudly cheered on by our pickets. The next morning we were greeted by numbers of strategically-placed police cars. A police inspector asked who was in charge and the others said it was me. He explained that there was no law against picketing but that it was the police's duty to ensure that other people who needed to go about their business would be protected and that's what the police would do.

We produced leaflets, written by me and helped by the Socialist Workers Party, with two of their members printing numbers of leaflets, which we distributed to local trades unions and trades councils with our arguments against a pay rise tied to productivity bargaining. Delegations joined us in solidarity, and collections were made on sites and in the trade union movement as we settled into what looked like a long dispute. The arrival of a tea and snack bar owned by one of our members gave proof to our determination. Throughout the dispute the pickets remained under our control as we bantered with our bosses, who saw themselves as victims of British government interference with their job of building a chemical complex. George, the second in command, told us after the strike that in the States such disputes would most times turn to violence. Franky (Ski) Gale and I remember spending time gathering mushrooms, which were then in season.

One a Monday morning we found that a sub-contractor had been hired and was on site; as far as we knew doing our work. Our answer was to march around the site shouting "Off, Off, Off". A couple of the "subbies" – when told of the situation – said they would all leave the site. I wouldn't say this was mine or the stewards finest hour but the use of what were scabs had to be dealt with quickly. An hour later all the stewards were called into the office of the labour manager to be told "This won't take long gentleman; you are all sacked!" The CEU Steward, promised that "the job will not be finished without us". Three days later we were reinstated.

Two weeks into the dispute the need to publicise our cause sent six of us on a mission to London. There the building industry was booming, and trade union organisation as strong as it could get. Our first stop was the London Communist Party HQ, where Bill Dunn the London Party industrial organiser fixed us up with contacts in London and beyond where we could stay.

Construction workers on strike against the capitalist yoke, working class heroes all, were feted by young students with whom we plotted the destruction of the capitalist class. One young man I walked with near the Houses of Parliament looked forward to the day it was burnt down; though this, even amongst our own Trots, was not what we were about just then. It was more about winning a dispute and providing for the families of our fellow workers.

I went first to the Horseferry Road Magistrates Courts, Westminster, scene of a year-long strike where the labour force was sacked. This work force were replaced with Sikh carpenters. A TGWU steward was the site chair, and the senior shop steward was Jack Henry, a well known Irishman and Communist Party member. We were warmly greeted by the stewards and took our place at the top table astonished to see rows and rows of seats filled with turban-wearing, brown-skinned, dark eyed people.

The men hired to do the work and those who'd been fired both had union cards, and Jack Henry seeking to build unity had a space set aside for the Sikhs' prayers. Indian workers, and Asians in general I have found, have a strong feeling for trade unionism and loyalty when in a struggle. Jack introduced me, and I did some explaining of our cause and its implications, particularly for construction workers. My words were received with not a murmur from the turbaned audience and I thought "they surely don't understand a word I'm saying" as I sat down to a wall of silence. Jack said "Well I'm sure you think, as I do, that Roy and the people from Shell Star have got a great case and deserve our support, and I suggest we will give them a five pound from each of us. So all in favour," then a pause and every hand in the room was raised, and for "those against" not one! I don't know whether it was in response to my words or loyalty to Jack and the stewards, but I didn't ask.

Next we went to the Barbican Centre in the City of London, where a strike by the civil engineering unions had lasted a year, ending with everyone but the shop stewards being reinstated, and they being sacked. This was the only way a return to work could be achieved, and those going back marched into work while the sacked stewards applauded them in. This time the audience assembled in the midst of a giant complex, where in 1982, Gladys and I would spend time on holiday weekends at jazz festivals, see Hollywood stars and go to a London Symphony Orchestra concert for £5.

The meeting was simply done, we knew we were being understood, and all went smoothly. We got our collection here, and as elsewhere we were given something for "a pint for yourselves". The others had similar receptions at the Shell refinery in Essex. The oration from our electricians shop steward, Harry Shaw, always began with the declaration that "silent protest evokes no response" in his Lancastrian bass voice. Later "H" became a Warrington councillor and its Mayor.

We returned to the picket line with substantial collections. These and other monies in the end did little good, in fact they turned sour on us, in the following way. With over a thousand workers in dispute we never had enough, we thought, to make a share out worthwhile. We decided instead on a strike fund, to be used when other workers on strike came asking for support. None ever did.

At the end of the dispute' we gave the money to another site's funds; some of our men believing though that we had pocketed some ourselves. In hindsight we should have shared it out, even if it only came to a couple of pounds per man. It became a blot on our record. In the third week we organised an open rally and mass meeting in Liverpool's Methodist Central Hall for our members, and support came from other sites, some of which took a half day strike to back us up. On another occasion we put our case to Barabara Castle at the Labour Party's conference in Blackpool, when we picketed the Winter Gardens, as visitors tickets allowed four of us to get inside the "hallowed halls" of the Labour Party's Brain's trust.

The first person we found was Mrs Castle herself, in the bar. She knew nothing of Shell Star or of our case, although she and her ideas on productivity bargaining were the reasons we were in dispute. We put our case, but it was obvious that she knew nothing of the construction industry because her response was "four pounds is quite a lot of money you know," and that was it.

After four weeks we had run the gamut of ways to win a strike. The pickets had remained firm and cheerful, although tension was showing when the stewards met to plan our next move to find we hadn't got one! The strike's effectiveness was in having an impact on the employers' interests as much as the workers. We were not fighting the employers, but a government determined to change the industrial climate, in favour of the bosses. It was a political and an industrial dispute. The Labour leadership's wish to weaken the shop floor organisation and its militancy was matched by a trade union's leadership that sympathised not only with Labour's economic strategy but could well do without shop floor trouble makers.

The only sympathy came from Chemico's on site bosses, who just wanted to get the job done, for which they told us they would pay. "It's not us it's the government" they told us in despair. Their solution was for us to accept 'on paper' small changes to working practices, but they would not put them into effect on the shop floor; nothing drastic would change. We were fighting against odds that needed an army rather than a platoon in a struggle. We shop stewards had to consider then to do a "backflip" and negotiate with Chemico on site. The vote to negotiate around what we faced was unanimous.

At the mass meeting we explained all of this, but added demands for no victimisation. It didn't satisfy everyone, after six weeks out the gate with little more than had been offered. There were recriminations and fierce arguments, but we came out of the meeting intact, although some people would never forgive. The vote overwhelmingly backed the stewards. We put this to those who had been in dispute, including two other contracting firms, and the deed was done. The unions' officials and the Ministry of Labour checked for productivity and accepted. The changes were never enforced on our site. We also demanded that these changes to the site agreement between Chemico and the trade unions at Shell Star would finish at the end of the contract. This meant for other contracts an end to the £4 productivity bonus, but with the changes in working practices taking place. Thus our good intent meant our successors lost out, so it was Pyrrhic victory.

One of our demands did happen through a "Big Sites" annual agreement on the
and conditions covering all major construction contracts resulting. at least for the shop
industrial action. The productivity agreements at Shell Star did little for productivity, so the Yanks
asked us to accept a measured work bonus scheme. This was turned down at a mass meeting, with
proposals from our side of the way to get the job done by paying us yet more money!

The bosses responded by measuring the work done, and paid us pay the money thus 'earned'.
A fortnight later the results of the exercise declared a bonus of two shillings an hour earned, which
would be in our next pay packets. An emergency stewards' meeting considered the outrage of this
'cynical' ploy by the management, but we were bound to consider what to do. One steward said
"give it back", "How?" said another, "take it out of the packet and throw it back through the pay
office window!"

The practicality of this proposal was discussed and abandoned with the lads being unlikely to
agree. Reluctantly we bowed to fate. That week our pay was over £1 hour, a rate that the workers
in the industry had been demanding. Our vow to just work normally prevailed but we appointed
our own bonus steward and, if ever the bonus dipped, a complaint made would yield work not
measured. It was then that shop stewards of ability – or those who were particular thorns in the
side of management – could be won over to take their place on the side of management.

This did not lessen our surprise, when on the Monday morning, a week after our return to
work, we walked into the labour manager's office to find Brian Meehan my fellow H&D steward of
the Friday night before, sitting next to our Yankee boss Bricker, who calmly introduced Brian as
the new labour manager!

This change from steward to labour manager was not new, but rarely on the same site with the
same workers. Strangely none of we stewards turned a hair, as "Bri", who was always a consummate
performer in the art of explaining away conundrums, told us how this was good for all on site,
bringing a less antagonistic situation. There were no cries of betrayal and or accusations of selling
out. Brian subsequently went to live in the US.

First steps in journalism During the dispute a chance encounter would be the key to a significant change for Gladys and me later. One day Jimmy Arnison, the *Morning Star* North West
reporter, came to report the dispute and talking of football I mentioned being an Everton supporter
and of reporting on football for the local papers. Jim said that the *Star* was looking for someone to
report on the games from Everton, Goodison Park, and he'd put a word in for me with Stan Levin-
son, the sports editor. The phone call came, and Stan immediately said yes, he would welcome me
aboard. However, I couldn't get a press ticket, and would have to report from the terraces, and
thus began forty-five years writing for the *Morning Star*.

My first report, on Sunday for Monday 1 September 1969 meant paying for myself and making
notes on the terrace. Later I was given a press pass for each match. I made my way through the
press entrance into the Everton FC Press Box and from that lofty position surveyed the terraces,
thronged with the people with whom I usually shared my views in the pub. This group was now
supplemented by the readers of the *Morning* Star via some purple prose. It put me amidst the most
famous sports writers of the day.

The first person with a cheery hello was the great English international, Tom Finney, who was
a journalist for the *News of the World*, and was reporting on the game. I thus found out that those
who had the most to boast about were in fact the most friendly. In football, and in sport generally,
as long as you were a fan of the game you were accepted as one of them. I never hid the fact that
I was from the *Morning* Star, and all knew of it, and most were glad that the *Star* covered the game.

Most of the journalists were NUJ members, but no one ever asked me if I was a member, nor
from 1969 to 1982 did I receive a fee or expenses. The 1969/70 season meant writing about one

of the greatest teams ever to grace England's top division, which was managed by Harry Catterick and based on the midfield of Colin Harvey, Alan Ball and Howard Kendall. I was transported into the players' lounge on the April day that Everton had won the league by nine points. It was a heady day for a part-time journalist, toasting his life-time club.

In those days the press met with mangers and players, with Northern Ireland's Billy Bingham, who succeeded Catterick, being out-going and amiable. There is a difference between then and now. Then it was the peoples' game and there was much more empathy and contact between the fans and the clubs, and much more with the media. A group of us North West-based reporters met with Bingham in a club bar for a pint, where a fairly forthright but friendly exchange of views took place. I never did lose the thrill of going through the Press Entrance into Goodison Park and up the stairs to the Press room and through the door to "The Box".

Comrade Tim Foster reported on Liverpool, who during the 1970,s under Bill Shankly, were winning everything. It was the rule that the reporter of which ever team was in European and national competitions ties and finals would report on those matches. So Tim got plenty of big games, and I got few. When Everton did get to Wembley in the League Cup in 1972, I was in the North Sea on an oil rig, where I listened to the game on the radio and was still there for the replay that Everton lost. On retirement, in North Wales, I was again reporting from Everton from 1995 to 2015. The Blues struggled most of the time in that period, but it was great to be there.

When Bill Shankly, the legendary Liverpool manager, retired, he came to games at Everton. One day when I going down the stairs, Shanks was walking behind me and he shouted after me "What paper son". When I replied the "*Morning* Star" he said "good, I'm a socialist you know," "I thought so" I replied. You never know whose on your side.

Back at industrial work   We got through the next months without much of a problem, but we were still not satisfying the "get up and go" Yankee bosses. In the July there was redundancy for a third of the workforce, for which we were able to negotiate higher than usual redundancy payments. A second redundancy got me, just. The stewards, seeing that there was a move to get rid of me, negotiated on the "first in, last out" basis. This is what happened when six fitters were reinstated this included me. We had been paid the redundancy entitlements, and this led nearly to a dramatic showdown .This was recorded by me in the *Morning* Star like this: "There were six of us sitting on the cold bleak site on the Friday before Christmas determined to get our just desserts, but beginning to wonder".

Re-employed on the site after being made redundant, we had worked for three and a half weeks. The rule was that you had to work for four weeks to be paid a week in lieu and redundancy money. We learned then that we would no get this. We were incensed, and decided we would sit-in until we had got the promise of our redundancy money.

The response of our work mates to this was not encouraging. Shop stewards pointed out our lack of negotiating power, and advised us not to be silly and to go home, but we were adamant. The site was about three miles from the nearest shops, so we spent the morning gathering together as many left over "butties", spare sugar, tea and milk as we could. We were ready for a long fight. When the time came for the departure our fellow workers showed little sympathy for our plight. Not only that, but they did not bother to tell the firm or the security guards what was happening, which was something that worked to our disadvantage.

We locked the doors and battened down the hatches. An essential ingredient to defiant gestures such as ours is that someone has to know you are making the gesture and being defiant. No one did. We had contrived to be left on a near deserted site, but thought that if we opened the door and stepped out, we would we be pounced upon by the police, so we stayed put. Then food supplies ran low. When I say low, I mean we had two butties, a small amount of tea, sugar and the milk had gone sour. Things got worse when we found we were nearly out of cigarettes. Some of us were visibly wilting when one saw the lone figure of a man some hundred yards away. We called, strangely in stage whispers, failed to attract his attention for some seconds, but fierce shouts brought him over.

We explained the situation, and he looked at us as though we were mad. However, he promised to tell the security man, and more importantly, gave us five fags. About this time some of our comrades were sitting in a pub giving thought as to our situation and decided that our loved ones should be told. Those assigned to the task were surprised at the reactions from the wives. Replies ranged from "well he would, wouldn't he" to "has he sent any money".

Back at the site, things had begun to move, A security man strolled to the window after trying the bolted door and wanted to know "what are you up to?" Without any sign of understanding he agreed to try and find someone in authority, although that "anyone with any sense would now be in the pub". An hour and five fags later George, the American second in command of the site appeared and listened to our case. He lay back and listened with the same conviction that we delivered our ultimatum. A compromise that was more a capitulation was offered, and this was to see us the following morning on the site. We jumped at it.

The fact that when we turned up the following morning the gates were locked, we will leave to one side. Honour we believed had been served, and we made our way home with assistance from a friendly tanker driver. Well not quite home; a traumatic experience such as this needed the consolation of a couple of pints and obviously a fag. When we arrived there, we considered whether our "sit in" could have taken its place among the greatest sit-ins of all time. If only there had been a cigarette machine handy. Such things are the stuff of history.

The marching years – 1960 to 1985 The Shell Star construction site was built in the middle of what should be entitled the twenty-five Marching Years, 1960 –1985. It was a time when somebody was on the streets, demonstrating and lobbying against something bad or for something good everyday, and mass meetings took place every weekend!

The causes were many and varied. The trade union movement was at the beginning of the sustained attacks by employers on hard-won rights, wages and conditions, and they were seeking to restore their dominance over their employees, helped by the collusion of successive governments of all hues seeking to curb the strength of the unions. Nevertheless there was enough of a left-wing influence to curb the worst excesses of the right wing in the TUC leadership, with a lot of this pressure coming from smaller more militant unions.

A move to change this was successful at the TUC Congress meeting in September 1983. Trades unions with more than 100,000 members, and mainly right-wing led, would gain automatic seats, and be eligible to nominate members without them being subject to a vote of other unions. Six seats were initially reserved for women.

This being adopted, the union rank and file at shop floor level countered this move. Industries and trade unions with "broad left" organisation formed opposition groups, with the TUC's own local trades (union) councils. London, Liverpool, Birmingham, Newcastle and Glasgow providing focal points for demonstrations.

The Communist Party was a prime mover in the opposition to this challenge to workers' rights. The most effective organisation was the Liaison Committee for the Defence of Trade Union (LCDTU). Its chairman was the indefatigable Kevin Halpin, a boiler maker once sacked from Ford at Dagenham with twenty-nine others, in an attack on the trades unions there.

The CPGB was the instigator of the committee, but involved in its leadership and organisations were left Labour stalwarts and prominent union activists. It organised through recruiting *bona fide* rank and file shop stewards' committees and trade union branches, trade councils or local union committees. I was then active in my union branch, the union's local committees and with the CPGB as a branch secretary, candidate which meant many a march and demo.

There was hardly a weekend without buses to Blackpool and train loads to London. Every May Day march and rally at the Liverpool Pier Head followed by visits to the pubs and clubs with the strippers. The men were macho then, but the women's movement was about to change that.

In the later 1960s arose the student movements, potent protesters all, which started in the US and spread to Europe and elsewhere, against the Vietnam war, but also to show solidarity with the working class. Thus the cry on many a march "TUC get off your knees and call a general strike" resonated across the country, and just once, it did.

April 1970 – unemployed I was the agent, unpaid, for the CPGB for Liverpudlian Barrie Williams, the party's candidate in the Birkenhead constituency in the general election of 18 June 1970. Barrie was a working-class intellectual of the top rank, his feet kept well on the ground as a boilermaker plater in the Camel Laird ship yard, where he was caught up in an explosion working inside a submarine. He suffered severe injuries to his face and body. He became a Boilermakers' union official. The election was the usual hard work getting across the Communist message to Birkonians.

Once when I was canvassing a block of flats, a man opened the door stripped to the waist and I jumped back, giving I thought a comical version of fear. The man thought not and came at me swearing, and I darted for the street. It was then I remembered the advice to those canvassing flats to always start at the top.

The comrades in our election office were great. A special person was Tommy Hadwin, a veteran campaigner, whose background included fighting in the First World War, the dark days of the twenties and thirties in Britain, and the Spanish Civil War. At the end of the campaign, in which our work brought us 360 votes and a stirring speech at the count from Barrie on our socialist future, Tom gave me a picture he had painted of "Hill Bark", described by him as a "old rich peoples' home" He thanked me for my work in the election during which he had been in the office every single day.

One day during the campaign I went into a telephone kiosk and found a woman's purse containing a fair amount of money. I took this to the police station, and was told there was the possibility of me having the money if it was not claimed, or at least of getting a reward. I never heard anything. Lightning though does strike twice, of which more later on.

Heath's Reign – June 20 1970 Despite, or because of the attempts of Wilson's Labour government to fix the economy in favour of the capitalist class, and his and Barbara Castle's attempts to muzzle the trade unions, the General Election of June 1970 was won by Edward Heath's Conservative Party by a majority of thirty seats. Most of the opinion polls, not for the last time, had indicated that Labour was likely to win.

Heath's 'One Nation' government was in favour of reducing state intervention across society and the economy, where he tinkered in all kinds of ways, to little effect.

His battle with the trade unions outstripped everything, but he lost, bringing his government down. The ground laid by Labour under Wilson and Castle, in the form of the Donovan Commission on Trade Unions and Employers Organisations, was the basis for Heath's 1971 Industrial Relations Act and included a sop to the trade unions with the introduction of a claim for unfair dismissal, but the Conservative government reduced the protection for workers, coupled with the suppression of the right to collective bargaining. The law limited wildcat strikes and promoted limitations on legitimate strikes. It also established the National Industrial Relations Court, which was empowered to grant injunctions as necessary to prevent 'injurious' strikes and settle a variety of labour disputes. This power threatened a trade union with extinction through the loss of its funds if it defied a court injunction, as some eventually did, leading to dire consequences when trade unions challenged the law.

For good measure along with high unemployment came high inflation, which Heath attempted to control in 1972 by the introduction of prices and incomes policies further fueling trade union opposition. Trade union reaction was such that the years of the Heath government proved to be among the most turbulent in the history of the British working class. This period and the role of the Communist Party's industrial organiser Bert Ramelson is expertly dealt with in *Revolutionary Communist at Work* by Sibley and Roger Seifert.

At last, one could say, the official trade union movement was galvanised into action against Heath's Industrial Relations Act. The Trades Union Congress (TUC) campaigned against the legislation with a nationwide "Kill the Bill" campaign. On 12 January 1971 the TUC held a 'day of action' in protest in London, where when 1.5 million people marched and lobbied parliament. It was then that I joined the trade unionists who thronged St James' Great Hall of parliament, attempting to contact our MPs, mine being Selwyn Lloyd, the Leader of the House. There was no chance of this happening, and things just developed into a heaving mass of bodies which police tried to control.

Somehow I got to be at loggerheads with those very police, by demanding my democratic rights, for which they seemed to take offence, and one of them, to my humiliation picked me up shoulder high and carried me to the great doors of the Hall and deposited me outside still proclaiming my demands for my democratic rights. It was to no avail; I was out. What do you do at a time like this? We went to the pub.

After the bill received royal assent, in September 1971, the TUC voted to require its member unions not to comply with its provisions, including registering as a union under the Act. Thus Heath's anti-union laws led to the Transport and General Workers Union being fined twice for contempt of court over its refusal to comply. However, some smaller unions did comply and thirty-two were suspended from membership of the TUC at the September 1972 congress.

The 1972 Miners' Strike, which was the first since 1926, was set in train when the 1971 NUM Annual Conference called for a 43% pay rise, and being a nationalised industry it would be subject to the Tory government's diktats at a time when the Tories' were offering around (only) 7.8%; heady days indeed!

During a parliamentary debate on the strike, in its second week, both Labour and Conservative MPs praised the miners for their forebearance shown during the mass pit closures in the 1960s, when their increases were so small that the miners went from the top of the wages league to near the bottom. On 5 January 1972, the NUM's Executive rejected a small pay offer from the National Coal Board, which two days later withdrew all pay offers. On the 9th January 1972, miners from all over Britain came out on strike. In South Wales, 135 pits were closed; fifty collieries and eighty-five private mines.

The strike was characterised by the use of flying pickets sent to other industrial sites to persuade other workers to strike in solidarity with the miners. This led to railway workers refusing to transport coal, and power station workers refusing to handle coal. Power shortages occurred and a state of emergency was declared on 9 February, after the weather had turned cold unexpectedly and voltage had been reduced across the entire national grid.

An offer came after the Battle of Saltley Gate, when around two thousand NUM pickets descended on a coke works in Birmingham, and were later joined by thousands of workers from other industries in Birmingham. The strike lasted seven weeks and on February 19 an agreement was reached between the NEC of the NUM and the government. Picketing was called off, and on February 25 the miners accepted the offer in a ballot and agreed a return to work on the 26 February.

The result of the strike was that miners' wages became almost the highest of any among the working classes, and demonstrated the importance of coal to the country's economy.

Substantial rises in other industries though saw the miners dropping down the wages league table, and in June 1973 the NUM's national delegate conference passed resolutions asking for a 35% wage increase, regardless of any government guidelines, and for the election of a Labour government pursuing socialist policies.

As inflation increased, miners' wages fell in real terms. In November 1973, the NUM executive rejected the NCB pay offer, but a national ballot on a strike was lost by 143,006 to 82,631. The overtime ban was implemented, with the aim of halving production. This action hurt the coal industry and was unpopular amongst the British media, although the Trades Union Congress supported the NUM's actions.

To conserve coal stocks, Heath, announced a number of measures on 13 December 1973, introducing a three-day week, limiting commercial consumption of electricity to three consecutive days each week. On 24 January 1974, 81% of NUM members voted to strike, having rejected the offer of a 16.5% pay rise and the strike began officially on 5 February. Two days later Heath called the February 1974 general election. His government emphasised the pay dispute with the miners, and used the slogan 'Who governs Britain?'. Heath believed that the public would side with the Conservatives on the issues of strikes and union power, but that was a big mistake. The general election on the 28 February 1974 ousted the Tories, and the new Labour Government and the miners reached a deal shortly afterwards, and the strike ended. Michael Foot was the Minster of Labour and the deal was 35%.

May 1971-1972 In May 1971 someone heard of work at the electrical and instrument contractors Smiths Industries, at its office in Blackburn and suggested I should try there. One Monday morning I hitched-hiked the sixty miles to Blackburn, and there I was taken on for what proved a tour of England and Wales, starting in Blackburn itself at the huge Mullards electronics factory, which manufactured televisions, employing hundreds of workers, most of whom were women.

The first thing to do was to find decent lodgings as cheap as possible, and I found a pub in town at a reasonable price. I had a "sub," an advance on my wages, enough for the digs, but it left little else to spend. It was customary when lodging in a pub to spend some money on drink in its bars. Scouser Albert Ellis advised "always take a sub, they may forget it," which proved right for me, when because of a wage clerk's illness, the sub I had was not reclaimed.

In Blackburn being short of the readies I eked out my money by walking around town to stop for a half of beer at one pub and then walk some more, with another couple of halves at other places, seeing the surroundings and its peoples.

That summer the Pakistani cricket team was playing England, inducing the children of Blackburn's burgeoning immigrant communities, then thriving in the cotton and electronics industries, to be seen on every available open space, with an innate grace posing as their cricketing heroes. These lithe and sinuous youngsters were to slowly to be gracing our county and international teams.

I'd return to the digs before closing time for the last pint of the night, thinking I had done my duty to the pub. After some five days the landlord called me to one side and told me "I've been watching you son! You're out getting pissed elsewhere and coming back for a lock-in. You can pack your bags and f*** off in the morning". I then found digs in the Gibraltar on a brow in Blackburn. A brow there is a very steep hill. The town then had within its bounds five famous breweries with 190 pubs, one on every street corner.

John, the landlord, was one of the best, so I'd go into the bar after tea until about nine o'clock, when the first of about ten regulars would arrive and take their own place behind, order a pint, and be served up in their own tankard which was hung behind the bar. This was a routine followed nightly. If a customer was upset, he would demand his tankard and stalk out. When the custom was thin and hardly any ale was being sold, John would cry "Sod it!, then drink himself into a stupor to be carried to bed by a staff member.

The Mullard workforce of hundreds women sitting at benches in long rows could be ribald in their communications to visiting male workers, and the occasional wolf whistle would head my way. I was there for the annual 'Wakes Weeks' – summer holidays when the factory workers and their families would head for Blackpool – and on the Friday pay day beforehand I was again in a telephone box where a purse had been left.

I took it to the gate man and handed it in. "Wow lad" he said "not everyone would have done that. You should get a good tip for that". On my way out I asked the gate man if anyone had claimed it. "Yes he said a young women came and I gave it her. She just took it without a word and went. Didn't even ask who had found it or say thanks. I thought you would have been OK for something". I didn't go unrewarded, for the next day the Smith boss let me know that he had been told of my good deed, and saying it was good publicity for the company, he added a day's pay, £5, to my pay. It was also clear that the firm trusted me in what became a tour of the country for it.

My next step in this activity was to Hipperholme, up the hill from Halifax, which because it was deep in the winter did not help its charisma. Its buildings, which were born in the halcyon days of the cotton and carpet industries, went unnoticed as I and a welder mate circled the pubs in the town square.

Piece Hall was once home of the wool merchants and the city fathers' 1860 masterpiece of a Town Hall were he site of a few pints. On stepping off the train there was the distinctive smell of Rolo and Quality Street chocolates, made there since 1898 by John Macintosh, from a family recipe of his wife Vera. The Halifax Building Society head office stood as proof of the Yorkshire town's diversity and history, set in a most unlikely landscape.

John Taylor's *Beggar's Litany*, a prayer, has it that "From Hull, from Halifax, from Hell, From all these three, Good Lord deliver us". On Hull and Halifax from my experience, apart from the weather, neither was particularly hellish; the people certainly weren't. No more of a contrast could there be between the Yorkshire moors and the mighty Thames and London's Strand works of Her Majesty's Stationery Office (HMSO), where I spent a few days. But it was also memorable for a weekend's work at Buckingham Palace!

In London I had your typically confident cockney as a labourer. We got on well including sharing a love of football. It was with him, his wife and baby boy that I 'digged' in Canning Town. Reporting at the Palace's Police Lodge Gates, we simply gave our names and were signed in and were then taken to the huge boiler room that catered for the Palace's heating and ventilation needs.

The Queen and family, unaware of a dangerous Communist within their midst, carried on business as usual. I managed a glimpse down a long corridor but that was it. We did our job and left, where a woman and her family were residing in a house with warm and well-equipped rooms, tended by hundreds of servants. In contrast we went to my mate's Canning Town terraced house, where the upstairs flooring was unsafe and uninhabitable. The ground floor was enough for two bedrooms, a living room and kitchen, and was a place called home to a man, wife and baby living with the danger of the ceiling falling in. There could be no bigger example of the yawning chasm that exists between the Queen and her subjects, living a Tube ride away from each other.

Next it was to the National Maritime Museum on the Thames at Greenwich, the largest museum of its kind in the world. There was the Royal Observatory, 17th-century Queen's House, and on the water the Cutty Sark tea clipper. Our grand tours of its historic halls of seafaring artefacts included the majestic *Ships of the Line* painting by J.M.W Turner and roaming the green swards around the Museum and Observatory.

In the workshop one day I told of being from Ellesmere Port, when a joiner rejoined "I come from the Port. My sister's a midwife there, Nurse Boyson," She was the person who tended Gladys, when she was having our youngest Elaine. In fact I left Nurse Boyson in charge when I ran away to work, when Gladys told me she was about due.

My next move was to Dorset, Thomas Hardy country, and the helicopter section of the Royal Navy Air Services to the west of the two-miles long Chesil Beach, later known as the Dinosaur Coast. There were Portland's cliff tops or the road through the middle to Portland Bill (like a crane's neck) and its lighthouse. The roads traversed the quarries from whence came the Portland Stone taken by Sir Christopher Wren, the Weymouth MP, to build St Paul's Cathedral.

The natural, and the man-made environment, and the proximity to the sea give Portland a quite distinct character.

The control room overlooking the helicopters' flying operations was where someone asked me where I came from. When I replied "89 Newnham Drive. Ellesmere Port" his reply was: "I come from 29 Newnham Drive Ellesmere Port". It is a small world.

Lulworth Cove, Dorset's most outstanding beauty spot, with its high cliffs, was just down the coast, with all the homes boasting thatched roofs recalling the visions painted by Hardy. At nearby Bovington Tank firing ranges – where crews practised bombarding wrecks – was the place from where, on the darkest Friday evening I've known, I stood at the camp gates with not a soul in sight, contemplating how to make the three hundred miles journey home. The journey would be via London to home in the early hours of the morning. I made it, but don't ask me how.

A weekend later I was in Sennybridge, in Brecon, Wales at an army camp housing paratroopers in training. The landscape is so hard it has killed a few, with the Beacons to the east and the Black Mountains to the south. Back at this market town I got lodging at the general store by the River Senni, and there were a couple more shops and a pub each side of the road; it was a holiday heaven for walkers.

I was to rerun the system's pipework from coal-fired to electricity in the troops' quarters and office buildings. Yes, from coal in the heart of Wales. A new member of the Smith's bosses' team, who had not heard of my honesty, directed me to the job, so the relationship was more formal and under more scrutiny.

Sennybridge's big day was Tuesday's Market Day, when the farmers came for the sheep and cattle auction; a day celebrated by the pubs being open from 9am to 10pm. Into the mix came as my mate, a little Irishman and with him at hand we started work. All went well until Tuesday, market day. We usually went to the pub for lunch and did so that day. After an hour I said authoritatively, "well let's be at it," he replied, "I'll just finish this and follow you up". Two hours later there was no sign of him, and I was struggling on my own, so I went to get him. Too late; Pat was in singing mood, so I just let it go. He didn't come back to work that market day, so I decided I'd leave him there and join him after tea for the night.

We were using galvanised pipe and had to use a torch. The sulphurous fumes were bad and we had no masks, and as I did the burning I got the fumes full blast. I was dogged by an ulcer and the fumes got at it, and I was fairly frequently sick. Our landlady was a good cook and her salads were a work of art, but I usually got into three bites before the sickness came on and I never finished a meal.

We hadn't finished the job before I was shipped out to the RAF's V bomber base at Marham, amongst Norfolk's huge fields of corn, under skies that spread for miles on summer evenings on a yellow carpet, providing the nicest walk to a pub you could wish for. The V Bomber Force was made up of the Valiant, Vulcan and the Victor, three bombers during the Cold War that were capable of delivering nuclear bombs and which, it was said, formed part of Britain's nuclear deterrent. The presence of a dangerous Communist activist it seems was never discovered.

At Marham I joined a gang of other Smith's employees from Haverhill, an expanded Suffolk

Market Town, where whole London communities were resettled from the devastation meted out during World War II. I never quite got on with the four on our job, but I don't know why. I was given a local lad as a mate, a young man from a nearby village who was a collector of glass bottles and things. When he invited me to his home, in the back garden, which was more like a field, stood an array of steam-powered traction engines that ranged from next to being scrap, to those that were dressed in engineering glory. He paraded them in agricultural and steam-engine shows all over Britain.

One of those involved in the rebuilding exercises was the local blacksmith. This was a trade I had come across in industry, but not in the village smithy, which has been written and sung about in British culture. However, in this case he was a small wiry man, rather than a mighty one, as a smith is usually portrayed.

This was then the less than grand finale of my work for Smith's Engineering, when on Monday morning in Swaffham's town square I waited for the Haverhill lads to be lifted to work. The gang boss leaned out of the car window to tell me I needn't go to work, and I could go home as my employment was terminated, (or words to that effect). I was left to my own devices on a glorious summer's morning in Swaffham Square. Never had I been sacked in such beautiful surroundings.

The chronicled events of travel to work included leaving bits of things all over the land and in my case the sea. At the helicopter base I ran a line from somewhere inside to a tank in a field that could be seen from the road which, later on holiday with Gladys, I pointed to proudly as my work. At the Regent Refinery at Pembroke, Bill Davies and I put the final piece of large bend atop a tall column, which whenever the refinery was in the news, could be seen in the view. As far as I know the pipe can still be seen.

In March 1972 I was working at the new EMI buildings, fitting piping to machinery turning out long playing records, including one by the Bonzo Dog Doo Dah band. I know because I pinched one. This was a job I was never happy in, with the other workers being from east London, who didn't seem to take to me, or I to them. Here at weekends I got to report on London footie games for the *Star*. The first was at West Ham, who were playing Notts Forest. After the morning shift, I put my overalls in a bag and over my shoulder and presented myself at the press entrance of the Bolyn ground. I showed my press pass and was directed by a steward, only to find myself on the pitch, with the bag on my pack identifying me as a photographer.

The West Ham press box then was the friendliest. The Hammers staff served up tea in a plastic cup and some butties. I did other games at that time, being more welcomed by the press gangs (and managers and players in those days) than by my workmates on the EMI site. On the job was "Big" John Wilson, who along with me found the pay not enough, so come the Whit Bank holidays, we decided that on our return we would try a bit of militancy to get more money from the job, only to find that when we came back we were sacked!

A fortnight of nights at Shell's Stamford Le Hope Refinery in Essex followed, where the welder on the job, who somehow had heard of me, commented on me being conscientious in my work, something that I thought I had been, and this was nice to hear.

I was the first one taken on a job in June 1972 in Edgeway, north London to work on the re-piping of the boiler houses that heated nine blocks of eight-storey flats. These residences had been built for working-class families from inner London. Edgeway though, had and has a large Jewish population, and Thais was brought home to me, when one day while we were cooking our own dinners from produce bought from local shop, we were puzzled by the taste of some sausages. Then it dawned on us that they were kosher.

I was able to get "Big" John a job and also for a couple of Londoners; one a fitter, kind of, and a mate. The mate, "Big" Malkie Stewart, if not a Scottish Highlander, he should have been. He was dark, squarely built of iron and, when posing as a crane, was able to grab giant pipes by their necks and hold them up in position, while we lesser men got the bolts in. Because I had been given the drawings and instructions, I was assumed to be in charge of things. This was enforced by Malky in any company introducing me as "My governor" so that was it.

On a daily basis, I had to deal with the 256 resident families, mostly young poor(ish) working class, and older people differing in affluence. To generalise, those with the least were the first to make you a cup of tea, which was drunk surrounded by numbers of inquisitive little kids. Most were civil, though we were put out a bit by an elderly Jewish lady, who guarded her exquisitely well-kept flat by spreading newspapers from the door to wherever we were to go to work in the house.

It being summer the heating was not needed and we completed four blocks. Winter's dawning meant it would be necessary to have all the heating on in a day or two; no chance. Having fitted the pipes and the radiators to thirty-six flats across eight storeys, bleeding the radiators of air in each flat was a nightmare. This was made worse as the work in the boiler house took on a life of its own. The joints would leak and had to be dealt with. There was cold water everywhere as we battled on cold wintery nights to get the job done. Worried women with children had to be assured it would be ok. This was said without conviction, and we unashamedly and hurriedly left.

Friday came as a relief, and with pay in our pockets we went to Edgeware's finest pub, where it was shepherds pie or corned beef hash, chips and peas, washed down with pints of bitter. People never having had a hard winter week's graft will not know of such delight. It almost made work seem worthwhile.

Malky stayed with numbers of people in one of the cheap run-down dwellings around Euston Station, with folks from all around the UK and Ireland there by luck or design, seeking gold or just an existence.

The Somers Town Coffee House, a pub across from the station, was where these characters assembled and there was a need to be wary. Malkie though made it clear to them that I was ok, in fact his 'governor'. At closing time these good folk would go to the Euston Station forecourt, where about midnight the vans of St Mungo's? charity would visit, whose menu of soup and chunks of bread and hot steaming tea was taken. Malkie insisted I join the queue, and when he insisted, you obeyed. I was hungry by now, and it was as great a meal as I have ever had, among good company. I offered the servers money but they would not hear of it.

I left the job before it ended; you can only be a boss for so long. The job did come to an end, but with others more expert than me doing it. I'm not proud of our shortcomings, but they were not the result of not working hard at what we did. Our hearts were in the right place.

While I was working in Edgeware I stayed with Bobby and Beatrice (Bea) Campbell in Cable Street in Tower Hamlets E1, in a nine-storey block of flats. These were then two of many Party comrades who showed me kindness many times over and above what I could expect.

Bobby was a former shipyard fitter and fiddle player, who in 1974 was on the *Morning Star* sports desk with Trevor Hyett and sports editor Stan Levenson and so were dealing with my football copy. He headed the *Star* features department, before finally going full-time at the *Sunday Times*, to become a chief sub-editor. He later returning to Scotland, where he became the chief sub and then associate editor of the *Scotsman*. He sadly died aged fifty-five, in 1997.

I remember Bob sitting on the floor and playing melodic fiddle, with visitors caught up and silent, before he changed pace with jigs and reels to much yelling and stamping of feet. I also got to carry the bags of Bobby, Trevor Hylett and Gordon McCullouch to folk gigs in London, that included the Sunday afternoons at a pub in the Holloway Road.

Beatrix (Bea), then a *Morning* Star reporter, came from Carlisle and from a family, Jim and Catherine Barnes, of committed communists. After the *Star*, Bea left to be a freelance writer and a leader of the feminist movement, the Women's Liberation Front in Britain. She was an enthusiastic campaigner and with that I became surrounded by Bea's comrades and the arguments of that movement.

It is written that Bea was one of a group of journalists on the *Morning* Star who in the early 1970s challenged the editor to break the paper's exclusive ties to the Communist Party and the trade union movement, and to open a dialogue with other social forces that included the women's movement. I can't remember discussing feminism with Bea, but I kind of recall that having a wife and three daughters didn't exonerate me from male chauvinism *per se*. Bobby and Bea parted in 1978, remaining friends, and none of the above altered their kindness to me.

I was working in London in July 1972, when five dock shop stewards were jailed for contempt of court, as the nation's dockers struggled to retain for jobs that were threatened by new technology; in this case the "stuffing" of containers in outside warehouses before being shipped to the ports. Dockers shop stewards Conny Clancy, Tony Merrick, Bernie Steer, Vic Turner and Derek Watkins were picketing one of the container yards when they were ordered by an injunction from the National Industrial Relations Court. to stop. When they refused, they were found guilty of contempt of court and were imprisoned on 21 July.

The jailings were met with immediate strike action on numerous industrial fronts. For the first time in fifty years, and never again afterwards, the TUC council called a general strike.

This so frightened Heath and his government, that the five were released by the Official Solicitor, a person nobody had heard of before, but who was a court official able to represent those unable to represent their own interests. He applied to the Court of Appeal for their release, and his appeal was granted.

I was in on the scene of absolute joy and controlled mayhem as the five came out, one by one to immense cheers and were carried shoulder high through the streets. I noticed, I don't know how, that there was no one there from the *Star*, so I rang the office hoping for a "scoop" but was told that Arthur Milligan was on his way. The strength of the working class was laid bare by the jailing and releasing of the five dockers achieved by the mass action of the labour movement.

How trouble in the Middle East oil got us a caravan In the late 1960s attempts by oil producing states to gain control of their local industries resulted in a need to upgrade refining plants in the UK. At Shell Stanlow, in 1973, I got work for the US firm Foster Wheeler that continued into 1974. This ended, and we were paid off and I took work with Smiths being posted to the St Athan RAF station in South Wales.

Foster Wheeler feared it could not meet its deadline at the pace we worked and we were gathered by the stewards and told that we had been offered £1,000 to finish the job in four weeks, which with some safeguards, we accepted. To pay out the two hundred of us in cash on site was done under the eyes of a security firm's men, in the biggest brown envelopes ever seen.

Gladys and I discussed what do with this big windfall, and decided the next day. At Millers Cottage caravan site at Towyn, North Wales we were running along the sands the proud owners (having paid a large deposit, with the rest on the never-never) of a caravan with mains water and gas, which was not common then. We paid insurance against not being able to pay because of sickness or unemployment, the latter lasting long enough for most of the rest to be paid by the insurance company.

We had many a happy hour there, once we had upgraded to a posher van for us and our families. Over a period of about six years we enjoyed sand, sea, mountains, bingo in the 'club' when it rained and the sing-songs in the Sandy Bay pub nearby. It was rented out early on, but worries of how it would be treated and our needs stopped that. Thus the Middle East oil crisis brought some benefit, besides helping the Sheiks.

The 1970s had swung just as much as the swinging sixties and with three teenage daughters our house was full of boy and girl friends and before long two grandchildren. These friends stood in groups in our front room, waiting to go out, as our girls got ready with many returning to take their place on our much used sofa for the night and sharing in the bacon butties cooked up by Gladys on a Sunday morning.

The music had moved on by then from Rock and Roll, with Bill Haley and the Comets (he had the teenagers dancing in the cinema aisles), to Elvis and the Mersey sound of the sixties Beatles, and on to soul, and in the 1970s the arrival of punk, putting me out of my depth. Politically the 1970s were crowded, as the Tories and Labour governments came and went, trying all the time to deal with one crisis after another, mostly by blaming the working class.

The Social Contract The election of Harold Wilson's Labour government in February 1974 by a small majority, and an increased one in October, saw the move from the Tories restriction on wage bargaining being replaced with the Social Contract, a voluntary incomes policy agreed with the trade unions, employers and government and it was a disaster.

Bert Ramelson argued that the Social Contract had its ideological attractions for many trade union leaders and activists. It was a trade-off, with union leaders agreeing a voluntary wage restraint in exchange for 'progressive' government policies, including economic measures to promote growth, with industrial innovation and the repeal of Tory anti-trade-union laws. Its language was appealing to many, with its reference to social justice and economic planning. However, there was an argument that the trade unions would have to give a lot, and would have little to gain in a three-way contract.

It did bring some progressive measures; a second state pension, maternity leave, ACAS, Income Support, Social Security payments and more. But wages fell behind inflation, unemployment grew and public spending cuts brought new and growing militancy, leading to the winter of discontent and the abject defeat of Labour in 1979. During the years described above I managed to remain active in the work in a number of ways, sometimes from afar.

I was chair of Ellesmere Port Sheet Metal Workers Union, secretary of the Port's Communist Party branches and on the Merseyside Area and the North West District Committees of the Communist Party. I had been a member of the Communist Party for ten years with more than the basic day-to-day party politics cut-and-thrust. The party provided a good framework for political discussion bring together working class activists and middle class professionals.

The debate centred often on the problems of the existing socialist countries. My conclusion was that we shouldn't accept criticism of what had gone wrong in the Soviet Union and its socialist allies with subjecting it to rigorous investigation but neither should be blind to shortcomings but that a system that gets people working together will be superior to one that depends on competition.

Social collaboration and common ownership are the basics. Controlling the means whereby we live and the means of production, distribution and exchange are the basis of socialism

My first reading was in economics and history in the writing of G.D.H Cole, where historical detail abounded with step-by-step accounts of the progress on various political fronts, and the forces arranged against each other in Britain in the late Victorian period, up to the outbreak of the Second World War.

When I joined the Communist Party in 1964, there were many comrades worth listening to on a wide range of subjects; theoretical, political and practical. Among these I particularly respected James Klugman. James was an historian born in 1912, with a double-first from Trinity College, Cambridge was a pioneer Communist student organiser when the Communist Party was overwhelmingly proletarian.

He became an anti fascist organiser, parachuted in occupied Yugoslavia to work with the partisans and headed the Communist Party's political education departmentand edited *Marxism Today* in its best years.

William (Bill) Alexander, born 13 June 1910, one of seven children of a Hampshire carpenter, studied at the University of Reading, then became an industrial chemist and joined the Communist Party. He was a prominent anti-fascist activist and was present at the Battle of Cable Street. Alexander joined the British battalion of the International Brigades to aid the republic in the Spanish civil war. He joined an anti-tank battery receiving a citation for bravery. Bill was made a captain and commanded the whole British force.

Bert Ramelson, who features elsewhere, was born in 1910 to a Jewish family in Cherkassy, Ukraine. He emigrated to Edmonton in Canada in 1922, won a scholarship to the University of Alberta, fought in the Spanish Civil War and was wounded twice. In 1939, he settled in Britain. In the Second World War he was a tank driver, and in 1942 was imprisoned by the Germans. He escaped from a prisoner-of-war camp to fight with the Italian resistance and became a second lieutenant and then acting captain.

At the end of 1976 the Port Trades Council lifted its ban on communists, and I was its chairman, a post I held until January 1982 when I left "the Port" and started work for the *Morning* Star in London.

The Port Trades Council, met in the Labour Club, its delegates coming from diverse and stable industrial and pubic services settings that included oil, paper, manufacturing and, since 1965, Vauxhall motor cars, which soon employed 12000 workers. We mustered between twenty and forty delegates at each monthly meeting.

The trades councils were involved early on in every issue of the day in support of their communities. In 1866 it was the trades councils, together with some trades unions that promoted the first TUC Congress held in Manchester.

Trades Councils in most cases take a more militant stance than union officials or politicians. One consequence of this is that the TUC has resisted trades council having the power to put motions to the TUC Congress. In Scotland's TUC they can!

The Port's trade council banner was held high in far-off London, Brighton and Blackpool. I went as a delegate to trades council conferences at Bridlington, where I was never off the rostrum, something the chairman, Terry Parry of the firefighters union must have noticed, for at Swansea the following year I hardly got called.

A year came when we decided on a May Day march and demonstration of our own. Starting slowly with few banners or people marching we followed a route around the town and its suburbs in an arrangement with the local police, with a meeting in the town's Whitby Park.

The speakers changed from year to year. One of them, Labour MP for Walton Eric Heffer, once a building worker, a joiner and a shop steward on an Ellesmere Port factory site, it was said insisted on the milkman serving the site having to have a trade union card. Eric claimed that honour to a cheering audience.Local Labour MP, Alf Bates, joined us, as did Brenda Dean, of the print and paper union SOGAT, who went on to become its general secretary and later entered the House of Lords. All of them did us proud, undeterred by our sparsely-attended marches.

At the last march and rally I attended in 1981, we decided on a much bigger event, ending in Whitby Park with all the fun of the fair. We provided a large tent for tea and refreshments, hoping for the chance of a healthy profit with a sunny May Day that never quite dawned.

We the organisers stood in the entrance to the tea tent as the rain started lightly and then got more heavy, and it never ceased for hours and hours until late. The rally and its speakers mirrored that, and it was less than inspiring. A few hardy family groups came and gave it a go, but trade was not brisk and we feared for our profit and were right. The fairground stall owners saying that it was hardly worth the journey, as they handed us a few quid with very bad grace.

Gathered at the dance in the evening we were not in great spirits, but then a 'rainbow' appeared in the shape of a raffle of a football signed by Liverpool and Everton players. On Merseyside it really couldn't fail. We cleared our debts from this useful idea. It may have been the best and only idea I ever had.

Unemployment Looms The 1970s was the decade when the rot set in and the promise was revoked that never again would mass unemployment take hold in Britain. Clement Atlee's post-war Labour governments from 1946 to 1953 took employment seriously while Churchill and the Tory government were careful to keep unemployment under control. In the immediate post-war decades the dark days of 1930s unemployment faded from the memory as capitalism followed its natural pattern of slump after the boom with a post war recovery.

Unemployment, at most 2.56% since 1946, rose in 1970 to 724,200; in 1971 to 804,300; in 1972 under the Tories to over a million. In 1976 it reached 1,331,800 or 5.7% under Labour. When it was on the rise for the first time since the war, including 4,000 Vauxhall Motor's workers sacked at the Port's factory, BBC North called upon me as the chair of the Ellesmere Port Trades council. I received a phone call from BBC Look North for some words on the situation. Amongst other things I pointed out that where once the traffic lights on a crossroads leading to Vauxhall would have stayed red as the traffic flowed into the plant in a morning, now it stayed red long after the traffic to the plant had gone.

The story was run on its six-o'clock news, and my interviewer used my words for his introduction to the piece. A week later the Open Door programme was shown late at night where the public discussed the topics of the day. *Open Door* was running a week of nightly programmes on unemployment, with five community groups putting their views on the subject, one group being six unemployed people from the Port.

We assembled in a semi-circle in the Labour Hall, I launched into a rambling speech, to be quickly silenced by the director who wanted a short intro. So I did it again, we did our stuff, it was 'in the can', and the following week we were on the 11 o'clock TV slot.

The fifteen minutes of fame manifested itself quickly when a woman passed me on a bike shouting: "Saw you on the Telly last night". She was a neighbour who had never spoken to me before and hasn't since. That went on for days. The concluding show was to feature two people from each group appearing on the Saturday night, live at the BBC Television Centre, and I was to be the chair! A Liverpudlian, Jimmy, was the other person. Among the other groups on the show were housewives from the Midlands and Yorkshire miners.

We were to take our wives, and on Friday Gladys and I and Jimmy and his wife travelled down to London (all our expenses being paid for by the BBC) to an hotel overlooking the Lords Cricket ground. On the Saturday evening we were at the BBC in Shepherds Bush and being taken to "hospitality", on the way to which we encountered Michael Parkinson, then a famous television celeb and on his arm was Hollywood film star Shirley MacLaine. We had arrived.

We were told that with BBC Two's Midnight Movie – films on TV were rare then – was on after us and our audience would be about two million. Something to conjure with as we went live at 11pm, six groups of two spread across a bare studio.

I had to set off the discussion, but once started it needed little from me, with the couples chosen for their gift of the gab. All I remember was that the housewives (of the middle class) were sympathetic to the unemployed, and the Yorkshire miners took the line that those on the dole didn't want work.

The BBC staff, who had worked with us, including the camera crew were happy with our efforts and much drink was taken in the hospitality suite into the early hours. We were joined by our daughter, Allison, who was working in London, and Paul Bonner, the series' producer, who was later to be head of BBC Two and who praised us for our work. The "Saw you on the tellly' cry was heard again among the citizens of the Port. My television career ended there.

The Ellesmere Port Trade Council followed the best traditions of these bodies close to the communities and was a proving ground for trade union delegates, many of whom, acting outside their industries, in this way learned the trade of conducting local affairs and producing leading figures. From these experiences came mayors of the borough and MPs.

October 1974 – February 1977 For the next two and a half years, from October 1974 to February 1977, my jobs were many and varied, and were mixed with spells on the dole, happily of not too long a duration. Alan Abrahams, a comrade, himself a joiner employed me to strip out a heating and water system. This went well until after I had replaced the pipework with new piping and turned on the water. There was water everywhere. How I made the repairs without the water scarring the ceiling underneath will never be known.

This was different from a period as a maintenance fitter in the brickworks in the nearby Wirral village of Hooton, which stood amidst the kilns and ovens that for a hundred years had produced the bricks for local and national use.

My past caught up with me with jobs abruptly ending at home and away. First was the locally notorious Cabot Carbon plant, producing the carbon for vehicle tyres and other black rubber products. Sited at the edge of two huge housing estates, the air around it carried enough carbon to paint houses a faint blue. I worked there for a week, having been given a chance by an old boy scout mate, turned entrepreneur. I was kitted out so as to minimise the oily blue carbon that coated the skin, no matter the amount of bathing you did. Sadly the management found out that an infamous red was on site, (the plant was in my council constituency), and according to my foreman had panicked, demanding my removal, which took place immediately.

I was removed from another job at Stanlow after being given a start by a shop steward mate, turned labour manager, when Shell, disturbed by my presence, intervened, and I was gone after the mandatory six weeks. My shortest stay in work was when I went with mates working on the steel works in Bilston, Staffs, about 70 miles from home, where I started at 8 a.m and was gone by the lunch break.

An attempt to add to my skills took me on a six-months' welding course, which paid more than the dole, and had travelling expenses to its Runcorn base. To tell the truth, apart from the money it did me little good , but a course for hairdressing came in handy. In the 1970s men's hair fashion was long haired, (the pop groups and footballers leading the way). I followed, and if I say so myself, my hair was luscious. I took my long locks once a month to the school's hairdresser salon, where I was what the apprentice barbers were looking for; and it was free!

October 1975 The Communist Party campaigned for a No vote in the Common Market referendum of June 5 1975, concerning continued membership of the EU. The electorate said yes, with 67% in favour, on a 65% turnout.

On March 16 1976 Harold Wilson resigned as prime minister, and James Callaghan, who was sixty-four, was elected leader with Denis Healey his deputy. This heralded a difficult period for the Labour Government, so nothing new there. Inflation stood at 16.5%, one of the highest figures since records began, and at one stage during the year inflation exceeded 24%. In December Denis Healey "successfully" negotiated a £2.3 billion loan from the International Monetary Fund on condition that £2.5 billion would be cut from public expenditure.

The demise of Heath was followed by two Harold Wilson governments, on 4 March 1974 a minority administration, and on October 1974 Labour won by three seats. In February 1975 Thatcher was elected leader of the Conservative Party after a stint as Heath's education secretary, during which she in famously ended free school milk for all children. Marchers chorused: "Thatcher the Milk Snatcher!"

By 1976 inflation was 20% and later was rarely below 10%. Unemployment was well over one million. This was because advanced engineering techniques required fewer personnel and this resulted in closures of "uneconomic" factories and coal mines.

In March 1976 Wilson resigned and was replaced by James Callaghan. In a year the Labour majority was eliminated and the Lib-Lab pact made in March 1977 governed for sixteen month. Callaghan's response to double-digit inflation and rising unemployment was to to cut public expenditure with a move towards Thatcher's monetarism. By September 1978, economic growth was firmly re-established and inflation was below 10%, at the expense of the unemployed, whose numbers were at a postwar high of 1.5 million. The opinion polls showed a clear Labour lead and Callaghan was expected to call a general election. He ducked it to pave the way to fifteen years of Tory government.

The workers fought back on pay, with widespread strikes by private and public sector trade unions during the coldest winter for 16 years. Thus came 'The Winter of Discontent of 1978–79', which was over-egged by the media helped by scenes of rubbish piled high.

In September 1978 in a strike at Ford, with all 23 plants idle, workers demanded in excess of 20%, and got 17%. TGWU lorry and oil tankers drivers struck and won between 17 and 20%. This encouraged groups of workers, particularly low-paid workers in the public sector into action.

In a twenty-four-hour strike on January 22, public service workers, in mainly in local government demanded a £60 per week minimum wage. It was the biggest individual day of strike action since the General Strike of 1926. ASLEF train drivers and NUR staff were on a series of 24-hour strikes, and on 18 January the Royal College of Nursing asked for 25% average rise for nurses. Ambulance workers then took action, wih the media announcing that 1,100 out of 2,300 NHS hospitals were only treating emergencies and that practically no ambulance service was operating normally.

Gravediggers' Strike When gravediggers, who were members of the GMWU, struck in Liverpool and in Tameside, leaving bodies unburied, it signalled any amount of horror stories of the consequences by the media. There were in effect no great problems as to the unburied bodies, although the relatives were concerned. The gravediggers settled for a 14% rise. The local authority workers' dispute was agreed, and workers got an 11% rise, plus £1 per week,

On a June day in 1978 I was working on a job on the Shell Site at Carrington, when the third most consequentially important episode in, by now, our lives took place. This was when Colin Clarke, a pipefitter from near Wigan, said to me "Listen Roy Jones, you have been travelling the country hitching lifts for long enough, I have a new car and I will give you my old one".

I took the car, a Morris Traveller, and at the age of forty-nine, passed my driving test and took off on thousands and thousands of miles all over England, Scotland, Wales and Ireland, and then sailed on ferries to Europe and drove through France, Austria and throughout Europe.

Approaching Thatcherism In March 1979 Thatcher made her move and won a vote of no confidence in Callaghan and his Labour government. The General Election on May 7 1979 returned the Tories. The result was Conservatives 339 seats, Labour 269 and the Liberals 11.

One of Thatcher's first acts was literally, the Housing Act 1980, which gave five million council-house tenants in England and Wales the right to buy their house from their local authority at a greatly reduced price. This is seen as a defining policy of Thatcherism. However, despite the local councils being promised the money gained by the sales to build more houses, they were denied it. This led to a shortage of houses for rent, and to a perception that those buying their own houses were superior to council house tenants. The endless struggle to ensure that everyone, no matter what their status has at least a decent home is a struggle that still goes on.

For the record, in 1981 we were offered our council house, which was valued at £5,000, which was a bargain, but which we refused, pointing out that it meant a shortage of houses for the poor, thus leaving some without shelter or still living in squalid conditions, and we were right.

By the time Margaret Thatcher left office in 1990, 1.5 million council houses were sold, or 67% of the stock. By 1995 the figure was 2.1 million, and as a result of the Right to Buy the Treasury received £28 billion.

On November 10 1980 Michael Foot was elected leader of the Labour Party. Foot was a journalist, a historian and anti war, and unlike most politicians was a giant intellect.

In January 1982, three years in from the Tory election victory, Margaret Thatcher's objective of shackling the trade unions and their ability to unite the working class was in full swing, and went with a move to 'liberalise' the British economy through deregulation, privatisation, and the promotion of 'enterprise'. A quote from an unknown source said at the time "The taming of inflation displaced high employment as the primary policy objective".

At the beginning of 1978 a lecture by Marxist historian Eric Hobsbawm looked to analyse the changes in the structures of Britain's productive capacity as: routine clerical labour was replaced by computer-aided information technology; the traditional bastions of working -class organisations were in rapid decline and financial services growing and; company and plant-wide bargaining replaced industry and sector-wide bargaining which undermined solidarity, and weakened the political and industrial coherence of the labour movement.

This led to *Marxism Today*, by then under the control of a CPGB faction whose argument was that new social forces were ascendant. This was understood to replace the Marxist view of the working class as the prime revolutionary force.

Thatcher started out by increasing interest rates to slow the growth of the money supply and thus lower inflation, with a preference for indirect taxation over taxes on income, and value added tax (VAT) was raised to 15%, a move which hit working class families hardest. It still does. These moves saw over two million manufacturing jobs lost in the recession of 1979–81. The industrial base was so reduced that thereafter the balance of payments in manufactured goods was in deficit. They have never recovered. Unemployment exceeded two million by the autumn of 1980, and soared further. It exceeded 2.5 million by the summer and was heading towards three million before Christmas. The government's popularity plunged. This then was the political and industrial situation when I joined the *Morning Star*.

The move into journalism In December a call came from Mike Pentelow, saying that the *Star* was going to interview people for a job on the industrial desk and did I want to apply. Two weeks later I was in the *Morning Star* offices in Farringdon Road, London along with one other candidate.

The interview panel was the editor, Tony Chater, his deputy, David Whitfield, Peoples Press secretary, Mary Rosser, the news editor Roger Bagely and Mike. This was a new process. Previously jobs on the *Star* either went with younger people on the subs desk or people placed through their party contacts.

At the interview Mary Rosser seemed uncertain of Gladys and I being able to settle in London; a point she made more than once. However, years later she took the credit for employing me, saying "I'm not sure all of my editorial comrades always agreed".

The job was on offer because the paper had been urged or bullied by the right wing grouping of *Marxism Today*, which was in the ascendency in the Communist Party, as per Eric Hobsbawm above, avowing that the working class was no longer the (revolutionary) force for change. The paper's "style and content" had been challenged, with *Marxism Today*'s clique looking for more of a Guardianesque style that would appeal to the new social forces more likely to be middle, rather than working class. The *Star* had followed these lines, only to find that the new social forces did not buy the paper and that many of the labour movement activists who had bought, and sold, the paper had stopped doing so.

This a note to explain that the decision to expand the industrial desk to three was quite a departure in that before it, Charlie Brewster and Mike Pentelow had together been covering the trade union and industrial affairs. Then Mike had done it alone, and this was an impossible task to do what the *Star* needed. Tony and Mary had decided the *Star* had to return the paper to its roots and to the support of the trade union and labour movements, financially, but politically as well. This put the paper firmly in conflict with the *Marxism Today* faction, and the administrative arm the CPGB's executive. I was being considered for my industrial experience and reputation (can't think of a better word) among the trade union rank and file, and some of its leaderships.

After the grilling I waited while the other candidate was being interviewed and when he left, I waited for the verdict. Mike came out and said "I think it will be ok", and Roger murmured something the same. It was Tony who said I had the job and added: "We will train you for six months and then decide whether you keep the job". Nobody ever did say whether I had passed the test and I never asked, and so off we went. I was over the moon, and agreed to start work at the *Morning Star* on Monday January 4 1982.

Settling in at the *Morning Star* I drove to London in blizzard conditions, with the snow lying thickly on the ground. I was at the office that morning taking my place at one of three desks that made up the industrial department. I felt strangely at home where some illustrious names had gone before. The fact that I had gone from pipe-fitting to journalism I explained as "the pen is mightier than the sword, and much lighter than a set of 36-inch Stilsons".

I never dwelt on this dramatic change of employment. Not having being formally educated in writing or grammar, I barely knew a noun from a verb. All my knowledge of how to write I simply absorbed from reading. It's a reason or a weak excuse that I was so eager to tell the heroics and some failures of the working class I didn't look to correct mistakes. I kept to my headmaster, Mr Stirk's maxim, "if maybe you are not good at something, don't say so, let them find out for themselves".

More than one sub-editor, jokingly or otherwise, was wont to point up the matter, and in a spoof front page of the *Star*, printed on my retirement after 13 years, the leading comment was that this would lead to the loss of four sub-editors' jobs. The doubt about my erudition was shown when, in a report from the TUC Congress about a charity cricket match, I wrote of "white flannelled fools" (Kipling). Back at the office Graeme Trickey, the chief sub, asked about this. There had been some discussion among the subs about whether I would know of the quote". When I replied "Kipling" He said "I said you would. know" There was no bet on it though. Mike (Pentelow) and Jo Stanley, later joining us from the features department greeted me with great kindness and help, and so we had lots of bases covered by this new regime.

I was found accommodation with a comrade, Sonia Williams, in East Dulwich in south London, in a fairly leafy suburb allied to working-class Peckham. I was welcomed by Sonia and a number of comrades there.

The *Star* office, at 75 Farringdon Road, London EC1 was a stone's throw from Fleet Street, and had been opened with huge acclamation in 1945, for the sum of £48,000 by its predecessor the *Daily Worker*, founded by the CPGB on 1 January 1930 (the same year I was born). Since 1945, it has been owned by the People's Press Printing Society. The paper's editorial stance was in line with *Britain's Road to Socialism*, the programme of the Communist Party of Great Britain. Its name was changed to the *Morning Star* in April 1966, again in an attempt to associate itself with a broader audience and to move away, by accident or design, from its dependence on working-class people for its readership and their efforts for its survival.

The décor was simple; faded green and shabby cream throughout. But it was a building where what was produced was more important, rather than what it looked like. Its heart was firmly in the right place with the oppressed of Britain and the world.

The building ranged over four floors, with a spread of administration, including the secretary, Mary Rosser's office, circulation, distribution, finance, The fighting fund, the cartoonist and graphics, maintenance, pictures, Part (Mantle) Alex (Apperly) and (later) Ernie Greenwood.

The editorial section was set in second-floor desks facing the street windows, including the sports desk, general reporters, foreign and diplomatic correspondents. Then there were industrial department and the news editor, and finally, left to right, Helen Bennet, Bill Wainwright then politicals Mike Ambrose and mostly Tony Clark. The subs sat on the right, at right-angles to the other desks in a line of two or three. The editor, Tony Chater's office had a door that was often closed. Now and again Tony would emerge, walk behind a reporter, and ask for 'a word with you'. Features was at the back.

One other person was the legendary Alf Rubin (Cayton), the racing tipster, a little Jewish man who had been with the paper for fifty years. On three occasions he had won the national newspapers' award Tipster of the Year, his daily naps making the most profit from a £1 bet during a flat or jump season. Punters winning from his tips would pass on money to the paper's fighting fund.

The basement housed the print workers, their wonders to perform, tending the printing press. Here they brought to print life the pictures, news and features from Britain and around the world that was sweated over and churned out on typewriters through the work of proof readers, typesetters and machine minders into what was , to my eyes. a more ordered thing of beauty.

It was a daily miracle, whose owners were its readers.

Once the editorial work was done, we would join admin and other staff in the Metropolitan pub next door, to await the circulation manager to deliver the first papers.

This was the result of our day's work which we then poured over, marvelled at, and then we moaned a bit at what we had produced. There is now nothing quite like it any more.

The *Star*'s print workers of the craft union, belonged to the National Graphical Association (NGA), and covering all the other staff, including distribution was SOGAT, the Society of Graphic and Allied Trades. The engineers, electricians and other crafts were covered by the appropriate craft unions. Each had fathers or mothers of the chapel (shop stewards). We of the NUJ were in the Farringdon Branch that included the *Times*, the *Guardian*, the *Star* and others, all meeting once a month. This for me was April 1982.

The pay then was £8,000, (the average wage in 1982), but I had to maintain myself and send monies home. The average daily paper journalist's pay was higher, higher still for specialists, of whom I was one, at least in name.

With Mike and Jo, I was a member of the Labour and Industrial Correspondents group, and within its ranks were all those claiming such titles on national newspapers, London titles, television and radio staff and agency staff. This was when 'industrials' worked together to cover the news and when industry, particularly manufacturing, was central to the nation's news. The group had mostly come through the ranks of local to regional to national newspapers and other media particularly, in huge industrial regions.

Comrades would question me on being part of this group (of the capitalist media). I explained that journalists, as with others, have to ply their trade for those who own the means by which they work. There were a number of left-leaning reporters working for right-wing newspapers because they had to; some were of the same minds as their employers some were not.

Reporting an industrial dispute for the *Morning* Star, a highly political organ, we had a mind to the workers "winning the dispute", which if they were big enough and important enough would weaken the ruling class's strength, even if only slightly. The Tory, anti-trade union legislation of seven Acts of Parliament between 1980 and 1993 was either carefully planned or made up as they went along. I think the latter, as evidenced below, but no matter it worked, I'm sorry to say. It was initiated by the Tory, Thatcher government, carried on by John Major governments, and maintained by the Blair government for good or ill. History will decide. Here's how it went.

Background to Tory anti-trade unionism Trade unions organisation and its practices effectively grew out of the struggle to advance workers' wages and conditions, against unwilling industrialists and governments. That they succeeded could be judged by the lengths taken to combat workers' advances.

The Tories main bone of contention was how votes were conducted in trade unions. Each union had its own rules but usually the election of trade union officials saw ballot papers distributed in union branches and at shop floor level, with branch officials and shop stewards naturally able to offer advice to union members. Voting for industrial action frequently took place in the workplace in order to quickly resolve issues locally.

Picket lines and and 'flying pickets' were usually peaceful but they were inevitably potential points of conflict. The closed shop was a workplace where a paid up union card was essential to secure a job and also to access benefits like strike pay or the union's welfare and unemployment benefits.

By the 1970s, the three powers were in play in the world of work; the government, the employers and the trade unions, were all concerned with shop-floor militancy, for different reasons. Trade unions had limited immunities in the conduct of their affairs and industyrial action going back to a compromise reached in the early twentieth century.

Taking account of the failure of both Edward Heath Industrial Relations Act and Barbara Castle's failed *In Place of Strife* proposals the Tories strategy was to conduct a prolonged 'salami slice' assault on trade union and employment rights.

The initial move was decreed that presidents, general secretaries and executive committees should be directly elected by secret postal ballots.

Closed shops were dealt with simply by making it unlawful to refuse a person employment whether that person is or is not a member of a trade union. Union affiars were regulated by the establishment of a Certification Officer, who oversaw an official list and schedule of trade unions and their annual returns, of employers' associations and their annual returns and could investigate complaints from union members. This put the power in the hands of the employers, including the government as employers, and barriers in the way of the workers and their trade unions.The Acts ensured that only disputes between employers and their workers concerning working conditions, wages, etc were legal. Support by others for workers in a particular struggle – that is solidarity 'secondary action', was made illegal. Picketing was limited to six people.

Threatening or abusive language, causing an obstruction and damage to property, could bring legal action. Trespassing, nuisance or being told to stop picketing by police and refusing, could lead to arrest. Immunity from civil action for trade unions was brought into line with that for individual trade union officials, making the trade unions open to damages with a maximum fine of £200,000.

Trade unions that ignored a high court injunction could be charged with contempt of court and fined, and if they refused to pay, they could have their assets seized. This gave employers a more immediate remedy than suing unions for damages, something that became possible again. The 1906 Trade Disputes Act had denied the employers this option. The employers, and others with grudges, real and imaginary against trade unions, used this ploy to great effect. This threat to union funds was the single biggest factor in curbing/ending trade union powers to act in advancing and defending their members by even the most militant-minded of the union leaderships, and there weren't many of them to start with.

In June 1984 most trade unions were still pledging "complete opposition to the Tory anti-trade union laws". In fact the Labour movement failed to muster its undoubted strength to fight effectively against the Tory aims.

The Employment Protection Act 1975 that established machinery for promoting the improvement of industrial relations; to enable trade unions to secure recognition for the purposes of collective bargaining was repealed in 1991. This decision led to wholesale de-recognition of trade unions in some industries, with a major decline in the wages and conditions of workers in those industries, and unions in industries escaping de-recognition were weakened in their ability to do just that. In The Employment Relations Act 1999 Labour introduced a new statutory trade union recognition procedure for trade unions with more than 20 employees, where a majority of the relevant workforce wanted it. This meant that trade unions could gain,or regain recognition at sites and in industries where a majority of the workers voted yes. However, unions still haven't retrieved the position they had prior to this anti-trade union law.

On 2 March 2010 the Employment Relations Act 1999 (Blacklists) Regulations outlawed blacklisting and discrimination in relation to recruitment or treatment. In 2014 blacklisting was proved against certain employers in the construction industry, and hundreds of blacklisted workers received compensation for such discrimination. This was a case of the biter bit.

The incoming 1979 Labour government kept almost every aspect of Conservative anti-trade union law; dubbing it 'fairness not favours', as if the right to strike was a favour." There will be no going back.

The days of strikes without ballots, mass picketing, closed shops and secondary action are over. The changes we propose will have Britain the most lightly-regulated labour market of any leading economy in the world". These laws remain the same today.

Although workers' collective action – including the right to strike – is a fundamental human right recognised in international law, guaranteed by the European Convention on Huma Rights it remains a focus of sharp conflict and persistent litigation.

In parctice British employment law has become, in the words of Tony Blair's boast: "the most restrictive on trade unions in the Western world".

Unions must hold a ballot of the workforce to go on strike; tell the employer of the timing and duration of the strike. Unions cannot carry out industrial action for a purpose unrelated to terms and conditions of the workers' employment contract nor take industrial action against anyone but the employer of the affected workers. Strikers must remain peaceful when conducting picket lines.

If those rules are breached, a trade union will be liable for damages to the employer for the cost of the industrial action, an injunction may be issued against the industrial action going ahead, and workers may be fired even for a good faith trade dispute.

Reporting from conferences and congresses On June 8 at the GMB conference Neil Kinnock told of leaked documents revealing that Thatcher's cabinet had instructions to settle a rail pay dispute, thus causing division, with the miners proclaiming that Britain was "moving towards the most centralised state in British history". He was making a plea for "democracy and liberty, as "the only way working people have made progress". Kinnock was again a man of fine words, but little action for those in struggle.

A TUC Special Conference on 5 April 1982, voted to support an eight-point plan to oppose the Act. It encouraged unions to refuse to vote in closed-shop ballots, to support other trade unions in disputes and to support any trade union facing legal action by an employer. A levy of ten pence per trade union member was raised to finance this campaign, which raised over one million pounds to 'Kill the Bill'.

At the TUC Congress on 7 September 1982 trade union leaders voted overwhelmingly for a militant resistance to the Act, including industrial action. This was quickly undermined when TUC general secretary, Len Murray. Miners' leader Arthur Scargill said "We will defy the law" and that "the way to change bad laws is change the government". In the event the fight to Kill the Bill never got to the first fence.

In 1919 the fierce industry-wide struggles had shown up the contradictions between the militancy, enthusiasm and solidarity in individual sectors and the isolation of each sector one from another. "An army in the field, whose component divisions operate as they think fit without any sort of kind of direction or central control, is not going to win battles" wrote Allen Hutt in his *The Post-war History of the British Working Class.*

A special congress of the TUC in December observed that time and again lack of coordination had caused vast financial and moral damage. The TUC had never been an effective confederation of trade unions; a national trade union centre. Originating as, and remaining a voluntary association of fully-autonomous constituents, it had failed to tackle the numerous new issues that had arisen. "Instead of being a legislative organ of the trade union movement, the annual meeting was little more than a combination of holiday parade and talking shop" wrote Alan Hutt. Some would say it never changed!

The special Congress did initiate a TUC general council of thirty-two members, representing sixteen sectors of the industries, and one for women, to "promote common action by the trade union movement on general questions of wages and hours of labour". But this was without the powers to enforce decisions on the trade unions. In fact it is renowned for curbing and denouncing action.

British Rail dispute 1982 In January 1982 I was into the thick of things, with a major dispute that had implications for the future underway. The British Rail Board (BRB), it was said encouraged by the Thatcher government, took on the train drivers union ASLEF. The BRB refused to honour part of a pay deal that had promised a 3% increase, backdated to August. Instead the Board said it would only pay up if the union agreed to 'changes in working practices'. After a month of forty-eight-hour strikes, bans on Sunday working and an overtime ban, an independent enquiry concluded that the Board had given a commitment that it should honour, and British Rail conceded.

This dispute got my first front-page lead, when the TUC general secretary, Len Murray told British rail to "Pay Up", and "on Tuesday night the Kings Cross rail workers lifted their ban on Rupert Murdoch's News International newspapers, when the *Sun* published articles by the ASLEF officials putting the case for the drivers". It would be hard to get that now, if not impossible.

At the heart of BR's demands for a "change in working practices," put to me by guards of the NUR at Kings Cross depot, was that the proposed "flexible rostering" would remove the eight-hour working time limit then in place, and would mean drivers having to drive trains back to the depot, from whatever distances they may find themselves, over and above the time limit. John Marks of the NUR said "It would mean that only the hours between midnight and five would our own. The job would be soul-destroying".

As late as 1900, one historian described the railway industry as "one of the bleakest spots for exploitation and lack of organisation". The eight-hour day was won in 1919, after eighty years of struggle. This dispute never went away, and in May 1982 BR's personnel director Cliff Rose said the company would not seek investment for rail until ASLEF had conceded flexible rostering. When the train drivers took strike action again, the BR Board escalated the dispute by announcing its intention to close the railway system on 24 July, involving the sacking of every employee taking industrial action.

The TUC would not organise support and the NUR's general secretary, Sid Weighell, was actively unhelpful. The union had no alternative but to call off the strike, which it did on 18 July, agreeing to negotiate on flexible rostering.

On February 26 I covered for the *Star* a strike by the British Airways baggage handlers at Heathrow Airport, for better wages and conditions. The handlers, overwhelmingly Asian, had been on strike for a month, when a mass meeting was called by their union, the TGWU. Its official then, Ron Todd later to become its general secretary, explained there had been no movement from the management, and it looked like a hard road ahead, but he asked them to continue with their action. There was some questioning from the floor and some speeches in favour of continuing that included criticism of BA. It was short and sweet, and when the chair of the meeting, white I think, asked for support every hand went up. The meeting closed and off they went. They won little from that dispute.

The precarious plight of the *Morning* Star was brought home to me when I was sent on March 24 to cover a mass demonstration and lobby of the Commons by 4,000 construction workers. This was against NormanTebbit's anti-trade union bill and the poor state of their industry. The piece appeared on an inside page, and with it a picture of the march, prominently featuring the banners and placards of the GMB general union. So it was that I got a tap on the shoulder and an invite from Tony Chater to "have a word".

The biggest union in the industry was the Transport and General Workers Union and it was nowhere in sight. Tony explained that the TGWU's London Region one of the *Star's* most loyal supporters of the fighting fund. Its secretary was furious at his union's non-appearance and the prominence of its rivals, the GMB and he was threatening to stop the London Region's funding. Tony then proceeded to savage my piece, and suggested this was why it was not on the front page, and warning me against such future failures. This highlighted the need to support those who supported us, or maybe it was a poorly written piece; I'll never know.

On April 26 a sign of Thatcher's things to come, the privatisation of public services featured at a meeting in Wandsworth where trade union leaders backed the council worker's move to take action against that council's plan to hive off their services. The right-wing council was riding the hobby horse that privateers, being competitive, would mean savings. Charles Donnet of the GMB told the meeting that "services must not be destroyed by private contractors only interested in profit and not quality". This was the trade unions' view and they were right.

NUPE's new leader, Rodney Bickerstaffe, added that profiteering through privatisation must be stopped". Being a nurse armed him with a wealth of knowledge of his subject and made his remarks trenchant and quotable. This applied to many rank and file speech makers.

The Falklands War On 2 April 1982, the Argentinian military junta, led by General Galtieri, invaded the Falkland Islands, a UK colony in the South Atlantic. The Falklands war began on 5 April, and Mrs Thatcher's government dispatched a naval task force, including the liners SS Canberra and Queen Elizabeth; two ships to engage the Argentine forces, to the cheers of the public on the quayside. The conflict lasted seventy-four days and ended with the Argentine surrender on 14 June 1982. This returned the islands to British control. In total, 649 Argentinians, 255 British and three Falkland Islanders died during the hostilities.

On the day of the declaration of the war the *Morning* Star's line had to be decided. To this end the editor Tony Chater, deputy David Whitfield and the diplomatic and foreign correspondents, Chris Myant and Sam Russell discussed the situation and decided to oppose the war. The alternative was negotiations.

The common belief that the Communist Party of Great Britain took its line from Moscow and

tar's from the Party was here disproved, in that there was not enough time to discuss the situ-
with anyone before going to press. Some in our office were for, and some against Galtieri,
who was a dictator who had made war on innocent British citizens. When the war ended, the
crowds returned to the quaysides, cheering and waving Union flags to welcome home the ships
and the troops.

On March 18 in Tenby I heard the arguments for and against the Falklands war when reporting
from the National Union of Seamen's biennial general meeting. These were the men and women
of the Merchant Navy on the liners Canberra and Queen Elizabeth II and the cargo-carrying MV
Atlantic Conveyor and *Atlantic Causeway*. They had been taken away from their normal work lives
and subjected to a close and dangerous view of the war.

The subject led to a heated discussion. I wrote: "The dilemma of the seafarers who face unemployment in their industry and who have friends in the South Atlantic made the debate an
emotional one". The meeting backed the Falklands operation on the basis of remarks from Jim
Slater, the NUS general secretary, on the basis of "getting the job done and removing our comrades from danger".

Delegate George Cartwright, a CPGB member and militant during the debates, raised the
question of British shipowners recruiting Asian seafarers at much lower wages and worse conditions than the British seafarers. The practice escalated later with the ship owners registering
their ships under flags of convenience like the West Indies. This practice was called "Flagging
out". This avoided conditions imposed on the company and its vessels under British maritime
laws. Delegates objected to the fact that the NUS executive had accepted this recruitment in return
for the union receiving forty pence (per week) for every Asian employed, called The Asian Levy,
and thus the loss of jobs for British seafarers.

"The Asian levy" did cease to be paid, but the British shipowners flagged out the vast majority
of their fleets and ceased the recruitment of British ratings, but not officers, until third-world staff
on worse wages and conditions replaced them. The word merchant seafarer disappeared as a job
title in Britain.

In June 1982 a meeting of the Farringdon Branch of the National Union of Journalists in the
Metropolitan Pub next door admitted me as a member, proposed by Paul Routledge of the *Times*,
and Alan Meale Press officer of the train drivers' union ASLEF. I was then allowed my byline.
This change of vocation and with it the change from overalls to suit and tie, was noted by the
Italian proprietor of the Windsor Cafe in Greville Street, off Hatton Gardens which I had frequented
wearing both. The cafe owner pointed to the suit and tie I now wore, and greeted it in Italian style
Mama. Maybe he was impressed with the change.

In April 1982 I was dispatched to my first Scottish TUC Congress in Perth, where I joined our
then Scottish correspondent, Martin Gostwick, who was an Englishman turned Jock, and was a
character! Martin needed to be enthused by the subject in hand to give it his full intention, but
once he fancied a story, he was able to put it together brilliantly, though I think I ended with the
more humdrum stuff.

He gave me a tip I never forgot, but sometimes never heeded. If a piece seems too long cut it,
or somebody else will. I had done a couple of conferences before and so had practice of taking the
notes and writing it all out before phoning the copy to the office. The portrayal of the reporter in a
movie being told a story, with Press in his hat band and reporting without a note is only for a reporting genius.

The Scottish TUC was never dramatic, but was though, never short of impressive oratory. A
left-of-centre majority of Labour and the Communist Party ruled, with the Communists edging the
influence, the general secretary, Jimmy Milne, being a CPGB member.

The STUC unions were big on solidarity at home, and internationally with particular support for those involved in struggle, as with South African's against apartheid, and the struggle between Palestinians and Israel. The debates were more rhetorical than real, and control on decision-making was kept in the hands of the STUC's executive council, where the biggest unions were the major influence.

Mick Costello, then the Communist Party's industrial organiser, who had been a *Star* industrial reporter, showed me how to make myself known, pointing to one general secretary after another, and by the week's end I knew half of the trade union leaderships!

The period 1977 to 1980 saw membership of the STUC peak to over one million, with eighty affiliated unions andforty five trades union councils. These were the halcyon days, although they were soon to be the prelude to more challenging and darker days that descended into very hard times.

Every union held social functions, covering the lunch, tea time and later evening "Dos". The one held by the Scottish NUM in the evening was, it was said, the "miners cocktail hour". The night would end invariably with a group in a big circle, and a singalong, featuring sad Scottish folk and revolutionary songs. No matter in what state they went to bed, the Celtic fringe would be at the rostrum first thing, giving forth.

The GMB union organised people who worked in the whisky distillery industry, and would arrange a trip to a distillery near to the conference centre. Pat Mantle, our photographer had an eye for these things and GMB delegates got seats on the coach. It was no ordinary event, as greeted by workers and management, we did a tour of the distillery, before sampling the goods, and then having dinner and speeches, and being presented with a goodie bag containing a bottle of the best the distillery could put in a litre bottle. When the STUC was held in Aberdeen, the trip was to the Lochnagar distillery, on a hill above the Queen's Castle at Balmoral. The guests included the "Queens distiller", who when I mentioned I was from the Communist" *Morning* Star, his eyes lit up; honestly. The "whisky trips" came to an end when the GMB's general secretary, John Edmonds, was invited on one, and though obviously enjoying it, he stopped there being any more.

At the Friday afternoon close of the conference, I bade farewell to Martin in the Salutation Inn in Perth, before driving home the 275 miles to Ellesmere Port where Gladys was still living, and I arrived home at about 10 p.m. I had a meal and went to bed, waking up as I remember, at about 3 p.m. on Sunday afternoon! I did about ten conferences in that first year, as did the other two, so we had gone some way towards the objective of re-introducing the *Star* to the Labour movement.

Move to London At the time we moved to London, Norman Tebbit, the then employment minister of ill repute, had told the unemployed that "like my dad, you need to get on your bike and look for work" and had backed this up with Tebbit's 'Mobility Scheme'. On finding such a job, as I had done, you went to the top of the local authority's housing list, in our case Camden, that is, where the job was situated. This was done by June 1982. The moving costs were paid and payments made of £200 a month for four months to help with fixtures and fittings.

Flat 32 Hasting House was in a newly refurbished block of ones built in the early 20th century. It was on the third floor, had one bedroom and was in Kings Cross or Bloomsbury, depending on how you felt, as it had the connotation for me of the literati of the Bloomsbury Set.

At the last count, the flat was in a block of twenty, council and privately-owned, cheek by jowl. It was crowded, as central London is, with Kings Cross and St Pancras stations, and buses adding to the traffic of the Euston Road which is possibly the City's busiest thoroughfare.

It was at Hastings House where our suspicions of police surveillance hardened. Gladys swears to hearing clicks on the line when on our phone. Once, when going to the local police station to pick up my daughter's Elaine's stolen bike I was greeted, I thought, with unusual familiarity.

At Hastings House we twice had our door broken down. We had two floors below and one above our third floor flat but we were the only residents to have our door smashed in half and robbed .The first time I had a tape recorder stolen, with my Jolson tape in it, and the second time a couple of items of Gladys's "jewellery". In fact she found them later!

We blamed the police, maybe looking for what we reds had under the bed. We thought later that the fact that no-one else was touched was suspicious. The first time it happened the police investigating the robbery told us "they usually come again". I don't know whether this was a threat or a promise.

Weeks after retirement to Colwyn Bay, a phone call from the police asked me whether I knew of a woman living at a Camden local address who had died without any known next of kin. She had been a *Morning Star* reader, so "we thought you might know her"!

Gladys joined me in June 1982, in what was one of those hot summers in a city where its buildings, like radiators, generated warmth to degrees not quite bearable. Gladys didn't like hot summers!

So from a three-bedroomed house with a garden back and front, in a small(ish) industrial town, with numerous children and grandchildren, mams and dads, and friends and neighbours in constant contact, Gladys now dwelt in this other place. On top of that I worked late hours, sometimes very late, and was even then away from home on jobs or at conference for a week.

Our next door neighbours were an oldish Bangladeshi man who spoke no English, and who worked nights in the Russell Hotel, and a youngish gay Greek man who was a hospital porter. Above us was a gay couple, one of whom would lock the other out, producing a cry of "open the door Richard". Below us was a young woman 'of the night'. We got on with everyone.

Shopping featured street markets, where fruit and veg were at their best and cheapest. We also went to shopping malls like Brent Cross, and to the department stores in Oxford Street and Tottenham Court Road. We walked most of the squares, gardens and parks of an infinite variety, from our locals; Russell Square, Covent Garden and Regents Park, and also London Zoo or to Hampstead Heath with its views.

Ken Livingstone was the Mayor of London, with the Greater London Council and individual boroughs, of which Camden was one of the best, promoting, or encouraging indoor and street entertainment galore. When the children and grandchildren came to visit, we were handy for galleries and museums, a magic shop and Hamleys, the toy shop, and trips to the seaside.

Gladys just got on with it and went to work, firstly as a chambermaid in a bed and breakfast by Euston station, from which she came home fuming at the owner's reluctance to change the sheets, and cleaning up after afternoon visiting couples. A note in a shop window told of a job for a publisher of a horticultural magazine, for which she applied and got. *The Grower* was in Doughty Street in a Georgian, terraced house next door to Dicken's House and the *Spectator*. It was near to home and with a working ambience as good as you can get in inner London. That would include the odd drink in the local, with any character that is always near at hand in a City, where celebrations of births, marriages and deaths are celebrated.

The magazine's owner, a widowed Mrs Stucken was the ideal employer. In winter she would tour the offices with cod-liver oil tablets and other aids to keeping well, and in the summer she came with seasonal apples and other fruit. There was an office "Do" at Christmas – once it was at Stringfellows night club – and trips in the summer, one being on the Orient Express.

As usual Gladys got on with people, and enjoyed the company of the girls, mostly younger than her, whom she mothered a bit. After being there a little while she was of the opinion that she was not being paid the rate for the job, so we worked out what the equivalent wages elsewhere would be, and she asked for, and got a rise; a situation that arose again, with the same result. The work environment then in an office for over twelve years was as good as you can get, and the time there was looked on fondly by most who worked there including Gladys. We were settled into what was a profoundly different life from what we were used to, and thinking of it now, such a change could have gone badly wrong.

It was the third year of Thatcher's government and in July 28 1982 and with unemployment totalling 3,190,000 the Labour and trade union movement's determination to resist was tested.

A major battle was joined when in June 1982 the health service workers made a claim for a 12% pay rise. The Tories imposed a 4% norm on NHS workers, despite inflation running at 12%. All negotiations on pay and conditions were on a national basis.

The TUC decided early on that the fight would call for unity and transferred negotiations away from the sectional Whitley Councils to the TUC Health Services Committee where representatives from all the TUC affiliates covering the NHS sat.

Research tells me that there was a three-day strike (or three days of action). My clippings tell me of three one day strikes. Here is a snatch of what I wrote on 9 June: "Health workers throughout Britain and Northern Ireland responded magnificently yesterday to a call for action in support of their 12% pay rise, and they received backing from other trade unionists".

"Hundreds of thousands of nurses, ambulance crews, technicians, laundry workers and cleaners marched and protested in the biggest demonstration yet of their determination.

"Social services secretary Norman Fowler, who gave a frosty answer to Labour MPs who called on him to negotiate over the pay, will receive a 10,000-strong petition today from people in Nottingham".

On June 24 it was the following: "Three quarters of a million health workers, joined by tens of thousands of other trade unionists, told Mrs Thatcher yesterday that they would not accept their miserable pittance of a wage and the bullying that went with it. The strikes were more extensive than ever, and marches, rallies and pickets sent out a message of no surrender"

"Ada Maddocks, NALGO's national organiser, told social services secretary Norman Fowler he must act now 'or reap the whirlwind'".

In a bit of editorialising, I wrote: "These actions should be a sharp warning to Norman Tebbit and his Tory supporters that his proposed anti-trade union approach will be ignored when working people are attacked". How wrong I was.

It was however, a truly awesome showing of trade union solidarity, bringing an offer that was increased to 7.5% for the nurses, and 6% to other staffs, and a review, all of which were turned down. The slogan remained; "The full 12%".

On the protests went then until September 22, when ". . . four hundred uniformed nurses followed Michael Foot and the TUC General council members when they took to the streets in a great solidarity march from Jubilee Gardens to Hyde Park".

At Hyde Park Michael Foot said :"This is the kind of demonstration that can save the country". Rodney Bickerstaffe said: "I believe for the first time in decades that the British trade unions have at last begun to understand the slogans on the trade union banners 'united we stand, divided we fall'".

It was heady stuff, and it lead David Basnett, the right-wing GMB general secretary, to say "We can stand no more, if we want more demonstrations we will have them, and if we want more days of action we will have them. We will not be put off by Tebbit's law".

A phrase used by a building workers' union leader comes to mind: "Fine words butter no parsnips". Certainly an air of defiance came with the NHS disputes, with a feeling that the ruling classes were wobbling, but in hindsight they were more biding their time.

One of my reports coincided with a strike of the print union workers in Fleet Street, thus closing down all the papers, with our management and our print staff believing it best to cover the demonstration. Our coverage accorded with and was helpful to the NHS staffs' demands.

At about 7 p.m., there was a delegation of print union workers at our front door, led by a CPGB member, demanding that we should shut down our presses, and after some discussion, that's what we did. So it was that my front page and inside stories of the day went unrecorded, and my purple prose, though printed, never got to the street or to readers. I had a copy for thirty years, but when I needed it for this book I could not find it!

When I was newly-arrived in London, I fell in with the Fleet Street branch of the Electricians Union the EEPTU, that met at Marx House across the road from the *Star* office. With a proverbial "flick of a switch", it had the power to close down all Fleet Street's newspapers. Its officers were left Labour and Communist Party activists. Its chairman, Len Dawson, was a CPGB member, with Sean Geraghty, from a Dublin militant family, being described as "of the left". This branch was the bane of the right-wing, virulently anti-communist EETPU leadership.

In August 1982: "Fleet Street electricians took the decision to take a one day strike in support of NHS staff, ignoring the law's outlawing of solidarity actions. The Publishers' Association sought and obtained an injunction outlawing the proposed action. It was issued to Sean and he went into hiding; concealed by a print-union official mate, while the strike went ahead. At seven o'clock one August night, two weeks later I was at the office desk and had a phone call: "Its Sean" a voice said "I'm in the Met", the pub next door to the *Star*. "I'm going to give myself up".

With a scoop on my mind I rushed to the pub where he showed me the injunction. I went back into our building and asked Alex, one of our photographers to photograph Sean. Thus we had a front-page lead with picture of Sean holding up the injunction.

Later in August Sean was charged with contempt and was to appear at the High Court. Ignoring a claim by my colleague, Jo Stanley, who deemed it her job, I shot out before I could be challenged. The courthouse was surrounded by hundreds of chanting workers pressed against the Court's walls. Inside, in the press gallery, we saw a crush of a bad-tempered public. Though ordered, it was truly menacing. The hearing itself was of very little duration. The prosecutor put the case and Sean was quickly found guilty of disobeying a judge; a very serious crime.

The judge summed it up with a phrase something like: "This not good enough Mr Geraghty". The punishment of a fine of £350 with £7.000 costs was derisory, for what is usually seen as a serious contempt.

There was more. The judge asked Sean's counsel if "Mr Geraghty could afford to pay the whole sum. The barrister consulting Sean briefly said "Well he has just bought a new house" which meant fairly heavy payments. But Sean was not looking to pay instalments. In fact, he had made it clear that he would not pay the fine or the costs. This would have meant jail, but somebody paid the fine and costs, and the best guess was the *Daily Mirror* owner, then Robert Maxwell, whose paper Sean worked for.

The truth is that when the ruling class sees signs of something that they can't control, and which may get out of hand, "Steady as she goes" is its motto. In the eyes of the law Sean had committed the greatest of sins, but here, as with the Pentonville Five, a quick retreat was the order of the day. When the verdict was heard, the crowd went wild, and Sean Geraghty was cheered from the court while the crowds went home and to the pubs. It should have been a lesson to the trade union leaderships as to the strength of the working class, but Sean's union leadership had washed their hands of him before he was in court, in case some of the blame would be put on them.

The one-day strikes and demonstrations were to be the height of the fight for the NHS in this case, and a ballot on an all-out strike became the consultation on the new offer. The rank and file fought until the end for a yes vote for indefinite action. The strike ended on 15 December when the TUC Health Services Committee voted to accept the offer of the two-year deal and the differential settlement. COHSE and NUPE voted against it, but were outvoted by the smaller organisations and Fowler won.

Norman Fowler for the government maintained that the action was "irrelevant to working Britain". Millions of workers knew differently. Thatcher had been extremely unpopular during her first two years in office until the swift and decisive victory in the Falklands War, coupled with an improving economy, raised her standings in the polls.

It was said that: "Labour's campaign manifesto involved leaving the European Economic Community, abolishing the House of Lords, abandoning the United Kingdom's nuclear deterrent by cancelling Trident and removing cruise missiles.

This was a programme dubbed by Labour MP Gerald Kaufman as "the longest suicide note in history". Events since then – Labour's near miss at the 2017 general election – seems to indicate that in fact Labour's stance then was pretty far-sighted.

At the beginning of July 1982 I was at the conference of the Confederation of Shipbuilding and Engineering Unions in Llandudo, where the Confederation pledged to defend any shop steward caught up in Tebbit's Laws. The Confederation was a force in the still immense British shipbuilding and engineering industries. With the twenty-three affiliates covering 2.2 million members, it concentrated on national agreements for its industries, on wages and conditions, including the hours worked. In 1989 membership still include two million members, but by 2001 this had fallen to 1.2 million members.

In the Confederation conference, Gerry Russell, an AEU executive member, spoke of a step by step attack on the trade union movement, telling delegates: "We shall be forced into hard resistance against this dogma of anti trade union laws".

Ben Rubner of the furniture workers union FTAT, and a Communist, proved to be prophetic, or just wise. He said that "many in this hall may be prepared to go to prison, but they (the government) don't want to make martyrs they want our money".

The steel industry The Iron and Steel Act of 1967 had brought the fourteen largest steel companies into public ownership, as the British Steel Corporation, representing about 90% of the UK's steel making capacity. On 2 January 1980, 100,000 steelworkers in Britain struck in an unprecedented display of national unity and industrial defiance. Until the 1984/85 miners' strike, it was 'the largest strike in post-war history', lasting over three months and amounting to the loss of 8.8 million working days. The steel workers' strike over pay was seen as a test of Thatcher's attempts to curb pay settlements and her attacks on the nationalised industries.

Government papers showed that it, the government, played a direct role in the strike's conduct, as a test of its new monetarist doctrine. It was a strike in which the workers were starved back to work. The steel workers, who "won" a 1% wage increase when they were seeking 20%, returned to work in early April 1980; the ISTC's general secretary, right wing Bill Sirs, declaring this a victory. Port Talbot and Llanwern lost 11,000 jobs shortly after the strike.

On August 21 1982 our front page lead chronicled the next chapter in the steel industry saga with the following: "Yesterday steel workers reacted with anger and determination to fight massive new redundancies in Sheffield and Scotland, with closures and mergers meaning at least 1,600 job losses. Scotland's steel union's ISTC official, Frank Lyons said "we intend to fight this to the bitter end".

In Sheffield, Cliff Wright, convenor at the River Don works, told management: "We will not accept, and we will fight for every job," adding that "with the jobs lost in the area, there is nowhere to go. If we have to sit in we will sit in".

These words were heard up and down the country, but no-one then could predict the extent to which industries were to be closed down by Tory policies. High energy costs and the failure to invest in new technology had contributed to the crisis. Thatcher's fixation with market forces allowed, even encouraged, the import of cheap foreign steel.

Margaret Thatcher's political philosophy and economic policies, Thatcherism, emphasised deregulation –particularly of the financial sector – flexible labour markets, the privatisation of state-owned companies, and reducing the power and influence of trade unions. Elected in May 1979, she was aided in this by her right-wing industry secretary, Sir Keith Joseph, and it was he who appointed Sir Ian MacGregor as chairman of British Steel Corporation in 1980, and he would be in the vanguard of the Thatcher government's programme of privatisation. The British government paid his then employers, Lazards, a £1.8 million settlement. Britain's workers in cars, steel and coal, where he held pivotal posts, were to pay a heavier price.

There was no transfer fee involved when in 1984 Thatcher moved MacGregor into the Chair of the British Coal but the miners and Britain paid an horrendous price for the promotion.

During the British miners' strike he observed: "I never thought the day would come when I wished I had some of my scruffy, sometimes ill-disciplined, sometimes loud-mouthed American police by my side in this country, and some of the curious ways of the law to back them up".

It could be said that the "loud mouthed American police" had nothing on the British Police in 1984/85 backed by the might of Britain's law makers and breakers when they waged war on Britain's miners and their industry.

At British Steel, the result of his four year's tenure was carnage. Against a background of mounting unemployment he savaged the traditional steel-working communities. By 1983, his stay at British Steel saw 166,000 staff being sacked and an annual loss of £1.8 billion. On 25 August 1982, I wrote: "The unemployed numbered 3,292,702 (13.8%), a rise of 100,00 in a month. Vacancies were 113,4400, meaning thirty people were chasing every job. Half a million young people were walking the streets.

Len Murray the TUC general secretary said "These are terrible and tragic figures. There seems to be no end to this government's capacity to mark new jobless records bring misery and despair".

In September a poll of steel workers taken without consultation with the unions asked if one of the big five steel works Ravenscraig, Redcar, Llanwern, Port Talbot and Scunthorpe were to close would they strike? This set in motion the idea that closures could happen breaking a promise by British steel bosses that it would not.

In September I picked up a dispute where people – in pursuit of justice for others – brought about great change in the lives of people worse off than themselves This was at the Rowton House Arlington House hostel in Camden, London.

"Fifty-six sacked workers at Britain's largest hostel for men, on miserable wages, face eviction threats from grim living conditions that could have come straight from the pages of Charles Dickens. The staff at the one-hundred year old, 1066-bed cubicle hostel share the same facilities as the residents, in rooms seven feet by five feet, with a bed, chair and small wall cupboard. Sixty five per cent of the mattresses that were in the hostel have been classed as unfit by the Camden Council Environmental Health Department. There were only 17 baths, 93 wash basins and 108 toilets, many without a seat".

The staff were paid £63 for a 48 hour week, out of which was taken £13 for a room and £24 for food credits, leaving £16 to spend. In January 1982 the staff organised into the Transport and General Workers Union, and in April after a two-weeks strike, they achieved union recognition.

In May the workers asked Rowton House for negotiations on a claim for £20 a week pay increase. On 2 September they said that if negotiations didn't start, they would withdraw their labour. They did so and they were sacked. The management tried to evict them, but with the assistance of the Camden Law centre the workers got an injunction allowing them to stay. Rowton House tried this trick again but failed.

Throughout their struggle, the Arlington House workers had the help of the Camden Centre staff that was led by Bernie Steer, one of the Pentonville Five jailed dockers. Left with no benefits, they survived on donations. The Centre provided one meal a day, and meals for 150 pensioners housed at the Hostel. Alongside their own struggle, the staff was demanding that the appalling standards at the hostel be improved. In September the Camden Centre took its first step to improve conditions and met residents on the hostel's conditions.

The titanic struggle went on for another 12 months, with the workers "resisting the sack, threats of eviction, physical violence and at times empty stomachs" (RJ *Morning Star* October 5 1983).

"The strike dramatically improved wages and conditions, and gave new hope to residents of Britain's biggest hostel for men". And "yesterday it was the owners of Arlington House itself who were evicted and taken over by the UK Housing Trust, which will run it for Camden Council".

And to the rousing tunes of *We Shall Not Be Moved* and *The Internationale*, 26 workers, accompanied by a big brass band marched back to work, celebrating a victory after a 13 months struggle. The TGWU convenor, Jim Cronin, called it "the greatest thing that has happened to the low paid", as he thanked the supporters, who had raised £20,000 "without which we would never have survived." And Kevin Raynor added "I'm proud that we have stuck together when some thought we had no chance of winning".

T&GU official, Phil Pearson, said "the Arlington situation has shown the need for public ownership rather than privatisation and this strikes proves if we fight for it, we can get it".

24 On September 1982 my front page intro read: "A possible pay strike by Britain's 250,000 miners came a step closer yesterday, when the union's executive unanimously rejected a slightly increased offer as 'wholly unacceptable'".

The NUM President, Arthur Scargill, accused the Coal Board of "acting on the instructions of the government and applying a cash-limits policy or an incomes policy by stealth, in answering the mineworkers claim".

A Special Delegate Conference would meet with Scargill in an opening shot in the battle for the hearts and minds of miners and the public. The delegates "will be asked to campaign for no pit closures and no loss of jobs in the face of what they believe are plans to shut a hit list of pits". In presenting the case on pay the NUM would seek a four-day week without loss of pay, and retirement at 55.

I think I underestimated what was to come. In November I was amongst the serried rows at the Confederation of British Industries, annual conference in Eastbourne, giving me the liberty, should I take it, of making fun at the expense of my once masters.

There was wishful thinking at my intro: "Bitterness felt by Britain's big business with Roland Long, a maverick I found out later, who said "it would be shameful if we stayed silent as British industry drifts down the drain".

Olé! Roland went on to say "without growth as well as increased productivity, the future of millions would be bleak". The heavily depressed North-west, said Clive Jeanes of Milkens meant "our region's industries being in danger of becoming an industrial graveyard".

The CBI – known as the 'Bosses Union' – was discussing a motion which said that "our voice, whether agreeable or disagreeable to other sections of the community, must be heard". (Presuming the "other sections of the community" are Tories, they will certainly be disagreeable".)

"The watchword of the CBI this year is competitiveness. Revealed in many speeches was the concern that after all the sackings they have achieved, and having, they feel, battered the workers into submission, the Tories are now letting them down."

CBI delegates trod carefully in the debates. Pointing to the decline in manufacturing and production as "the worst since the war", the CBI's economic chair, Ronnie Utigar, asked for the National Insurance surcharge to be delayed, a cut in energy bills and a cut in local authority rates".

One thing that did go down well at the conference centre was the free cider on tap in the vestibule, of which the man from the London *Evening Standard* took enough. At the CBI and other bosses' gatherings I found it hard sometimes to take a great dislike to them personally, but managed, I think, to adjust enough, to remember what their role was in capitalist society and to work up some rancour.

In the middle of November 1982, belatedly the Save our Steel campaigning decided on an action against one of its main enemies; imported cheap coal. Bill Sirs announced a blockade of Ports in an effort to draw attention to, and ultimately stop, the importation of cheap steel from South Africa, by mounting pickets at the ports unloading such steel. Thus, hearing of South African coal due at Immingham docks in Lincolnshire, and of pickets being mounted to stop its unloading, I was dispatched to the east coast to witness the event. I met the local CPGB secretary and ex steel worker, Dave le Purple, at Scunthorpe Labour Club in the early afternoon. The news of the steel shipments and blockade was unknown to him and to all the ISTC and steel workers' contacts, and there were many.

We worked out that if there was to be a blockade, we would have to organise it, and Dave rang his contacts again. At 7.30 a.m. the following day, we managed to get about a half-a-dozen who were prepared to picket Immingham docks, which was about ten miles from Scunthorpe, and to assemble outside the dock gates. We explained to a sympathetic, though puzzled gate man about our mission. He said that the best he could do would be to pass a message to the T&G shop stewards to come and see us. The stewards in turn knew nothing of a shipment of steel or its blockading. They called their local officials, who talked to their union officials, but they told us "not today". We quickly called off our picket, and repaired to the Scunthorpe Labour Club for a couple of pints. The following day there was a limp intro that; "Pickets at Immingham Docks Humberside yesterday were partially successful in halting the import of cheap South African steel into Britain. TV crews publicised the protest".

"An agreement was reached between the unions (ISTC, T&G, rail unions ASLEF and the NUR) and management that steel without a customer would be held in the port, but steel with a customer would be unloaded and let through. In return for lifting the pickets on steel with customers, the ISTC is to be given the names of the firms so that the ISTC general secretary or an national officer can call on each one and ask it why they found it necessary to buy steel from South Africa rather than the British Steel Corporation". I never heard from Bill how he got on!

At Aylesham in Kent at the end of 1983, I got up close to Arthur Scargill, then sporting a ginger Afro-like haircut, at a meeting held about the possible closure of its Snowden pit. The headline said: "Strike to defend Kent pit, Scargill tells miners". It could be said and was said that this was Arthur's answer to everything industrial. It wasn't that the threat would sometimes would be enough. The next bit was also to become familiar: "In a powerful speech that received a standing ovation from a packed hall, Mr Scargill said "you are fighting for your jobs and your right to live". This was a statement that under the Thatcher regime was likely to be actual rather than speculative.

Arthur's speeches were well prepared and rehearsed, with an opening attack on the media and an impersonation, usually of posh sounding protagonists, but with the facts and figures to back his arguments. He was ignored by his detractors, but had taken a number of TUC courses and listened, and he learned well from Communist Party stalwarts. He was worth listening to, but there are those who will not see what they don't want to see. Thus we repaired to the pub. Arthur packed up his papers and left.

In 1983 I was at a rally of Conservative Trade Unionists in Bristol, attended by none other than the prime minister, Margaret Thatcher, backed by a row of shadowy figures, as she launched a new project to put up "moderate candidates for key trade union posts". Mrs Thatcher told of the political activities and the obsession of some trade union leaders that had damaged the interests of their members and the firms they worked for. She blamed the workers themselves for unemployment because of their insistence on excessive pay demands and the reluctance or refusal to accept new working techniques.

I noted that "a lesser mortal", Tom Peet, from the National Union of Mineworkers no less mixed the obligatory attack on Scargill with the amazing claim that miners were always better off under the Tories. The renowned miners' libraries have clearly not acquainted him with the Tories in the twenties and thirties, and the starving out of whole communities in 1926.

"What would have astonished other trade unionists" I added "was the gathering's willingness to applaud their own downfall or even more, help to bring it about".

My coup-de-grace was as follows: "Appropriately the Conservative trade unionists will be followed at Bristol's Colston Hall by The Stranglers. Although the Conservative Trade Unionists were not strangled at birth, they made little headway in their quest to take key or any other posts much in the trade union movement, and slowly sank in the west, a night in Bristol only a way towards oblivion.

Settling in at the *Star* : The Water Industry Strike January 1983 was the start of my second year at the *Morning Star* and it featured the water workers strike. This was one of the most satisfying episodes of the trade union and labour movement in struggle in which I was involved both in its characterisation and its outcome.

For the water workers the bleak midwinter of 1983 was an ideal time, and for a writer no less ideal, as it was enhanced by a successful outcome, a victory for the working class.

My addiction to Dickens paid off, as in the fifth paragraph of my story with the following: "The workers in the industry struggling to maintain a decaying water and sewage system at times in the most vile conditions are incensed that the value of their work is not recognised. Dealing with life and death emergencies in flooding, repairing Victorian sewers in dank and dangerous conditions, and keeping clean water supplied to the public the workers are asking for justice".

Alongside is a picture of two dark figures in a snowstorm, balancing on planks, overlooking a blackened trench, where an even darker figure struggles up to its waist in water over a pipe's outlet.

The strike involved the 29,000 manual water workers of England, Wales and Northern Ireland; the Scots had their own set-up. The water industry was publicly owned, with ten regions and the National Water Council, whose board was responsible for wage rates and conditions agreements. The trade unions concerned were the GMB, representing two-thirds of the manual workers, NUPE and the TGWU.

There were twelve months of peaceful bargaining before, in September 1982, after another seven weeks and a 24 hour strike later, the National Water Council offered 4%, which was rejected. It transpired that Tory Environment secretary, Tom King had directed the Water Council Board as to what it should offer. £100,000 was spent on national advertisements, cajoling and condemning the water workers and their supporters for their actions, in attempts to beat off their challenge.

A demand by the employers for compulsory arbitration was countered by Ron Keating, of NUPE, and chair of the trade union side with the following: "At the centre of any arbitration would be the four million reserved army of unemployed and the idea that you are lucky to have a job." In November the unions decided on a ballot for strike action. This brought an improved offer of 7.3%, spread over six months, which was rejected.

On January 7, my introduction went: "Once again Tory policies are pushing a group of the nation's vital industries towards a national confrontation. This time to their first national strike in their history." On January 8, the day of the ballot result, I was at the Hampton pumping station in Surrey, where the workers were up for the fight. Ernie Eldridge, GMB shop steward, with twenty-five years service, summed up the mood with "we have toed the line for thirty years and have been kicked in the teeth". Fred Hunter said "we have the best water in the world, but it is going backwards. Where we once had ten inspectors, we now have three, and when we go on jobs, we have to take our tools on the bus".

A front page warning that "a strike may mean sewage in the streets as water workers land Tories in a mess". And: "If raw sewage pollutes Britain's houses, streets and rivers as a result of striking water workers, the Tories will be to blame".

The ballot for action was passed by 4 to 1. The strike began on Sunday 24 January, with UPI reporting: "Britain's 29,000 water and sewage workers went on strike today for higher pay, prompting health warnings to millions of Britons, leaving some homes without water and threatening disruptions in industry".

Water authorities urged Britons to boil water for at least a minute for cooking, drinking, cleaning the dishes and even brushing teeth". I piled it on: "Gloves off in water industry fight" was a *Star* front page on 27 January. "Six million people are having to boil their water, families are walking to standpipes, 120,000 could be without water by 10, and millions of tons of raw sewage were being pumped into rivers". And "troops were training!"

"Raw sewage" was our favourite theme. We forecast it and told of it daily, but truth to tell, we couldn't find any, nor any major incidents. The power industries, relying on water, were left virtually untouched, although "Blyth and Shelton power stations were affected".

Some smaller operations had difficulties, such as water supplies to fifteen industrial units on a Warrington estate being cut off. The same with the public, mainly affected by the need to boil water, or being cut off for short periods, or as in Eastbourne a 12 inch main pipe burst, causing the road to collapse.

Redundancies at that time had meant that "the workforce had got younger. This younger workforce saw the need to organise and unite for change and this was the time! The action this week reflects our determination to get a better deal".

Over the second weekend talks at ACAS were looking for a formula for ending the dispute. This was said by the employers to produce from £5 – £10 extra but by the unions' own calculations it offered only about 50p: "angering trade unions and officials who felt totally conned".

Into the third week and: "The leaders of Britain's 90,000 power workers pledged their full solidarity with the striking water workers". Then the representatives of the four trade unions in the electricity supply industry do the same, as I report "the dispute starts to threaten electricity supplies". At 6 p.m. on February 12 1983, a Press Association tape landed on my desk giving us what we had been seeking; proof of raw sewage flowing in the streets! It was on the streets of Funtington, near Chichester. A frantic search to local newspapers, local radio and TV stations near Chichester, as to where is Funtington, produced nothing; not even Funtington; but it was there. Thus the intro read limply that "The strike by workers in the water industry led yesterday to sewage in the streets of Funtingdon, near Chichester but the Southern Water Authority was quick to play down the threat to health".

In the same piece we noted that going into the fourth week "the effects of the strike are reaching into every area of the country's life; homes, industry and the environment, with the water workers blaming it on the government, and the government and the media blaming it on the water workers".

Britain's water and sewage systems were laid down over 100 years before the strike and were at best primitive.

During the strike Thatcher threatened privatisation, this she partially carried through in 1989 by selling off the regional supply companies. This meant that when the European Commission issued its edicts as to water, sea and river standards and sewage treatment and disposal rules, it was the private companies that demanded increased water rates.

The four weeks of the strike meant many hours waiting until deadlines in the National Water Council offices that were housed in a plush Georgian, Grade 1 listed building in Queen Anne's Gate. It was well looked after by the Council's staff in one of the most elegant parts of London. It also housed London's oldest public house. It was called the Two Chairmen, named after two sedan chair operators of yesteryear. Its publicity retells: "Rebuilt in the mid-18th century, features include oak beams and ornate fireplaces. There are also chandeliers, wood panelling and comfortable leather furniture, making it a pub experience in which to relax and enjoy our food and great range of drink and cask ales".

It was the biggest industrial story in town, and drew a sizeable chunk of the media's best. Plying our trade between pub and offices, we badgered Water Board and trade union officials alike; the latter mostly in the pub.

At the end of the fourth week a Committee of Inquiry was set up at ACAS. Its decision was a payment of 7.3% on basic pay; about £6, and on overtime £3.55. In addition, there was consolidation of a £5 bonus into the basic hourly pay, £3 on overtime pay, and a service increase paid after two years, down from five years (£2). An increase of £14 .50 on hours worked. A £75 lump sum (a week's ages) for wages paid through bank, an hour off the working week and an extra day's holiday.

In Parliament, Tom King tried to belittle the result and the workers' struggle as achieving nothing very much by striking. To which Gerald Kaufman MP said: "the House will have listened to the Secretary of State's sour and ungracious statement with a good deal of distaste. Flavoured with the arrogance and insensitivity that provoked the strike in the first place".

The water workers had beaten off Thatcher and the Tories' demand to peg the rise at only 4%. They had stood firm, and this against the whole might of government, the employers and the media. On the day of the announcement of the settlement that was accepted, it was my Sunday off, so that Mike Pentelow got to do the story of this famous victory for Britain's water workers. Blast!

Trades union offices In 1983 the trade unions' head offices wore the trappings of great days, Their London locations were decked in oak or mahogany panelling from floor to ceiling, and balconies aping the chapels once used by union pioneers as cover for clandestine activities. The Furniture union FTAT's West Hampstead branch was suitably decorated, and the National Union of Seamen's offices at Clapham, mirrored a Cunard liner. In Euston Road there were the marbled halls of the National Union of Miners and the National Union of Railwayworkers and in Gray's Inn Road the Iron and Steel Trades Confederation. There was black and white marble from floor to high ceiling, with murals depicting their history etched with gold leaf.

Local government union, NALGO had a nine-storey, concrete edifice at our end of the Euston Road. It was sold off, when as, Unison, it moved to its present modern nine-storey block on what was the Elisabeth Garret Women's Hospital. ASTMS general secretary, Clive Jenkins, in Camden Road, built new offices, with his office on the top floor with an adjacent roof garden!

More mundane were the Transport and General Workers Union offices in Smith Square, Victoria and the AEU at Peckham. All had local pubs, where the press were briefed. At these, offices not pubs, I did one-on-one interviews with the ruling general secretaries. I would be shown into the room by a PR person to meet the great man; rarely a woman.

The trade union leaders' rooms housed a vast desk, and desk furniture, framing whoever it was I was to talk to. I was left with no doubt, in most cases, that it was a privilege for me that I was being so honoured.

In times of an industrial crisis, we went to the TUC in Great Russell Street, by way of the British Museum, for briefings from the general secretary, at that time Len Murray or for the general council meetings, when we were briefed by the press officer. Titles got more high-falutin later, with Brenda Barber later becoming Lady Barber. Other talks with trade union officials were in the Bell, or Museum Tavern pubs.

The giants of British industry were represented by the Institute of Directors at 116 Pall Mall, with its Greek-columned portico, and inside was nothing short of a palace, befitting only the greatest money-makers, or some who lost money. Nothing there would make a person aware of working class needs, although some of its denizens claimed to do so.

The CBI had a suite of offices in Centre Point, Tottenham Court Road. The main government offices for me were the Departments of Health, Industry and Employment, or whatever their titles were at any given time. They were in Victoria where we were given employment and economic statistics monthly, briefed by departmental press officers.

One PR person was leftward inclined, and told of ordering his department's daily newspapers and ensuring a goodly supply of the *Morning* Star. One employment secretary, Michael Howard, had queried whether so many needed to be told; "Well, yes" was the reply, "it's important in our field we all know what it (The *Star*) is saying". So the order stayed the same.

More stories at the *Star* Work at the *Star* was hectic and on a grand scale and different from construction work. I was caught up in a rush of passengers and pedestrians with the pace set by an unknown pacemaker. Routine meetings at trade union and employers offices and great institutions took place at a trot.

The *Star's* office proved that writing – pounding the typewriter – about the nation's affairs, may sound pompous but from the workers' side dealing with major industrial crises and their consequences on a daily basis of was seriousness work.

I was now in the company of and in the same position as men and women trained and experienced in journalism from youth with many having worked through the ranks of local, regional and then national newspapers, some but not all, after university. I may have considered my position among them, but I don't remember. I was just too busy.

I'm sure my background was touched upon sometimes during my 13 years at the *Star* but working at a daily newspaper develops a number of skills. There is something about working at a paper where idealism mixed with the day to day chores that made work a cut above working at a purely commercial enterprise. I best remember the help and kindness of the people I worked with at the *Star*.

On 17 February 1983 I was back to work to write that 2,800 jobs would go with the closures of the British Rail Engineering Workshops in Shildon, County Durham and Horwich in Lancashire, marking a further step towards the end of yet another of Britain's skill-based industries.

The things that led to this appalling end were many and varied; either by design or incompetence, as the railways and the rolling stock needed did not disappear.

The familiar prose, mine, reported that: "The two towns have been the home of the railway's engineering industry since its beginning 150 years ago, and with the loss of 3,800 jobs the closures will produce another unemployment desert".

Russell Tuck, the NUR acting general secretary, said: "The NUR is not going to stand by and let it happen. We stand by our policies of no closures and no redundancies".

The 1962 Transport Act, had disbanded the old British Transport Commission (BTC), and established the British Railways Board (BRB). The result was 16,740 employees sacked, and twelve works closed. The Lord Beeching reports of 1963 and 1965, closed 2,363 stations and 5,000 miles (8,000 kms) of railway line were marked for closure, with 55% of stations and 30% of route miles being lost. This was at the added cost 6,000 jobs.

We also saw the UK government's fanatical emphasis on road building, under Ernest Marples, the Tory transport minister from 1961-1964, with the refusal to allow the railway workshops to compete for orders with the private sector.

The 1980s were the worst years in the history of the railway workshops, and the damage to the communities, supply chain and economic stability of the country was portrayed almost nightly in television. Between 1982 -1988, 27,500 jobs were lost and seventeen works closed.

Michael Martin, MP for Glasgow, Springburn, said in the Commons "Not long ago my community had four British Rail engineering workshops and some private. In their heyday, 10,000 highly skilled engineers worked in those workshops. Sadly, now only one loco shed remains at Eastfield. The position is very serious".

Between 1990 -1993, 2,861 jobs were lost, with only three works remaining, and all were closed after 2002. By 1993 the last three that were British-owned were sold off to the Canadian company, Bombardier, and to Germany's Alstom and Siemens as support facilities in the UK. This is a brief history of what was a great industry, built in conjunction with the first rail network in the world, by Britain's engineering pioneers; men of genius such as Brunel and the Stephensons.

This Tory government can only be described as fools caught up in a web of incompetence.

The SDP The Social Democratic Party, SDP, was founded on 26 March 1981 by four senior Labour Party moderates after Labour committed the party to unilateral nuclear disarmament and withdrawal from the European Economic Community. The SDP enjoyed a honeymoon period with the press, before joining the Liberals to become the Lib Dems. Labour leader Michael Foot, blamed the SDP–Liberal Alliance for siphoning support from Labour in the 1983 election, allowing the Conservatives a triple-digit majority, leaving Labour with 209 seats.

People's Marches for Jobs In 1981 and 1983 there were two People's Marches for Jobs. One was from the Labour Movement; the idea and organisation owing much to the Communist Party. These two biggest demonstrations against unemployment came from the North-West. Both were very successful as protests, but had little or no effect on Thatcher and the Tory government.

The 1981 march was the product of the North West Region of the TUC, together with the Liverpool Trades Council. This started in Liverpool's Pier Head, from where 500 unemployed marched 280 miles to London. It had a joint statement in support of the march by the Anglican Bishop of Liverpool, David Sheppard and the Catholic Archbishop of Liverpool, Derek Worlock. The march drew comparisons with the Jarrow March of 1936. The march cost £70,000, estimated as the most that the organisers could afford in order adequately to clothe and feed the marchers. It ended on 1 June, with a rally outside the Greater London Council, a lobby to Parliament and a party in the evening, before the 500 unemployed dispersed. The marchers handed the government a petition with 250,000 signatures calling on it to change its policies to ensure full employment. And that was that.

The 1983 Peoples March for Jobs was the brain child of the Scottish and Welsh TUC regional councils. The main march route was Glasgow to London, but feeder marches were organised from Lands End, Great Yarmouth, Liverpool, Hull and Halifax, so that many more localities could be involved in the demonstration.

Sixty marchers set off from Glasgow on April 23, but the numbers had grown to 500 by their arrival in London on June 3. There was a festival at the Crystal Palace on June 4 and a rally in Hyde Park on June 5, attended by up to 100,000. The march itself brought together a goodly mix of working people, whether they worked by hand or brain, carrying their flags and banners from every part of the country and engaging people in meetings along the way.

Both were propaganda successes and in line with the Communist Party's policy of extra-parliamentary activities, blunted as always and limited in its effects by the media's indifference to any such event that did not have any disruptive element. It did highlight the trade union and Labour movement's organisational abilities and the workers' willingness to take such actions. I took no direct part, other than selling some *Morning* Stars in the 1981 March.

On the March 1983 march I wrote the intro of the *Star's* account of the march's beginning, but little else. The writing was done by John Haylett on the march itself and by our local reporters. It was named as the Daily Paper of the March, subsidised by trade union organisations.

The June 1983 Election The march of Margaret Thatcher was not halted, and on 6 June 1983 the Tories were re-elected with an increased majority. Conservatives won 397 seats (42.4%), previously (339 seats, 43.9%) with 13,012,316 votes while Labour won 209 seats (27.6%) previously (269 seats, 36.9%) with 8,456,934 votes. The Lib Dem Alliance gained 23 seats (2.54%), up from the Liberal 11 seats, 3.8% 780,949 votes.

This was despite record post-war unemployment, rising from June 6 1979 when it was 1.3 million to December, when it was 1.4 million, then to May 1982 and 3 million. For the next six years, up to 1987, unemployment was always over 3 million and 10.5% or more. It was not just about the workers on the dole either, but poverty in work, and the introduction of poverty plus to many areas of Britain and Northern Ireland, as they are to this day.

Labour's campaigning suffered from its concentration on outdoor mass meetings, featuring Foot and hundreds of (mainly Labour supporters), while the Tories made the most of TV and millions of viewers to get their messages across. Foot's position was undermined every inch of the way by a vitriolic media that criticised everything he said and did. Foot's turning up at a First World War Remembrance Sunday Parade at the Cenotaph in a regular overcoat was flagged up as an insult to Britain's dead.

When politicians stand for election they will talk to anyone, even Roy Jones of the *Morning Star*, in some cases especially him! Our backing did no harm to some who were seeking office. After the elections were over, most didn't want to talk. I remember chasing Neil Kinnock around buildings after the election, whereas beforehand he was only too willing to have a word. I put it no higher than that.

The election of Foot with the move left exacerbated divisions within the party. When we consider what an economic mess the country was in June 1983 the notion that the Falkland war was what kept Thatcher in office, seems feasible. It paved the way to another thirteen years of Tory rule, and the very heavy price that we was paid.

Shipyards April 1983 On 2 April 1983 I was getting reporting the plight of another industry in trouble. It was Tory-inspired, though helped by willing, hand-picked assassins. British Ship Builders announced the shedding of 9,000 jobs throughout its yards. The literature on the demise of British Shipbuilding 1950 to 1980 focusses on the technological, institutional and political or economic reasons of its decline.

British shipyards failed to modernise and increase productivity when compared to the competing yards in Japan, West Germany and Sweden; i.e. it's the bosses fault! Relationships between unions and management, were fractious in British yards when compared to Japan and West Germany, hindering the development of British shipyards. i.e. it's the workers fault!

Economic analysts argued that governmental failures exacerbated the problems of the industry and did not address the industry's concerns; i.e. it's the government's fault.

You know what my viewpoint is. The shipyard bosses owned the yards and controlled the introduction of new technology. Dealing with the workforce was in their hands. The ideas and experience of those who built the ships, the workers and their trade unions, were not taken into account nor consulted about what the introduction of new technology would mean. The workers saw only machines taking their jobs.

In 1978 there were 78,000 people building ships in the UK, about 40,000 of whom were building merchant ships. Ten years later that was down to 3,000; the prime years of the Thatcher governments. As the UK's industry foundered, others took to the new markets. Germany concentrated on container ships, while other European nations went upmarket, focusing on cruise liners or complex vessels such as gas carriers. Britain was left retaining only a capability to build military vessels, such as the aircraft carriers under construction in Rosyth, Scotland. Even so, the UK's entire maritime industry was worth £10bn to the country's economy, and its employees – ranging from seafarers to ship brokers, welders to naval architects – numbered 90,000. The production of warships at yards such as Barrow was kept going when others were losing work to foreign shipbuilders.

A report of April 2 1983 by British Ship Builders announced the shedding of 9,000 jobs throughout its shipyards. Sackings in warship yards followed. Jim Murray, the chair of the trade union side, proposed to fight the cuts, it being the biggest crisis to date.

It was to get worse! It had been planned. In the 1970s the Ridley Report devised a policy for Thatcher's shadow cabinet for breaking up the public sector through privatisation and dismembering the unions. Privatisation was, at first, subordinate to other policy aims, above al,l wage suppression.

In her first term, from 1979 to 1983, the first eight flotations were all commercial and/or industrial enterprises operating in competition; Cable and Wireless. National Freight, bits of British Leyland and Britoil, together with the right to buy council houses. These were followed by coal, iron and steel, gas, electricity, water supply, trucking, airlines and telecommunications. On top of this came Rover, Rolls Royce, Jaguar Cars, and British Steel and British Aerospace. Electricity transmission and distribution companies were sold by John Major in 1991, and Railtrack in 1997.

It was not just stimulating private sector investment, but was also a cultural change to 'popular capitalism'. Thatcher's way of making capitalism popular did meet with resistance, and I was on the picket line with two hundred British Telecoms staff on April 14 1983, outside its new plush headquarters, as they clashed with its chairman, Sir George Jefferson.

A meeting of 2,000 members or so, of the Westminster branch of the Post Office Engineers Union, welcomed their union's pledge to campaign against the move. Tony Benn read from the Labour manifesto its pledge to re-nationalise the industry.

It was not   Tony's fault but this is a promise that was never kept. Labour's answers to such Tory measures have been almost completely unsuccessful.

The official legend is that the early 80s recession begat privatisation as a solution based on the discipline of the marketplace. Privatisation would make the large utilities more efficient and productive, and capitalism more competitive with rivals. And pigs might fly!

The man and woman in the street did buy shares and sold them off for a one-off profit, but popular capitalism, US-style never made it, and inevitably the shares ended up with the big banks and investors.. Since then foreign interests, including government-owned companies have bought into nationalised and public industries, including communist China.

The John Major government continued with selling off British Rail.

The CPSA in Conference 1983 On May 13 I was in Brighton at the then Civil and Public Services Association conference. With a membership of 200,000, the CPSA was the biggest of five civil service unions, covering staff in the social security, employment, tax and other departmental offices in the nation's high streets. Its members were likely to face some very angry and desperate customers. The delegates were young and the worst paid. Nothing much has changed for them.

In the 1960s and 1970s, our Labour Exchanges had been places of decorum, the staff of three or four elderly people attending to a few unemployed from open counters. In 1983, under the weight of untold numbers of unemployed, the "dole" was much more rowdy, and could become a bear garden. The staff retreated behind protective barriers.

In common with other civil and public services' unions, until then the CPSA had an advantage over industrial unions in organisational and monetary terms, in that dues were on check off, deducted directly at source. The union branches had offices in their department premises from, which the staff reps would do business. The 2010 Conservative government's anti-trade-union stance did away with check off end a number of legal battles since have seen union victories for the merged Public and Commercial Services Union under Mark Serwotka.

For delegates, the Annual Delegate Conference meant time off with pay, and the same applied to the number of apprentice delegates attending to learn the ropes. The delegates had little political nous, but a majority of backed the Broad Left.

Growing militancy amidst Tory Opposition The 2,000 delegates were up for a fight. They cheered their favourites and jeered the right wing leadership. There were loud comments and raucous behaviour from the hall, stirred on by the literature given out to delegates daily in news papers, including the *Morning* Star, and propaganda sheets.

Resolutions were passed demanding militant action over more pay and better conditions. In print they made a good story. Most of them came to nought. .

The conference did not reflect its membership, and their problems were not properly addressed, never mind solved. Nevertheless the elections for the union's full-time top officials and of a president, two vice presidents and 26 executive seats made page leads, together with any swings from right to left. The competitors for office were the right-wing Moderates and Broad left slates. The Broad Left, included the trotskyist Militant Tendency, then at the height of its disruptive powers, Labour left and Communists Party members. The press waited with bated breath for the election anticipating Britain's biggest civil service being taken over by 'Militants'.

Thatcher and the Tory government took an interest and the *Guardian* sent Richard Norton Taylor to investigate. The right-wing won on this occasion, I recorded with suitable sarcasm, but frankly it was not going to help or hinder Britain's destinies.

In 2017 the *Morning* Star exclusively revealed that John McCready, a CPSA official, and a member of Militant had been targeted with a government file and exposed how the Thatcher administration had plotted to undermine him following his 1986 election as the general secretary of the union. Ray Alderson, a Communist Party member, who in 1982 had lost his vice-president's seat, as a member of the Broad Left, analysed the Left's problems: "The left are not doing enough to convince the members of the correctness of our policies. Not for the first time the arguments of the activists were failing to register because they were simply loaded down with the cares of their jobs and providing for their own".

I don't know if Ray's words were taken on board and worked on but in May 1984 the conference headline read "Left sweeps to victory in the CPSA" in "a complete reversal of last year's election to the executive council".

A note at the bottom reports that "Every one of the 150 copies of the *Morning* Star on sale on each of the five days of the conference were sold". So our aim of winning back the trade unions to support the *Star* was working.

All the conferences of the civil and public services and nationalised industry unions were well attended, and delegates were more militant than their membership. They were in the second tier of trade union organisation, and although some were involved in early struggles, were reasonably free from strife. None of the civil service unions was affiliated to the Labour Party, but lots of their leaders were individual members and active often on the right wing. The civil, and public service unions, NUPE, NALGO, the nationalised Post Office and Post Office Engineers; the public trade unions above, all met in large halls with similar numbers.

A group, including the NUM, the AEU, the NUR and ASLEF and UCATT and the Boilermakers met with a small number of delgates. These were the unions with long traditions of earlier struggles when meetings were forbidden by law, with dire consequences for those disobeying. The AEU's policies were made by fifty-two delegates, never addressed by name, but only by numbers assigned to each. In the AEU this also worked in favour of a right-wing domination in most of its period after the Second World War.

On 16 May 1983 I was in Scarborough for the National Union of Public Employees, NUPE, which represented the 'other ranks' in local government and the NHS. Its membership grew from 250,100 in 1966 to 693,100 1977; Britain's fifth largest. Rodney Bickerstaffe, born in London but bred a Yorkshireman was its general secretary and of the left, and with him a journalist was never short of an intro and here it was a choice: "It is whether to accept the harsh, cruel and biased society of the Tories, or the caring, compassionate and working-class society that is our choice. The Tories have taken on the slogan of 'Forward to the eighties not back to the thirties' but they mean the 1830s". Bickerstaffe shunned a peerage and on retirement became president of the National Pensioners Convention, and afterwards of War on Want.

On July 14 Gladys was with me at the Iron and Steel Trades Confederation, ISTC that was still trying to find a way to fight against closures.

This 'stand and fight' theme was expanded in an exclusive interview with Arthur Scargill.

The paper reported Scargill "tells Roy Jones that political education, class commitment and struggle are essential to winning socialism". I told him at the end of the interview that I could not put it better myself.

Reading it now, Arthur's message was well thought through and clear sighted. He laid heavy blame for setbacks for trade unionism on its leaders, including those of the NUM, who "over the last 20 or 30 years" could have shown better leadership qualities "through struggle".

He was not then looking to take on the government in a fight to the finish, at least not yet but he was considering the question of winning socialism, but not off the backs of the miners.

The interview – a month after Thatcher's June 1983 second general election victory – gave plenty of evidence of how far Thatcher would move from the liberal consensus of Labour and Tory government's to a market-driven economy; one protected by barriers raised against the ability of the trade union and labour movement to struggle effectively".

How far she would go in using the state apparatus against any threat to her objectives, as in the miners' strike, could not then have been imagined.

Arthur said a start had to be made with "a programme of re-education to change the fundamental weakness of our movement – the politicisation of the working class". "When we can persuade the mass of working people to accept an alternative radical programme, only then will we be able to move towards a socialist system of society. We need to politicise workers and bring real politics back into the centre of the arena". There was no indication of a quick fix to a socialist society here, or that it would be achieved by a strike by Britain's miners.

"Far to often people in the trade union movement see the essential arguments of going for wages and conditions, but fail to comprehend the political impact of a lost job". "It's the responsibility of the movement to educate and to show people that there is a need to struggle against that lack of understanding. Workers are taught the three Rs, but they are not educated in the political sense".

All of what Arthur said is classical Marxism. He said: "I had my lessons in political education in politics in 1972, when I had been involved in politics and the labour movement since I was 15, and spent a great number of years in the Young Communist League".

"At no time did I know what I was meaning by political education until 1972, in the miners strike. Then I saw miners become more politically aware in 48 hours than in the 48 years in seminars and tutorials".

"That strike led to the downfall of Heath's Conservative government, but it made no difference to the way trade unions thought, or to an advance in the way they conducted themselves. It did lead to Thatcher's plans to see that it didn't happen again, and led to a fundamental change to the trade unions' ability to fight and win in the struggles that lay ahead.

Arthur concluded: "You have to fight on wages and conditions, but begin to relate that to the system whereby we live, and show how the two are interconnected and where the structure operates against the interests of the workers.

"Not that I think we are going to change things overnight, but the fact that I am talking about this fundamental change in our approach is at least a demonstration that we are beginning to think about it".

Throughout the interview he emphasised that the workers were nowhere near politicised enough to make any great change to society through strike action. The 1984/85 strike to Scargill was about saving the mining industry, not about revolution.

Gladys and I stayed with a couple in St. Helier, Jersey, who were members of the Jersey branch of the Communist Party who when young lived through the German occupation in World War Two. They told us of life on the island as a tax haven and related this in the *Star* feature: "Millionaires wishing to take up residence in the Jersey Island paradise now have to join a queue". And why was this? Because its success as a tax haven was beginning to put what could be intolerable pressure on resources and its citizens, so that the Jersey States government had said "no more".

Applicants seeking sanctuary would have to have an income of at least £80,000 a year, and be able to buy a home for at least £250,000, a price which, 35 years ago, was astronomical. It was also the case that: "While the tax exiles lap up the luxuries of Jersey, the island's other inhabitants are left to struggle, on long time waiting lists for houses, in a poor state and with high rents."

Cheap foreign labour on low wages was matched by appalling living conditions with many in barns on farms. Cheap labour meant fewer jobs, and poor pay for locals in farming and tourism. "Looking at Jersey's economy, which was based on financial institutions, backed by tourism and farming, where the unemployed get parish relief, and health is based on the ability to pay, the question arises: Will there soon be a parallel over the water"

In November 1983, the Post Office Engineering Union POEU, which had included strikes in fighting the privatisation of British Telecom, scaled back other action, including 1,000 other engineers being instructed to go back to work.

On 15 March, three months before the June 1983 election, the Thatcher government's Chancellor, Geoffrey Howe raised tax allowances and cuts taxes by £2 in the budget. But then on July 7 the new Chancellor, Nigel Lawson, announced public spending cuts of £500 million.

September 8 brought another giant step in Thatcher's plans for Britain's future, when the NHS cleaning, catering and laundering services were to be privatised, in a move which Social Services Secretary, Norman Fowler, predicted would save between £90 million and £180 million a year. This did nothing good for the NHS's finances, but filled the pockets of the privateers, and worsened the wages and conditions of the staff involved. This was repeated throughout the public services industries, to the detriment of the workers and of the services themselves.

A story in July of merchant seafarers and travellers said that: "Tens of thousands of peoples have had their holidays saved following a dramatic last-minute climbdown by Townsend Thoresen shipping bosses yesterday.

The National Union of Seamen's members at Felixstowe, Cairnryan and Larne, who had been on strike for 14 days, won a 5.4% pay rise, after a threat to escalate the action. It was to herald, though, another sad tale for the workers concerned. Time was running out, and in the 1990s, the Ferry Companies, following on the merchant shipping companies "flagged out" its fleets by registering them in foreign ports. Thus the greatest merchant shipping fleet in the world, together with most of its jobs, ceased to be British, and sailed under foreign flags, even if the vast profits from it still flowed into British owners hands.

On August 7 1983, the end of Britain's coal industry was signalled, when the Mergers and Monopolies Commission Report on the National Coal Board, was said, by the NUM, "to be engaging in what can only be described as a political attack on the nationalised coal industry".

"Miner's President Arthur Scargill said "The report does not make sense economically, politically or morally. The recommendations reduce mining capacity, close down pits and coke works, and shed jobs on a massive scale; and how many? "It was now investigating efficiency on narrow financial grounds" Scargill said. This was to be the nub of the argument around pit closures, in that the social costs to communities were never considered. "We are determined to fight the pit closure plans", he said. "In closing pits" Arthur Scargill said "the Board are acting as agents for the Tories and carrying out their political decisions". The government was also legislating to open the way to selling off BT, through a share issue to the general public; something they achieved in May 1984.

Without winning the argument for privatisation, Thatcherism so comprehensively demolished the militant left and trade unions, that there was nothing to prevent New Labour from abandoning all promises made in opposition to take back into public ownership the industries sold off by the Tories.

I had words with the new, "highly-paid" boss of British Shipbuilders, Canadian Graham Day, at a press conference on September 1 1983, noting that his installation provided "no joy for the workers in the nationalised industries".

"The £80,00 a year made it brutally plain that if the country's shipbuilding industry is to have a future it will be on the backs of the workers". Jobs will go and yards will close unless there were "a change of attitudes". Day added that "there would be no rise in basic rates of this year's pay, while demanding productivity increases to enable British yards to compete in 'the market place.'

In July 1983, six NGA members were called out on strike, and sacked, at the Eddie Shah-owned Messenger group's Stockport plant. This related to the company breaking the closed shop agreement, and it was deemed a contravention of the Employment Acts 1980 and 1982. Shah had signed the closed-shop agreement for his new printing works at Stockport, but when he opened two more print works in Warrington and Bury, he used non-union labour at cheaper rates and picketing started at the Warrington site.

In late November, the site became the battleground for the first test-case confrontation over the new union laws. On Tuesday November 29, a call for a one-day strike and demonstration at the Warrington plant, with mass picketing being mounted, was met quickly by mass policing. Eye witnesses said that "Until 5 o'clock the police were content to pull pickets from out of the front of the line. They didn't arrest them but just gave them a good thumping. This was followed by baton charges to disperse many hundreds of pickets. Police reinforcements left the pickets in no condition to fight back.

A leaflet published by the London Workers Group said that "The police (had) foolishly smashed up the NGA control van, causing union officials to lose control of picketing workers.

Moving into December, actions in support continued from the print workers and other industries when Shah used 1980 and 1982 Employment Acts to try to prevent both the boycotting of work and advertising, and secondary picketing at his other plants at Bury and Warrington.

The NGA ignored the court's instructions to stop the secondary picketing, and on December 9 the High Court pronounced it in contempt of court, so that I reported the following: "The anger reverberated through the ranks of the trade union movement yesterday, as the news spread of the staggering half a million fine on the National Graphical Association".

Should the NGA refuse to pay the fine, its funds could be subject to sequestration and thus it would be unable to pay staff, and not able to protect its members. A special conference of the NGA's Fleet Street members met on December 11, where there were calls for action that would shut down their papers.

On the following day, December 12, the NGA national council called a strike for the following Wednesday, backed by trade unionists from every industry and most parts of the country, who urged the TUC to back the print workers. On the Wednesday evening of December 14, the TUC general secretary, Len Murray, said that the TUC general council members had recommended that the NGA leadership should purge its contempt and pay the fine, because the TUC Wembley Conference had not backed breaking the law. Thus the decision was branded as a "betrayal" of workers in struggle.

On Wednesday 18 January 1984 members of the national council of the print union, the National Graphical Association, agreed to purge its contempt of court in the Stockport Messenger Group, effectively ending support for the dispute. This was thus another blow to the procedures built over decades, when in this case the workers used the craft status to win and protect better wages and conditions within a close shop. Because of new technology, it enabled less skilled workers or those with none to take on the work, with of course less pay. As the employers would see it, these were demarcation lines that stood in the way of using machines efficiently.

It was the beginning of a process of which the print workers were the most graphic example. (Sorry!) The workers failed to get their fair share in wages and conditions from new technology. They helped what many practices had been designed to avoid, unemployment by the millions. On March 14 1977 inflation had risen by nearly 70% within three years.

Confederation of Shipbuilding and Engineering Unions and Tebbit's Law At the beginning of July 1982 I was at the Confederation of Shipbuilding and Engineering Unions conference in Llandudno, where the twenty three unions of the Confederation pledged to defend any shop steward caught up in Tebbit's Laws. The Confederation was a force in the shipbuilding and engineering industries with the twenty-three affiliates covering 2.2 million members, and concentrating on national agreements for the above industries on wages and conditions including the hours worked. Its biggest unions were the AEU, GMB and EEPTU, the construction union UCATT, the white collar union TASS and the TGWU's white collar section. There were also a number of smaller craft unions.

At the Confederation conference, Gerry Russell, an AEU executive member, spoke of a step by step attack on the trade union movement (by the anti-trade union laws), telling delegates: "We shall be forced into hard resistance against this dogma". Ben Rubner, of the furniture workers union FTAT, and a Communist Party member), proved to be prophetic, or just wise, when he said that "many in this hall may be prepared to go to prison, but they (the government), don't want to make martyrs, they want our money".

In a speech that, as usual, was analytical, humorous and inspiring, Michael Foot, warned delegates that the Tories had taken "a crazy, mad, dangerous, monetarist economic course".

In other subjects discussed at the conference, a delegate spoke bitterly of a government minister's statement that he "saw no objection to the successor to the Royal Navy's *Atlantic Surveyor* transporter, that had been ship sunk in the Falklands war, being built in Japan!"

Ken Cure of the AEU put the reasons for the lack of women trade union representatives. He explained that "a lot depended on men's attitude to women". This was one of the six, all-male, AEU's right-wing, executive council speeches, with mostly progressive answers to the industrial issues. A glance at their progressive scripts would show them in double-spaced large print, which were delivered with aplomb, but written by staff member, Julie , the American wife e of Sid Brown, the *Star's* graphics man.

The Boilermakers On 20 October 1982 in Torquay, the annual conference of the Boilermakers Society proved to be its last after 120 years of independence. The delegates were startled, when their business coming to an end; the doors of the Torquay theatre were thrown open, and David Basnett, the GMB general secretary with flags flying, led in a delegation of the general union, the GMB, to formally declare the merger, or take over, making the two unions one.

The merger was unusual then, but not thereafter, in that the two unions had been born and grown up in two different strands of the movement. The Boilermakers emerged from the guild tradition of craft unions formed in the 18th century. The General Workers Union was just that, one of the "new" general trade unions. The GMB was the godchild of some of the great trade union leaders of the Victorian era, the foremost of whom was Will Thorn. He organised first in the gas industry, where wages were poor and conditions appalling. The favoured way forward for the progressives in the early trade unions was for industrial unions.

Union trip to Bulgaria In late December I was an invited guest of the British Bulgarian Trade Union Association, in a group of fourteen trade unionists that flew to Sofia where we were given celebrity status by way of the VIP lounge and a stayed at Sofia's best hotel.

The meals seemed to include vodka from breakfast onwards, tempered by bottles of Coke, which disguised it enough for an older Yorkshire miner to imbibe enough one night to be found naked on the front lawn. When I was in Bulgaria a year later, following in the Soviet Union's path, the government had introduced a ban on drink. Luckily it was still allowed in tourist hotels.

The first week was spent travelling by coach to the most beautiful places, including a farming enterprise where we ate in the barn and danced furiously about the table. We were shown a lakeside, mountain holiday village, where workers deemed special cases were housed. We were shown the heroics and achievements of Bulgarian workers celebrated in stone or metal in towns and were fed and entertained by adult and children's choirs and dances, at centres old and new.

Wherever we went there was always a man accompanying us, whom we soon knew to be a Communist Party official, who engaged with us little. A talk with him in a town square revealed that an imposing building in the square was where he had been imprisoned for four years under a fascist regime.

We came across little sign of discontent in the Bulgarian populace, although we were closely supervised, and those who spoke to us were at meetings arranged by Communist officials.

In a second week, at the Bulgarian Trade Union Centre, discussions were led by its director. We did meet trade union leaders and workers when visiting factories, an oil refinery in Plevin and an aluminium smelter in Shoumen. Our "linx-eyed" group members looked for any possible violation of the health and safety code, at skilled jobs and poor products.

I wrote that the group was "determined to get at the truth of what we were told about (Bulgaria's) society". We had some difficulty in relating to the different roles of a trade union in a capitalist and a socialist society.

"In Bulgaria the ownership of the means of production is in the hands of the workers. So the relationship between the workers and the management is qualitatively different. In Britain it would be viewed with suspicion by most trade unionists".

I concluded though that "the most striking impression of Bulgaria is of a country going forward. Things are improving". In light of developments not, it seems, one of my best conclusions.

In 1987 I was at the Bulgarian TUC's annual conference in Sofia, when the Bulgarian Communist Party had followed the path of glasnost and perestroika following Gorbachev and the Soviet Union. This opened the country up to greater transparency and open discussion on the good and the bad. The workers from the rostrum told a challenging story of life for Bulgarian citizens at work. Trade union delegates told of mismanagement, poor work conditions, poor production levels and inferior products. A convenor from a large factory turning out railway trains and rolling stock, warned the delegates against travelling in them.

My conclusion was that although there may have been 'a unity of purpose', trade union bodies need to be independent of the government with the right to withdraw labour if all else fails.

This lack of trade union muscle in the Soviet Union and the other socialist countries – to challenge what they thought unacceptable on the shop floor – was a weakness with profound consequences. The collapse of the Soviet Union came about through the actions of politicians while the trade unions, the representatives of the workers on the shop floor, were unable to influence what has followed in Russia since.

Another side of Bulgarian life was featured at the Congress, in the reception for foreign guests in the magnificent Hall of Culture, which was about a hundred yards long and twenty yards wide, dripping with drapes and chandeliers, sculpture and paintings, with French windows all down one side open onto gardens that were lit up, as a full orchestra played.

Tables were piled high with food and drink, which was served to us by the partner of a print union official from Glasgow, lately Glasgow's winning beauty queen. A six feet tall, blond woman swept elegantly from drinks to each of us, as every Bulgarian official, young and old wondered at this vision.

At the Congress, Pavlina Mincheva, an instructor at a woollen mill, told delegates of: "A heavy bureaucracy, and how the multi-level structure of the trade union system often thwarted good ideas". Another delegate told of filling in "a multitude of forms" and that "it would be good for producers and managers to spend a month or two in the shop. Let them spend a day or two addressing the justifiable complaints about quality instead of us doing it".

But it appeared to be too late for the socialist revolution in Bulgaria, the Soviet Union and its European socialist country allies. They have all gone, but "if only!" is left.

The Miners Strike

Introduction The year long "Miners' Strike" was an epic, as 160.000 miners from across Britain's coalfields fought to save an industry that had been at the heart of Britain's industrial revolution, and which had fuelled the building of Britain's empire over three hundred years.

It was not, as has been written and said, a spat between egocentrics, in Tory prime minister, Margaret Thatcher, and National Union of Mineworkers president, Arthur Scargill.

It was about how to treat honest, hard-working people decently. The 'Great Strike' from 6 March 1984 to 6 March 1985 showed how the mining communities – with the support of organised labour and many individual citizens, were able to sustain themselves, standing in unity for a year against the might of a state apparatus and its allies in the media and among employers.

A great thing had happened to mining in 1946 ,when the Labour Government nationalised coal production. This civilised the industry with better pay, holidays, and sick pay and conditions. This progress was recorded on film by images of new pithead baths ending the practice of miners bathing in a tin bath in the kitchen of their homes.

In the 1960s hundreds of pits closed without a fight of any kind. In contrast, in 1972, a pay fight was won, a government fell and a giant awoke. Not since the 1926 General Strike had the NUM taken national action. But fighting for the survival of their industry proved much different than fighting over pay.

The miners' strike was for me and my comrades at the *Star* a year of high drama. Reporting it was a challenge that could only be met by the wholehearted support of all the staff at the paper and it was. Not one person in the building or in the field failed. Jo Stanley had left the industrial department, leaving Mick Costello and me. One person Graham Atkinson joined us in the field. Those of us at the paper were aided and abetted by volunteer contributors throughout the country, particularly in the coal field areas, so that almost anything of note was covered.

For the most part I was not in the coalfields. I spent more time at Hobart House, the home of the National Coal Board, just behind Buckingham Palace. Here, visits from the NUM's president, Arthur Scargill, vice president, Mick McGahey and newly-elected general secretary, Peter Heathfield, were joined on high days by coalfield and pit officials and miners. On one glorious occasion, Kent Area miners occupied the building for the day, parading their golden torsos from high windows, to cheering crowds outside.

In contrast to most of the capitalist press, the *Morning Star* was able to capture the high order of heroism shown by the miners, their families and communities from within, and from their supporters without great examples of working class solidarity.

In the early skirmishes between the NCB and the NUM, there was a strike on 14 September 1983 over the planned closure of the Monkton Hall pit in Scotland, and on 11 October, 560 miners walked out at Cronton pit after being told it was to close. On 18 October, miners throughout Scotland staged a one-day strike in support of a five-week stoppage at Monkton Hall.

Three days later, on 21 October, a special delegate conference of the NUM voted for an indefinite overtime ban, with MacGregor warning that this would lead to pit closures. The ban started on 31 October, and was never to be lifted.

On 3 November the NCB presented a new 'Plan for Coal', which Scargill said would be catastrophic for the industry. This it proved to be. On Tuesday 13 December the two sides came together again to discuss the plan.

I wrote that: "The NPC policy presented at yesterday's meeting, according to Scargill clearly commits resources to long-life pits and new mines, and that it's clear that the Board accepts the government's intention to cut investment. This means that every pit producing coal at more than the average cost per tonne faces the threat of closure. This is 60% of them". New pits, in this case a super pit at Selby, North Yorkshire had, according to the NCB, set new standards of engineering that are the best in the world. The problem for the other pits, I reported, was that Selby effectively defined all other pits as 'uneconomic'.

Part of the plan, not spelled out at the time – but which was always in the mind of the government – was that the pits calculated to be economic or profitable (enough) would be ripe for privatisation. 'Uneconomic pits' were the buzz words used by Thatcher, the Coal Board and their supporters from the start of the strike, and they gathered momentum as the days went by.

Lawrence Cunliffe, miners' MP for Leigh, led a debate on the strike in the House of Commons on 19 December. He asked: "What is an economic pit? How is an economic pit to be defined? I am not talking in terms of pounds and pence. Nor shall I talk about the NCB's accounting system. I worked for the NCB for 30 years. Even then, we manipulated the figures. The figures were not distorted or untrue. It was a matter of presentation. It is quite easy to do. The NCB does it when it fiddles the books, It must be more expensive to make miners redundant than to invest properly in the coal industry".

"In keeping twenty pits open, the costs to the NCB in subsidies would be £275 million per annum. If they are closed, the Government will lose a maximum of £480 million a year in redundancy payments, supplementary benefit and lost tax revenue. Plus the cost of job losses in industries that supply the mining industry. A figure of £130 million a year is spent on pensions for past employees, and for that there is a subsidence charge of £245 million a year. Nothing to do with operating and production costs. The Board has always made an operating profit".

What should also be counted were costs of the loss, to the pit village or town, of the social, cultural and educational activities serviced in buildings all funded by the monies of the miners.

The dominance of mining in these local economies led Oxford professor Andrew Glyn to conclude that "no pit closure could be beneficial for government revenue".

In London's County Hotel, Mick McGahey explained, tongue in cheek, "I think what both sides were looking for was a word other than 'uneconomic' that would be acceptable to both sides, and without being exactly that, if you know what I mean".

One night at the Sheffield Meeting of the NUM Executive, McGahey was explaining this to a group of journalists all fresh from the pub, and wondered if there was a word to be had that could be used instead of 'uneconomic'. industrial correspondent Patrick Wintour, then at the *Guardian*, said helpfully "that a thesaurus could be useful in finding an answer".

Mick, who, from his childhood, was one of the best read-people – brought up in a house where his father was himself a well read communist, said "no", pretending ignorance. Patrick volunteered to look it up. I don't know if he had a thesaurus with him, but somewhere along the way he caught on to the fact that Mick was joshing, and was, I think, suitably, chastened. On consulting the Thesaurus I found the alternatives to be "not" economic or "unprofitable". No help there then.

On 20 February 1984, in a ballot, Scottish miners rejected an all-out strike call, but agreed to strike at Polmaise colliery against threatened closure. Pictures of Polmaise miners picketing the Scottish NUM meeting were a glimpse of the anger that was to come from the miners themselves.

These early events suggested there was to be a confrontation between the Thatcher government and the miners, and was further borne out by the following points:

Firstly, Thatcher's belief in markets forces led to buying cheap coal from abroad, mined as Scargill said, by children in South Africa and South America.

Secondly, the move of Ian MacGregor on 28 March 1983 to chair of the NCB from British Steel, where he had been responsible for "a remorseless programme of plant closures and redundancies, damaging many traditional steel-working communities".

It was made obvious then to Arthur Scargill and the NUM what was being planned for the industry. What was not known by the NUM and its allies was that Thatcher had plans prepared to beat the miners struggle, and how to do it, almost at any cost.

It was said "authoritatively" that the government strategy designed by Thatcher, was threefold: to build up ample coal stocks; to keep as many miners at work as possible; and to use police to break up picketing of working miners.

The NUM leadership's strategy lay in its confidence in the miners to struggle and win, as it had in pay strikes of 1972 and 1974, by striking for as long as it takes and relying on the solidarity of the Labour and trade union movement.

There was also an expectation that a cut in production would lead to shortages of coal to industries fuelled by it, and that power-station workers would either refuse to use 'scab' coal by direct action orr by picketing it deliveries.

Trade unions rank and file support was magnificent as was the response of the general public, of which, more later.

In January 1945 the National Union of Mineworkers was founded replacing the Mineworkers Federation of Great Britain. The federation status was maintained, though with each coalfield having a president, general secretary, and with headquarters having a huge degree of autonomy, including the authority to initiate strike action in their own coalfields, which they often used. One historian noted: "Different areas varied as to how militant they were, and it was not uncommon for animosity to exist between areas". This turned out to be an understatement.

This was a potential recipe for disaster, and as much as anything it was Arthur Scargill's powers of persuasion, rather the media portrait of him as some kind of Svengali, or a dictator, that the NUM leadership commanded the support of so many of the NUM areas.

This was testimony then to his ability and that of the NUM leadership as well as the justice of their cause. That a majority of the miners in the Nottinghamshire coalfield were not won over to the cause, considerably helped Thatcher in maintaining some coal production. A significant and heroic minority of NUM loyalists in the Notts coalfield did support their fellow strikers and suffered much abuse.

The NUM National Executive was made up of representatives of seventeen coalfields, of craftsmen, cokemen and staff sections. At the time of the strike the NEC was left-leaning with a number being left Labour and Communist. There were sufficient centre and right wing members to make radical actions a challenge sometimes but most played an honourable part in the strike.

Where there were major issues to be argued and decisions taken, the NEC would usually call a special delegate conference of rank and file pit delegates. This was what happened when the vote for a national strike originally required a two-thirds majority in a ballot of members. As this proved near impossible to achieve, the majority was reduced to 55% in 1970, and to 50% in April 1984.

In considering the question of the decision not to call a national ballot before or during the strike, one South Yorkshire activist Dave Douglass, said that: "Whatever the reasons for not having a ballot initially, and there are many sound ones, as the strike progressed it may have been opportune to call one". He speculated :"All the pundits and opinion polls, judging both strikers and non-strikers results, suggest we should have won something like a 70 – 75 % yes vote nation wide, and even 42% yes in Nottingham".

Douglass argues that the suggestion that a ballot was not held because the NUM leaders would not be bounced into a ballot by the Tories, the reactionary press and pressure by their allies in the Labour and trade union movement was wrong: "It was a decision of the rank and file at mass meetings at Welfare Halls, and mass assemblies all over the country which made that decision, not the leaders".

In truth, some in the rank and file suspected the leadership were trying to sell them out with such a call – that they were looking for a ballot defeat in order to call off the strike.

Whatever one thinks of Arthur Scargill's role during the strike, and I think overwhelmingly favourable, it wasn't Arthur who denied the ballot; he was chair of the conference, and didn't express a view, let alone cast a vote.

The Miners' Strike starts The call to 'get to your marks' came on 6 March 1984, when the miners' leaders met the Coal Board bosses in London, and were told of an intended cut in capacity nationally by four million tonnes, and the closure of twenty pits, with the loss of 15,000 jobs. The trigger was pulled that day with the news that the Yorkshire area's Cortonwood, and Scotland's Bullcliffe collieries were to close, prompting the executives of the two areas to call out all their members on strike. This was "In opposition to Board boss, Ian MacGregor's butchery of Britain's coalfields".

Mick McGahey, NUM vice president, and Scottish president predicted a "domino effect", with more and more pits striking against closures. This concept was taken on board by the workforce and areas, and was allowed to blossom without discussion at NUM national executive level. No-one could claim that it went smoothly.

On 8 March, I was in Sheffield at the NUM headquarters, to where the NUM had recently moved from London.

Following the Coal Board's plan to cut four million tonnes of coal production, an NUM executive committee meeting took place in the morning and continued into the afternoon, as we waited, following a Yorkshire pudding lunch and a couple of pints. Also there were hundreds of Yorkshire and Scottish miners vociferously demanding strike action in support of their pits and jobs, the loss of some of which was imminent. They also let us know what they thought of the press, which wasn't complimentary.

In reporting from Sheffield I noted: "Not even the last despairing efforts of government and the Coal Board to buy off miners at £1,000 for each year of service are likely to put a brake on the anger of Britain's miners.

The demonstrating miners could be heard all morning and afternoon, with four or five lending a menacing presence to the press conference following the executive deliberations.

We were first entertained by Arthur's view of the reporters' intellect and ability to understand much at all. Arthur announced that the executive had "unanimously given its approval to a strike by Yorkshire's and Scotland's 70,000 miners starting tonight, 8 March".

He blamed the Coal Board for "a further savage programme of pit and plant closures, a provocative action that had led to a rapidly deteriorating and a spontaneously escalating situation". This was greeted rapturously by the miners, who were threatened immediately with their pits closing and the loss of their jobs.

The NEC, he said, had extended in advance approval to any other areas taking similar action. This move left it to the individual coalfields and sections to vote and decide on their actions. Thus the road taken by the NUM to the strike was 'pragmatic' to say the least and depended on the actions of miners in their own areas deciding, in their own way and never nationally, how they would conduct the dispute. The only nationally coordinated actions in the 1984–85 strike were the mass pickets at Orgreave.

Some NUM areas were subjected to 'friendly picketing' by 'flying pickets'. In truth this was messy, with the intended 'domino effect' not always successful , and most especially in the Nottinghamshire area. On March 14 the law entered the dispute, when the NCB was granted a high court injunction to stop Yorkshire miners from picketing pits other than their own. Splashed by the *Star,* I reported that Arthur Scargill said that the use of the courts would only strengthen the miners' determination. I also wrote that three quarters of Britain's pits were closed on the third day of the strike. Not a word of which was noted by the rest of the media who were too busy reporting dissension among miners.

The NUM's failure to hold a strike ballot before declaring strike action was deemed by a judge to be against the law, and the NCB was granted a high court injunction to stop Yorkshire miners from secondary picketing at pits in the Midlands, the North-east and North Wales. On March 17, the NCB was given leave to bring contempt action against the Yorks NUM for defying the injunction against secondary picketing.

Energy minister, Peter Walker, forbade Ian MacGregor from invoking this judgement, as the government considered it would antagonise the miners and unite them behind the NUM. Instead the emphasis was on mass policing rather than court action, which might have solidified the strike. As it happened the (anti trade) union law and the mass policing both played a major part before the strike was to end.

On March 15, I reported that Yorkshire, Scotland, Kent, South Wales, Durham, North Derbyshire, North Wales, Lancashire, Northumberland, the Midlands, North Wales and South Derbyshire; the staff, coke and craft sections, spread over all areas, seemed to be onside with the strike.

This impressive result was achieved through differing means. Where they had voted against a strike the executives of the coalfields and the sections recommended them to do so, and they did. Where there was reluctance, the miners themselves decided to do so anyway, with flying pickets from neighbouring and distant coalfields picketing their colleagues out. A lot has been written about the flying pickets, and no doubt there was a good deal of intimidation aimed at those who were not on strike, and it got worse when it came to miners returning to work. But it was to all involved a fight to the death.

On 15 March, at Ollerton Colliery, it was literally so, when a miner, David Jones, aged 24 was killed during heavy picketing of the Notts pits, where miners were going to work. On March 25, I reported in the *Star* that "Interference with pickets blamed for pit trouble", with Jack Taylor, the Yorkshire Area, president saying that his executive never condoned violence.

An eyewitness reported of "miners returning to the Barnsley NUM HQ from Ollerton pit Nottingham, with many of them splattered in blood".

About fifty police confronted a hundred and fifty pickets, when thirteen police carriers suddenly appeared in a column, carrying around 130 extra police officers. There were at least two carriers from the West Midlands among a column of 88 officers who marched straight into the centre of the pickets clearing a way through to the colliery gates.

Taylor protested that "pickets have been on the end of unprovoked violence of picketing procedures, with young inexperienced lads being roughed up by police", and pointed out that "only injuries to the police were reported by the media, but the injuries to miners go unreported".

This complaint was a running sore felt by the miners throughout the year-long strike. was the fact that the police had been mobilised before the strike, not only locally, in county forces, but centrally, using other police forces prepared for action nationwide.

The flying pickets not only sought to 'peacefully' picket out their mining comrades still working, but included any other enterprise that used or carried coal, coal-fired power stations and steel works, the ports where cheap foreign coal was landed, and road haulage and rail companies carrying coal, including from open-cast British mines. On March 19, I reported the "tightening of the coal blockade" by unions, which at this stage was more about intent and preparation than action, which this turned out to be sketchy at best.

The power industry trade unions, the strongest being the right wing's Electricians and Engineering Unions, (EEPTU), and the AUEW, put a huge damper on actions by ruling out support of any kind. Massive police presence in Notts helped to ensure that forty-two collieries in the Midlands kept up production.

The NUM leadership looked to history, and pre war instances of the Triple Alliance of miners, transport, and steel workers, but the response was poor. One reason being, in steel the adverse long-term effect a shut down would have on their industries and their jobs. Where steel was made with the use of blast furnaces, the cost of shutting them down and their consequent cooling would be heavy, and in some smaller mills would mean the end of steel making. Thus we were reporting on the preparation and intent of industries rather than action. So we made the best of the fact that: "Forty T&G Northern delegates and stewards, representing lorry drivers, passed a resolution not to cross pickets lines", which was "expected would affect power stations. Eventually," then representatives of 7,000 T&G open cast miners were to meet in support".

British Rail depots, in Dover and Faversham in Kent, pledged not to move coal that undermined the strike. The Southern region and London trade union councils planned a major event that brought miners, rail and print to increase solidarity. Ron Todd, the T&G docks officer. toured docks, seeking his dockers' help for the miners. There was also retaliation: "BR warned rail crews they will be sent home without pay if they refuse to cross picket lines".

The TUC general council was by now boycotting the joint industry body in a move not liked by general secretary Len Murray. The TUC strategy was decided by its employment policy and organisation committee chairman, SOGAT print union leader, Bill Keys, a steadfast supporter of the miners throughout.

On 27 March the NUM went to court to defend the decision taken on Arthur's instigation, to ban finances from the Coal Board/miners' pension scheme from being invested abroad; an action the union eventually lost. Arthur took the opportunity to warn of most power plants being "virtually out of coal" and that "the NUM would not allow special dispensation asked for by steel industry chiefs". At this time reports of steel works being hit by the strike were numerous. On 27 March, it was: "Scunthorpe steel works production halved", but denials were plentiful too. At Bidston Docks "thousand tonnes of coal lay at the quayside, and if any more was delivered, dockers would boycott it".

A report in the *Star* told of coal stocks so low there were only "Sixty days to blackout Britain". This was denied by the Central Electricity Board and chairman, Sir Walter Marshall, who said of the coal stock position: ". . . he could not be happier, and there would be no power cuts to the autumn". He didn't know that the strike would go on for another six months after the Autumn.

Ray Buckton, general secretary of the train drivers union, ASLEF, and the railwaymen of the NUR, now led by Scot, Jimmy Knapp, were the most successful in organising trade union support. ASLEF instructed its branches and local officials "to black completely the movement of coal and coke from any source" as it recognised "the serious repercussions which would arise for the trade union movement if the miners were defeated".

Near the end of March, I reported: "An MP has complained to the Home Secretary, after four miners returning from picketing in Nottinghamshire were arrested in a village pub".

Mick Welsh said that Herefordshire police burst in on the four, who were on their way home to Doncaster from the Clipstone pit. Where were you safe from the cops! I wrote "Police have now virtually sealed off Nottinghamshire to miners attempting to put their case to colleagues, and save jobs from Coal Board Boss Ian McGregor's axe".

I saw for myself something of the goings-on in Nottinghamshire, or more accurately was prevented from doing so, when joining flying pickets at the South Yorkshire NUM's Barnsley Holiday centre. The report put it thus: "Five police vans stretched across a flyover on the M1 in South Yorkshire were the first sign that Big Brother was watching yesterday, as I travelled with a group of Durham miners to Nottinghamshire.

"The pickets were travelling by van from Barnsley, to persuade their Notts colleagues to join the strike. They were new to the daily cat-and-mouse game taking place between police and pickets during the last three weeks, Their innocence was not to last long. On the road police cars were always in evidence. In the short strip through Derbyshire we saw about fifteen police vans streaming over a flyover. At yet another junction police had closed off one of the roads.

"A police van passed by, headlights blazing, leading a convoy of intercepted miners carrying men back home. Behind that was another police van. Suddenly it was our turn. A small group of police was waving us down and signalled us to stop. One asked the driver where we were going and where he had come from.

"From Durham, I'm going to give leaflets to miners in Nottinghamshire" the driver said.

The policeman told him: "There is a dispute going on, and I must warn you if you proceed, a breach of the peace may occur. I will be taking your details and if you are seen in the area today you will be arrested".

The atmosphere was good-humoured, but the threat was still real. It was decided to turn back. Our van joined a convoy that was escorted miles back in the direction of Barnsley. Then the police drove off and left us to our own devices.

At other places in Notts that day numerous arrests were made of pickets who had got through the cordon. When I left, the Durham miners were preparing to return again to Notts. For one of them, it would be his third trip to Notts in twenty-four hours". This time he might just make it".

"At Eggborough and Drax in Yorkshire, two pickets, who were in Blyth power station, were arrested on March 30. Since the strike began, the total number of pickets arrested was 484. The police said that there were 2,917 pickets on duty at 139 sites, and 5,750 police deployed.

Trade union leaders sympathetic to the miners cause sought to rouse their members with the explanation that a defeat for the miners would be a defeat for all.

Urged by Arthur Scargill to impose a ban on coal movements, Aslef's executive committee backed this and added "from any source". On April 2, the NUR executive called on all its members to put a block on all coal movements within their compass. Three days later the NUR and the TGWU were to make the same pledge.

The ISTC's Bill Sir's though, said that he would not support the miners "to the extent of losing jobs. I will not let the steel industry be crucified on someone else's altar" was his warning.

Mick McGahey told a rally of "a new industrial disease – Ballotitus" of which he said: "Most of Fleet Street is willing not only to provide the ballot paper but set the question as well".

On April 2, I wrote a piece on the strike that paid little notice to the news, but was biased in support of the miners. The headline read: "Mac the Knife's stab at running NCB".

"Even by his own high standards, Coal Board boss, Ian MacGregor has made a spectacularly disastrous start in his latest business venture; the National Coal Board being set to end the year, which closed on March 31, with losses of over £750 million.

"Mr MacGregor took over in September last year 1983, and it has been downhill for the NCB ever since. The arrogance of his 'take it or leave it' pay talks and his refusal to negotiate with the National Union of Mineworkers over pay, and the loss of jobs are now plain to see".

MacGregor, with his guns-at-dawn approach, brought disaster. Pat Lowery, the then chairman of the conciliation service ACAS, told me later that MacGregor thought he could beat the miners into submission pretty quickly, and was never into conciliation as a means of resolving disputes.

On April 3, the Nottinghamshire area leadership called on its members not to cross pickets lines and to join the strike, in order to restore dignity to their coalfield, where massive police actions were harassing pickets. This decision had to be ratified two days later at the area's Mansfield HQ by its lay area council. This was by no means a certain outcome. Even so I wrote: "It will be difficult for the council and those Notts miners still working to ignore the sacrifices that other unions are prepared to make to save miners jobs.

"Already train drivers have been sent home by management after refusing to move coal from the coalfields".

The National Union of Seamen executive had on that day instructed its members to stop all movement of coal around Britain's coasts.

On 5 April , I was jammed inside the gates of the Notts NUM HQ's courtyard in Mansfield, together with pickets from Notts, Yorkshire, Northumberland and other areas, and as many policemen awaiting the result of the delegate meeting. Five hours of debate took place to the sound of a mass picket's calls of "Out,Out, Out". The decision – etched on the grim-faced council delegates – made clear the result. This was confirmed when, by 186 votes to 72, the council voted against joining tens of thousands of their fellow miners outside the pit gates. Devastated pickets first stood in stunned silence as the council delegates walked out through the ranks of miners and police, before booing and cries of 'scab' rang out.

With 7,000 miners on strike in the coalfield angry miners reacted to the vote with the claim that the vote was ". . . not the end of the Nottinghamshire miners' story". But the Notts coalfield produced coal throughout the strike. Ray Chadburn, the favourite of the right-wing press and Notts area president, who twice lost to Scargill in the contest for the NUM presidency, said it had been a hard meeting, in which the executive had tried to get support for its recommendation not to cross picket lines, but had failed.

The Notts EC was still looking for a national ballot. It never came. Not only was the vote a bitter blow to the NUM', but Nottingham and a group of its miners' officials became the centre for anti-NUM strike activities and a propaganda base for national newspapers and others to mount attacks to undermine the strike.

Another blow to the NUM came on 11 April when the mining supervisors' union NACODS voted by 7938 to 6661 to strike against the pit closures but failed to get the three quarters majority needed. Their help was vital, but not forthcoming.

A month into the strike the background of a titanic struggle had been sketched in, as the two forces, an immovable object for twelve months met an irresistible force in pitched battle.

There was Thatcher, her government, MacGregor, and the law newly reinforced to fine trade unions deemed to have broken it. There was also the ranks of helmeted police, already lining up behind shields a with batons at the ready and the Notts 'working' miners and from the start a group of right-wing trade union leaders.

The Tories were clear-sighted and determined. In the early days, Neil Kinnock and Labour leaders stayed in tune with the NUM. Kinnock accused Ian MacGregor of trying to starve the miners back to work. Later he changed his attitude claiming: "We want to sustain the industry, but we do not want the atmosphere poisoned. Get round the table and negotiate within the new financial environment" he advised. In practice Kinnock advised the miners to give in. And in the divided Communist Party while its members wholeheartedly backed the miners elements in the leadership prepared to abandon the struggle.

By way of a writ issued in the High Court on 25 May, by Colin Clark from Pye Hill Colliery, the law forbade the Nottinghamshire area from instructing that the strike was official and to obey the strike call. Similar actions were successful in Lancashire and South Wales.

On 30 May Scargill himself was arrested for obstruction on a picket line at the Orgreave coking plant.

Against this Arthur Scargill and the NUM leadership headed an army of striking miners, their wives and families, key trade union leaders plus politicians for the Labour Party and others.

There were thousands upon thousands of activists and the ordinary public supporting the miners including the *Morning Star* and its staff.

There was no area more militant than South. Its miners picketed anywhere that had anything to do with coal or its movements. They targeted power stations, steelworks, docks, open cast mines and haulage lorries. They moved in their thousands outside of Wales, particularly in Nottinghamshire. This eventually led to a High Court injunction, sought by two haulage firms, and served on the South Wales Area ordering it to stop its members picketing at power stations in Wales and England. In consequence of the picketing continuing, the High Court fined the area £50,000 for contempt of court. When it refused to pay, the area had its £707,000 of its assets seized by a sequestrator.

The heroes in this dispute were undoubtedly the great majority of the industry's 160,000 miners, who were on strike at 150 pits, and their families. During the strike they lead changed lives – from being well paid, with a full social life – in facilities financed and maintained over the years by the mining communities themselves.

They valued a good education for their children, which meant for some boys, an alternative to going down the pit, and many enjoyed holidays abroad. That they went from that to the loss of the weekly wage, struck not only at the family but the community.

In the aftermath of the strike the losses would increase five-fold when a pit, on which a town or village relied for its main employment shut down. The area then became, in time, all but destitute and took years to recover. Some never did. The miners and their families could see this coming; Thatcher and her crew didn't care and therein lies the reason the miners fought so hard for the survival of their pits.

In all of this, women were to the fore. They were heroines. Sixty miners wives from South Yorkshire, whose husbands worked at Edlington and Hatfield near Doncaster, picketed Ollerton pit in Notts because: "We want to show our support for the men on strike" at Ollerton, "and will picket to try to persuade other miners from going into work".

On April 1, no less, a major demonstration by miners' wives and their supporters in London shouted defiance and "Coal not Dole". Betty Heathfield, the march organiser said: "Today we have put the truth across. People should listen to the miners' wives instead of the BBC. The tremendous solidarity here has given a magnificent boost to morale".

The women remained active on picket lines, were involved in confrontations with the police and travelled the country, speaking at political meetings. Nationally, women organised the Women Against Pit Closures conference and, following the National Women Against Pit Closures rally in London on 11 August 1984, handed a petition to the Queen.

Frank Watters; Yorkshire coalfield organiser for the Communist Party and by the time of the strike Midland party secretary said of the women: "They were different than in any other strike, particularly the Women against Pit Closures, blossoming in every coalfield, joining their husbands and boyfriends on the pickets lines, speaking for the first time at public rallies, and in Barnsley on 8 May 1984, organising the biggest demonstration of women".

The financial plight of miners was answered with its own finance industry, as the miners and their supporters organised to fill the void left by the lack of pay. The average miner's wage in 1984 was £200 a week (some miners would have earned more). This multiplied by 150,000 equals £3 million a week going into the mining communities.

How to match that during a strike? The miners and their supporters tried.

I wrote that "Miners from all over Britain are on the stump drumming up support, and wherever they go, people are responding. Miners, Tommy (Inky) Thompson and Kevin Hughes of the Yorkshire NUM EC, and Bob Morrison from Kent met Fleet Street electricians, where *Daily Express* and Associated Newspaper Chapels gave £600". It was said that a number of miners campaigning in big cities were so enamoured they never returned home!

Miners Support Groups (MSG) were formed at work and in communities. An early selection of contributions were: Hampshire MSG (where there was nee'r a pit), collected £763 and then £1,000 for South Wales Miners. T

rade Councils were to the fore: Corby TUC £167 to Snowdown colliery, Kent, and Bristol £300. Clubs and pubs were invaded; an Easter tour of Wigan Clubs by a T&G pair realised £1,024. Massey Ferguson's Manchester Plant collection was £170, CPSA Customs members £61. The print union SOGAT's London clerical branch, gave £1,000, the Machine branch £1000, and also set aside £3,000 to finance publicity for the miners' cause, while NUPE donated £50,000".

Not only money was collected, but also masses of food parcels, clothes and accessories, toys to sanitary towels were paid for, collected, sorted and transported from town and city centres to Britain's coalfields. "A Manchester MSG delivered food to the Chesterfield HQ of the NUM Derbyshire".

In pit towns and villages the miners and their families were organised mainly by women through Women's Action Groups, to ensure people's needs were met. They distributed food parcels and organised sophisticated soup kitchens, feeding meals to their children in the miners clubs and welfares during the day, and to the menfolk before and after picketing. In the evenings these venues staged charity concerts, where well-known artists of the day would turn up at Christmas and other high days. The idea was to make life as normal as possible.

Later on, international support was also evident, as lorries brought Christmas toys for striking miners' children from Germany, Belgium and France, and some children went abroad to spend Christmas holidays in Hungary. Local Labour councils provided breakfast and dinners free to children, Fife guaranteed support, Blaenau Gwent Council spent £14,000 on food vouchers for the borough's miners. Glasgow Labour Party pledged full support for the miners, declaring "MacGregor is after turning the Scottish coalfield into a Culloden".

On 9 June 1984, the war of words continued. The NUS seafarers were instructed not to unload any oil that would keep powers stations in production, and ASLEF drivers in conference endorsed the decision of six transport unions to tighten the coal blockade, including moving coal to steel plants. There were reports of one of Britain's four major, oil-powered stations being vulnerable to a blockade. A further £15,000 was provided from ASLEF to the NUM, making it a total £45,000. On the same day a meeting between the Coal Board and miners' leaders was arranged in Edinburgh, with Scargill and MacGregor in attendance. "A number of areas of discussion were explored without there being signs that either side had moved its position," I added.

Confrontations escalate On Friday 15 June, an underground worker from Kellingley Colliery, named Joe Green, was killed whilst trying to dissuade lorries from delivering fuel to Ferrybridge power station. On 18 June, Orgreave saw a violent confrontation between police and pickets at the British Steel Corporation coking plant. It was a pivotal event in the strike, and one of the most violent clashes in British industrial history. It was "a defining and ghastly moment" that "changed, forever, the conduct of industrial relations and how this country functions as an economy and as a democracy". Most media reports depicted it as "an act of self-defence by police, who had come under attack". Civil liberties group, Liberty, said: "There was a riot. But it was a police riot".

The NUM deployed 5,000 pickets from across the UK, who by sheer numbers planned mass picketing to prevent access to the works by strike-breaking lorries that collected coke for use at the BSC mill in Scunthorpe. The miners faced at least 6,000 armed officers at Orgreave, equipped with riot gear, and supported by police dogs and 42 mounted police officers.

Lawyer, Robert East, in the *Journal of the Law Society* in 1985, wrote that rather than maintaining order and upholding the law, "the police intended that Orgreave would be a 'battle' where, as a result of their preparation and organisation, they would 'defeat' the pickets". Lawyer Michael Mansfield said: "They wanted to teach the miners a lesson – a big lesson, such that they wouldn't come out in force again".

The police operation was as organised as Wellington at Waterloo. First corralling the pickets into a field, the police positioned officers equipped with long riot shields at the bottom of the field, and mounted police and dogs to either side. A railway cutting at the top of the field made retreat by the pickets difficult and dangerous. When the pickets surged forward at the arrival of the first convoy of lorries, South Yorkshire Police Assistant Chief Constable, Anthony Clement, ordered a mounted charge against the miners, with them responding by throwing stones and other missiles at the police lines. Clement retaliated with two further mounted advances, and the third advance was supported by "short-shield" snatch squads, who followed the mounted police, "delivering baton beatings to the unarmed miners".

By now "massively outnumbering" the pickets, the police advanced again and launched another mounted charge. The police pursued the pickets out of the field and into Orgreave village, where Clement ordered a "mounted police canter" and an "out-of-control police force, charging into pickets and onlookers alike on terraced, British streets".

Following the confrontation, 71 pickets were charged with riot, and 24 with violent disorder. At the time, riot was punishable by life imprisonment. The trials collapsed when the evidence given by the police was deemed "unreliable". Gareth Pierce, a solicitor for some of the men, said that the charge of riot had been used "to make a public example of people, as a device to assist in breaking the strike", while Mansfield called it "the worst example of a mass frame-up in this country this century".

It is a frame-up that has not yet been rectified and the police concerned charged with violent conduct or perjury. In June 1991, South Yorkshire Police paid £425,000 in compensation to 39 miners for assault, wrongful arrest, unlawful detention and malicious prosecution.

In 2015, the Independent Police Complaints Commission reported that there was "evidence of excessive violence by police officers, a false narrative from police exaggerating violence by miners, perjury by officers giving evidence to prosecute the arrested men, and an apparent cover-up of that perjury by senior officers".

Solidarity from other trades unions On June 23 1984, I was at the heart of the miners' struggle in the village of Tonyrevail, in South Wales, witnessing a moving encounter, when Fleet Street workers delivered food worth £7,000 to the pit village "under Tory siege".There was a coach-load of print workers with lorry-loads of food and groceries weighing nine tonnes.

"What you have done for us today will live in our memory for a lifetime" miners agent Emlyn Jenkins told the visitors. "The links being forged between miners and the workers supporting them in their struggle would not be forgotten for a generation".

The *Daily Telegraph* SOGAT 82 night machine chapel and the *Financial Times* members responded with the assurance that "Your fight is our fight". The reception given to the print workers by this mining community was simple, but deeply felt. Ron Busby, depot father of the *FT* Chapel, declared it had left him 'overwhelmed' and humble. Derek Lloyd, the *FT*'s FOC recalled that in 1926 the NATSOPA (by then SOGAT '82) workers had refused to print an article in the *Daily Mail* criticising the miners. "That was during the General Strike and today a new bond is being forged", he said.

As the packages of meat, beans, vegetables, fruit, soap, washing powders and many other good were being unloaded at the community centre, women from the surrounding areas described the atmosphere in the valleys. Without the gifts that are now beginning to flow, they have had to rely for 12 weeks on their own communities.

Ann Drummer, from Rhydyfellin, a miner's wife with two children, said people were always reassuring them: "If there's anything you need you just have to ask". Nancy Dean from Glyncoch said that the previous day she had been offered cabbages and rhubarb from growers who were picking crops. Tonyrefail Labour Party ward member, Enid Jones, a miner's daughter, told of the unselfishness of the miners. Those not in urgent need always insisted that families with children should come first. John Nicholas from Coedely is responsible to the NUM for servicing the food centres in South Wales. A thousand packets a week are being provided, and only those in real need came to the centres.

"The Fleet Street workers, who live and work far from the Welsh Valleys, yesterday showed there was no difference as they met the miners and their wives in common cause. The Welsh place names they encountered in their morning journey mystified some of the Cockneys, but the understanding that was there in the afternoon needed no words".

On 27 June, Salford strike breakers had asked Justice Caulfield at the High Court, in Manchester, to rule that the NUM's strike actions at Agecroft colliery were unlawful, and this was upheld. It was declared that the NUM could not call an official strike without a ballot of members.

At the end of June 1984, I was at the NUR conference in Llandudno, which was dominated by the miners' strike, and which demonstrated the NUR's support for the beleaguered miners. Its general secretary, Jimmy Knapp, told of his union's help to its own members. Those suspended without pay for not crossing picket lines would have their pay made up. The meeting also decided to put £6 million, (a quarter of its funds!), into a provident scheme, in an attempt to avoid sequestration under the then current Tory anti-trade union laws.

Legal judgements On 1 September, Lord Justice Nicholls heard the two cases that were to prove crucial to the NUM's cause. The first was brought by miners at Manton Colliery in the Yorkshire area but geographically in North Nottinghamshire, when the Orgreave Colliery was threatened with closure, and this prompted a two-week strike. The NUM executive approved the decision in Yorkshire, relying on a decision from January 1981, in which 85.6% of the members voted to strike if any pit was threatened with closure on economic grounds.

In the second, North Derbyshire miners argued that the (national) strike was illegal, both at area level, as a majority of its miners had voted against, and at national level, as there had been no ballot. Mr Justice Nichol said that in both cases the NUM had breached its constitution by calling a strike without holding a ballot. In the case against the Yorkshire Area he said that the 1981 ballot result was "too remote in time, [with] it now being two and a half years later". Scargill called the ruling "another attempt by an unelected judge to interfere in the union's affairs". He was fined £1,000 (paid by an anonymous businessman), and the NUM was fined £200,000.

On 1 October 1984, contempt of court papers were served on Scargill and the NUM. On 4 October, despite NUM lawyers arguing that the case should go to a full trial, the High Court gave the NUM five days to obey the interlocutory injunction and to call the strike off. This not being obeyed, on 26 October, the High Court ordered total sequestration of NUM funds. In early November 1984, the NUM executive voted to co-operate with the court to recover the funds, despite opposition from Scargill, who stated in court that he was only apologising for his contempt of court because the executive voted for him to do so.

On 18 December, Lawrence Cunliffe, the Labour MP for Leigh, told the House of Commons that: "The handling of the strike in legal terms is significant, in that the rule of law is being used against the legitimate views and actions of a trade union, aspiring to fulfil the aims and objectives of its members as represented in its leadership. A paramount symptom is the Government's attempt to suppress the rights of that union and its members, with all the vigour that they can muster.

"The law on sequestration, and the apparently prejudiced interpretation of it by the courts is rapidly leading to the erosion of civil liberties. In the view of many of us, that will be the result of court decisions based on bad law".

A pundit reckoned it was "a defining moment in British industrial relations. The NUM's defeat significantly weakened the trade union movement, was a major victory for the Conservative Party, and the Thatcher government was able to consolidate its economically liberal programme".

The saga continued. The NUM sought to beat the sequestration by moving the vast majority of its funds to banks abroad setting off a rush to grab the money. Price WaterHouse Cooper was one high profile firm that the NUM resisted, as its application to return union assets to the UK from Ireland failed on 7 November. A Dublin Court ruled that £2.75 millions of NUM funds remain frozen and not be given to the sequestrator.

On 30 November 1984, arising out of the failure to seize the NUM's overseas assets, a Receiver, Mr Brewer, a Tory Party official from Derbyshire, was appointed to control NUM assets and funds, and started his abortive trek to get NUM money. On 9 December 1984, the Receiver and Sequestrator tried to seize £4.6 millions of NUM funds from Luxembourg, but again the NUM's application successfully froze the account.

According to Mrs Thatcher's papers, it was only tip-offs from the Security Service MI5, based on telephone taps and surveillance, that enabled Price Waterhouse, without the NUM's knowledge, to take control of £8.7 millions deposited in banks in Luxembourg, Zurich and Dublin.

At the outset of the strike a fund was set up, with donations going either to the NUM HQ or to coalfield area offices, but after the high court ruled the strike unlawful, the Miners' Solidarity Fund (MSF) was set up to ensure hardship money could not be sequestrated. The MSF was then administered from Headland House, the then headquarters of the Agricultural Section of the TGWU (now where the NUJ is based). This was funding from at home and abroad that "did more than anything else to raise hopes and sustain beleaguered mining communities".

With the sequestrator seeking to plunder every NUM penny, tales were legion, as monies were making their way to Gray's Inn Road by cheque, in buckets and in bags carried there at dead of night from sympathetic trade unions. enabling the NUM to continue the struggle.

Even more bizarre was when Roger Windsor the NUM's chief executive was accused of damaging the image of the union by visiting Libya (as reported by the *Sunday Times*), despatched there, it was claimed, by Scargill to meet its Colonel Gaddafi either seeking funds or in an attempt to put NUM funds beyond the reach of the Government. Windsor met Gaddafi, and film of the two men embracing was shown on British TV! What was achieved by the escapade is anybody's guess.

Before and after this episode, Gladys and I spent hours and many late nights with Mick McGahey at the County Hotel, Euston near where we lived. Most of the year of the strike the right-wing press corps and the anti-Scargillites in general sought to portray Mick as being at odds with Scargill's conduct of the strike, and being someone who would have looked for compromise from early on. In all that time I never heard Mick disagree with how the NUM's or Scargill's actions were prosecuted. Indeed he was heavily involved in the most criticised tactic, of the "domino" effect by the strikes by militant areas provoking strikes in other areas. He ridiculing the cries for a ballot of all miners after the dispute had started which he labelled "the ballotites disease".

Only once did he indicate displeasure with Arthur. Mick always referred to Arthur as "the young man" and on the night the Gaddafi incident was on the news, he simply raised his eyes to the heavens saying "Young man, Oh My Goodness". And that was it, as we raised our wee dram to all miners.

Subsequently, in 1990, the *Daily Mirror* owner, the disgraced Robert Maxwell, took on board reports alleging Scargill's misuse of, and receipt o,f funds from Libya, based on Roger Windsor's evidence. The story was initially reported on the front page of the *Mirror* and in the Central TV programme *The Cook Report*.

Later, Gavin Lightman QC, was requested to undertake an enquiry into the manner in which NUM funds and the £1 million donation by Russian miners were used, allegedly, for the refurbishing of the homes of Scargill and Peter Heathfield, during and after the miners' strike.

There was, Lightman said, evidence that Scargill had failed to account properly for substantial amounts of money, including bank accounts but there was no evidence of misuse of funds. It is little wonder, given the chaotic situation that the NUM was involved in trying to keep the union afloat as its funds were being plundered, that the greatest propriety was not kept.

The experiences – of the NUM, the South Wales miners and the NGA print union – of the anti-trade union laws which lead to the sequestration of their funds as they attempted to prosecute industrial disputes, exposed the Achilles heel of modern trade unionism. Where once the e only things we have to lose was our chains by 1984 trade unions were giant organisations employing hundred of workers.

The livelihoods and pensions of these workers were put in jeopardy and the ability of trade unions to carry out actions in defence of members' wages and conditions was in jeopardy. Unions a were threatened by sequestration of their funds, leaving them with little alternative to surrender to what was lawful blackmail.

All may have been different for the NUM if NACODS' 17,000 members had backed their NUM colleagues who were fighting to keep the pits open including for NACODS members. If they had taken action from the very first day of that strike, conditions in every pit would have started deteriorating despite the efforts of the colliery managers. With the maintenance staff also on strike-putting the majority of pits would be in danger of enforced closure.

In April 1984, by a small majority NACODS had voted to strike in support of the NUM, but without the two-thirds majority that their constitution required for a national strike. On 28 September 1984, for the first time in their history, NACODS members voted to strike by 82%. This was a momentous decision, greeted with joy by miners who saw victory ahead of them.

These hopes were dashed, when a deal negotiated between NACODS, led by general secretary, Ken Sampey, and the North Yorkshire NCB director, Michael Eaton, persuaded the union to call off the strike action in return for the introduction of an independent element into the coal industry's review procedures for threatened collieries.

What had happened was the subject of dispute for many years, until in 2000 a *Guardian* obituary of Ken Sampey, the NACODS president, by industrial journalist Geoffrey Goodman, said that "Arthur Scargill and the NUM turned away from Sampey's plan". Because Scargill and the NUM wouldn't accept the proposal, "NACODS' leaders then decided to settle separately and call off their strike threat".

In a letter to the *Guardian*, Scargill disputed this version and wrote: "This account of events is completely untrue. The 80%-plus vote for strike action, if implemented, would have been sufficient to save pits and jobs, and win the dispute, but was ignored."

"An ACAS invitation to a meeting, to the NCB, the NUM and NACODS, to see if there could be a negotiated settlement with the NCB proved futile. The NUM and NACODS held a separate meeting, and agreed a joint proposal outlining their final position. This proposal was submitted to the NCB with a copy to ACAS. It would have settled the strike and stopped all pit closures other than on safety grounds or exhaustion of coal reserves. It was emphasised that if the NCB did not accept the joint proposal, the NACODS strike would go ahead. The NCB agreed to consider the proposal."

On the eve of the reconvened discussions, I learned that the NACODS leadership had reneged on its agreement with the NUM and had decided instead to put forward a proposal for an "independent" non-binding element within the colliery review procedure, and if this proved acceptable to the NCB, NACODS would call off its strike action", and this is what happened.

Scargill wrote: "No explanation was given for this u-turn, in which Ken Sampey played a leading role. The NACODS decision, like all sell-outs, was shameful, with terrible historical consequences, leading as it did to the virtual destruction of Britain's mining industry. Scargill and the NUM and NACODS' leadership later worked together, for what it was worth, at national and local levels.

While all the above was being played out, the miners and the police were at the pit gates and throughout the land. The miners were still backed by the support of millions of citizens.

On 9 July, I joined and reported on a march of over 20,00 miners and supporters at Saltley Gate Birmingham, where in February 1972 mass picketing had led to the closure of its fuel storage depot. This turned the tide in the national miners' strike over pay, and led to a major pay rise for miners and the downfall of the Ted Heath Tory government.

At Saltley Gate the march held a short meeting that included two minutes silence for Joe Green and David Jones, the miners who had died on the picket lines. Red roses were hung on the Saltley gate; with the march turning to song of "Here we go! Here we go! and then to "We will win! We will win!"

The symbolism was palpable, fuelling the fervour of the march to Birmingham City Centre on a hot summer's day, with the short sleeved, by now bronzed miners and the women in their summer dresses. They and their supporters marched behind banners bright.

Arthur (Scargill) and Mick McGahey were at the front of the march, accompanied, I hope it's safe to say on such an emotional occasion, by some adoring nurses of the Birmingham Blood transfusion Service, ("Who happily were not needed" I quipped!)

As with such gatherings, the good humour increased, as the heat and the derisory jokes about Thatcher, MacGregor and the bosses increased in intensity. For the whole day the accompanying police guarding us were chided as to "whose side are you on".

At every step the sense of the power of the working class when on the march increased, and there was the feeling that with this power, after 18 weeks of facing increasingly hostile actions by the state, victory would be ours.

"Birmingham bubbled with the confidence of triumph for the miners, as 20,000 people marched, led by the Maerdy (south Wales) pit band. There was a mass of colour, with 550 banners that billowed and bounced along through the housing estates and into the crowded city centre.

"The miners' group banners were matched by a wives support group with Maerdy and North Staffs "preferring to be a picket rather than a scab'. The leader of the miners' wives, Betty Heathfield, said: "we see it as our struggle too".

"The reply from the miners ranks was 'we could never have done it without you. There is nothing more inspiring, surely, than joining thousands of comrades who are in a struggle, on the march, particularity when the sun shines down!" I concluded.

On 9 July, I wrote of "Anger at scabbing may halt dockers," at the port of Immingham, where contractors were brought in by British Steel to load iron ore onto lorries, which was then shipped to Scunthorpe steel works, after ASLEF train drivers had refused to cross picket lines.

There was a chance that T&G members might help the miners' cause by hampering coal movements. Immingham was registered under the National Dock Labour Scheme (NDLS), and the use of contractors was a breach of the national agreement. That they were scabs only fuelled the anger of the nation's 20,000 registered dockers.

Dockers "from Scotland to Penzance" took immediate action followed by Liverpool, Bristol, Tilbury, Southampton and Humberside, the home of Immingham and Hull. There was a total stoppage on the Manchester Ship canal. Not only that, but the dockers joined the ranks of pickets at steel works entrances. Simultaneously The Port Employers' Association and the union, whose national officer was John Connolly, were meeting, but without any result.

In a House of Commons debate, Thatcher threatened the loss of dockers jobs if they did not return to work. On the 11 July, a special T&G dockers conference decided to stop all movements of cargoes in and out of British ports.

The registered ports dealt with 70% of goods into Britain and Northern Ireland, and on 13 July the port employers told the union that it was "willing to fully honour its obligations under the national dock labour scheme,and this would enable the union to recommend a return to work".

The talks broke down and the strike action continued and widened. However, both sides accepted an invitation from the conciliation service ACAS, and on 18 July, sixteen hours of talks produced "an agreement to end the eleven-day-old dockers' strike ensuring, that there will be no breach of the NDLS through the use of other than the permanently-employed, registered dockers at registered ports".

The agreement meant that no matter the dockers' wish to help the miners, that scabs would not again be used where the TGWU had managed to take actions that had stopped the movement of iron ore or coal into individual steelworks. The dockers could do no more.

It was also stated on the T&G side: "The response to the strike was presumed to have stopped attempts to abandon the Dock Labour Scheme, which gives job protection to registered dockers". This was not to last for long.

The summer brought added pressure to ensure that miners' children in every pit village and town, had a happy holiday. The loss of school meals and milk was replaced by those, mainly women, already serving their communities from kitchens with doubled workloads to provide meals for lively youngsters. Many local councils provided free packed lunches for all its mining family children. Gateshead gave them free bus passes as well.

Wakefield Council provided free meals. Barnsley, Doncaster, Rotherham and Wakefield reduced council-house rents and local tax rates for striking miners, but the Conservative Selby Council refused any assistance.

Community facilities were used to entertain kids for six weeks, with family holidays for those on strike pay who were unable to pay for them. The money came from supporters, but also from the striking miners themselves, like those from Worksop, Nottinghamshire, a thousand of whom worked in Yorkshire pits. They walked 250 miles to London, over two weeks, on their way collecting money and sponsorship to 'feed their kids'.

Holidays were arranged throughout the land for women and children such as in Devon and Cornwall. Miners working from the GMBATU offices in Plymouth collected £9,000 in the South West, from where £3,000 worth of good were sent to South Wales. The mini bus that took the food, also took three wives and seven children for a week's holiday with Plymouth families.

There were holidays abroad with French miners of the CGT union organised pits "taking Britain's pit striking children into the hearts and homes". Two hundred miners' children from all over Britain were taken on the trip using funds raised in France and Britain. The coaches to Dover were provided by Transport and General Workers Union regions in Scotland, Wales and the North West and Eastern England. They were driven free of charge by the T&G drivers, and the National Union of Seamen arranged discounted fares on P&O Ferries.

The fighting did not stop, and in July I reported: "Chaos as pickets block Humber Bridge" and on actions in South Wales and Scotland: "Thatcher's hate campaign and actions against them and their leaders left reverberations around Britain yesterday".

The Bridge was blocked in the rush hour, when drivers drove on to the world's longest suspension bridge and left their cars there, stopping attempts to move iron ore from Immingham reaching Scunthorpe's steel works. The police alleged that 3,000 miners had been turned back from the bridge during the day.

At Port Talbot, South Wales, five women and three men were arrested as a mass picket tried to stop lorries taking supplies to the Llanwern steel plant, and in Bilston Glen, Scotland's biggest pit, police violence was said by an NUM official to have "reached unprecedented proportions". Five working miners got in, and thirty-five pickets were arrested.

"Miners President Arthur Scargill said on television yesterday that "We are absolutely certain we can win".

On 26 July the NUM executive announced a special delegate conference to see how the NUM could "tighten the knot we have, so that we can win this dispute quicker".

It was at this time that a man nicknamed by the press as the Silver Birch was supposed to be organising a return to work. The state propaganda machine painted a picture of hundreds of the strikers beginning to go back to work, a media theme that persisted to the end but without much substance.

At the end of July, the National Graphical Association was savaged in court yet again over its dispute with the Eddie Shah *Stockport Messenger* news group. The NGA was ordered to pay £125,000 "to the infamous anti-trade union boss" for damages incurred during the six-month dispute over the victimisation of six of their members.

On the same day, the South Wales miners were found in contempt of court for not paying the £50,000 fine imposed. This happened when one, Judge Park observed a report on July 18 in the *Daily Express*, that the area appeared to be trying to avoid paying the fine by seeking to move its money into a private account of its officials.

Into August and "City gents yesterday began their dirty work of tracking down the assets of the South Wales miners in the bid to grab the £50,000 fine imposed for contempt of court. The four doing the work for Price Waterhouse, may not even have to leave their offices to find the money."

Seventy Welsh miners were barricaded into their NUM offices in Pontypridd, sleeping on the floor, in order to stop the bailiffs from lifting any of the office equipment. A Price Waterhouse spokesman explained that they would be in touch with the institutions where the NUM have their funds and would be taking control of their funds.

I reported that three of the four Price Waterhouse men, working to seize the South Wales miners' money, also worked on the *Stockport Messenger* grabs, and I named them.

At the *Star* we were part of a never ceasing propaganda war, handicapped in that just ourselves and the ultra-left news outlets, were on the side of the miners and their families, against the capitalist and state media.

One aspect of this was to give as positive a picture as we could of the official trade union movement, which in truth was pretty mixed. There were those in support of the NUM, those against it, a few ambivalent and some openly hostile.

The TUC general secretary was by then Norman Willis, whose elevation coincided – unluckily for him some would say – with the start of the strike. Willis had been an amiable T&G and TUC official. Some said too much so with his speeches being spattered with badly chosen jokes. Norman was 'a fixer' in its clearest sense but Arthur and his immediate colleagues showed no inclination to be fixed. Files later made public showed that the government had an informant inside the Trades Union Congress passing on information about negotiations.

Norman's one distinctive move – to get a settlement in June by drawing up a plan to end the strike with a compromise – was shunned by Arthur and the miners with Arthur sweeping the document off the table whilst metaphorically spitting on it.

The quick glimpse of it that I saw, would I believed, in normal circumstances have given the miners time to regroup and save some pits for some time. Events I think proved me wrong. The South Wales miners' take on Norman's efforts at conciliation was revealed at a meeting in a miners' welfare where his speech was answered graphically by the lowering of a noose from the ceiling.

It was the unions and their individual leaders that decided policies. The TUC had s neither the ability to sell out or take the lead.

The Nottingham area situation apart, a mostly a slow return to work occurred. This the media embellished in overly dramatic fashion, as the few working miners were bussed, in what were dark, meshed windowed, armoured vehicles under police escort, illustrating a sinister and stark representation of the strikes' most bitter aspects.

We had one of our best days, on 5 August 5 when my splash said: "Britain's striking miners blew the biggest raspberry at the Coal Board yesterday as they defied the blackmail and blandishments and stayed away from work". The Coal Board had made a great effort to entice men back to work with special buses "that lay unused or ran empty, with the police having few miners to escort through picket lines on a dismal day for the Board and a victory for the miners' union".

The NCB had timed their campaign to coincide with the end of the miners' annual holiday, and to weaken the stand of the special miners' delegate conference on the Friday, that aimed at stepping up the dispute.

International support for the miners On the same page there were pictures of "children of striking Kent miners on their way to Bulgaria, and twenty children of South Wales miners off to Zurich to spend three weeks in the mountains of Switzerland".

This example of international solidarity with the British miners struggle was to become a great feature of the strike. Internationally, trade unions went to extraordinary lengths to express their solidarity. NUM figures for donations to the Miners Solidity Fund, from July 1 1984 to May 1985, show that Denmark, Norway, Sweden and Finland contributed £690,327.97. Miners in the Donbas in the USSR gave £50,000 worth of roubles, Swedish miners 700,000 Crowns, Finland's trade unions SAK £13,300 and French miners delivered £61,000 in cash.

The news of the strike went as far as Japan, whose trade unions asked for, and got, an NUM international delegate, one John Burroughs, the Derbyshire NUM treasurer, who from an official, sixteen-days visit to that country brought home £25,000; and another £25,000 came later.

In May, a delegation from the Communist-led CGT unions were so impressed by the miners' solidarity that – in a symbolic act on the night of 23 May – coal wagons with 16,000 tons of coal were dumped in the railway siding at Calais. French miners travelled to Britain with a 30,000 francs (£3,000) collection.

The *Bulletin* of the World Federation of Trades Unions – which united left wing unions in capitalist countries, the Third World and the Socialist countries – described a Danish ship the *Libra*, docking at Hull with hundreds of thousands of tonnes of food and clothing, manned by volunteer Danish seafarers. First loaded in Rostock in the GDR (East Germany) with clothing and food collected by trade unions in the Soviet Union, Bulgaria, Czechoslovakia and the GDR, it then went to Copenhagen for clothes donated by Danish seamen. The French CGT unions donated 35,00 tonnes of food and toiletries, delivered by the French themselves to British coalfields, and there was a shipment of 100,000 chickens that came from Denmark. The Italian unions linked to the West Midlands, from where construction union UCATT's secretary, Ken Barlow, visited Milan and Brescia in July, returning with seven million lira (£3,500). Ken Loach's film *Whose side are you on?* was shown all over Italy, stimulating interest when shown in Communist Party clubhouses. One hundred artists donated paintings, which were sold for £7,285.

Australian trade unionists took solidarity to its bosses, with the Miners Federation's general secretary, Barry Swan, advising the coal owners not to export coal to Britain during the strike. The coal was stockpiled until the end of the dispute. The Australian Seamen's union stopped tugs in Brisbane from berthing the *Crystal Transporter*, attempting to pick up 130,000 of coking coal bound for Britain. Details and statistics of international solidarity were collated in *Pit Props*, edited by Granville Williams of the Campaign for Broadcasting Freedom.

In July 1984, the Australian Miners Federation flew out Malcolm Pitt, Kent NUM, and Austin Fairest, North Derbyshire NUM, to tour Australia. It brought an avalanche of donations, raising £66,000 and a £10,000 donation from the Seamen's Union. Queensland miners levied £86,000.

New Zealand's 3.2 million population was outstanding, with its seaman's union to the fore in raising £32,582 from its 1,300 members. Kevin Hughes and Derek Frances, from Yorkshire NUM, toured New Zealand in October and November 1984 raising £24,000.

The large amounts were matched in Yemen, Bermuda and Palestine, accompanied by messages of solidarity. Citizens of Ireland, France and South Africa remembered the support of British miners in the past. Tom Sibley, the organiser of much of the international support through the WFTU, reckoned that international support came to 20% of money raised for Britain's miners. An international march from County Hall, London set off for Dover with fifty marchers from fifteen countries represented, including organisations from Chile, Iran, El Salvador, Pakistan, Lebanon and the Sikh community in Britain. An example of solidarity from Granville Williams told of "£15,316 contributions from the 30,000 inhabitants of the Faroe Islands; a striking testament to the way the miners' struggle inspired people across the world".

Paul Mackney, president of the Birmingham Trades Council during the strike, summed up the support for the strike, which involved more people,at a greater pitch of activity, over a lengthier period than any other campaign in the history of the labour movement. It would not be an exaggeration to say that it represented the biggest civilian mobilisation in Britain since the Second World War.

The NUM special delegate conference, on 10 August 1984, in Sheffield, rejected the Coal Board proposal to keep open five of its threatened pits out of 70, and agreed to step up the action. Scargill said the NUM would take its case to the floor of the TUC Congress in September 1984: "There we will be asking for total support for our dispute".

I wrote that the reporters there "Pressed him to attack his members for violence on the picket line. He replied that he was not prepared to condemn those whose only crime was to fight for jobs. "Over 2,000 of our members have been injured on picket lines, two have been killed and one man is in intensive care in Northumberland with a fractured skull. Don't talk to me about violence". he said.

The TUC at Brighton gave broad support for the NUM and its striking members, looking to the power, transport and steel unions to further curb the transport of scab coal, and stop the crossing of miners' picket lines and activities undermining the strike. The TUC was to consider an interest-free loan for the miners' union and a cash appeal was to be launched.

The most heart-warming event was in the traditional pre-Congress cricket match, between the TUC General Council and the industrial correspondent hacks. This transformed into a miners Children's Gala day at the print union SOGAT's leisure centre at nearby Rottingdean, where the kids were staying.

I wrote that "While the white-flannelled fools (including your reporter) flung bat and ball the Yorkshire miners' children played games and swam, the local jazz band played and Welsh miners' choirs and brass bands rent the air. I ended with a joke that "the barracking of the journalists by Durham miners may have affected the game (in favour of the TUC), "but no police presence showed on the wicket line"!

There was a clarion call, (my interpretation) to 'Dig Deep for the miners', to help relieve the hardship now being caused to the mining communities in the 28th week of the fight against pit closures. Unions were also asked to give donations or interest-free loans to the NUM, which was still having to meet administration costs of £150,00 a week. Talks between the NCB and the NUM on 22 September broke down.

The 30th week of the strike ended with an upbeat Scargill, and the NUM leadership buoyed by the support, said that: "Promises made by the TUC Congress are coming through in an increasingly fruitful way, and that "This contrasted with the signs of panic by the government". On 10 October, EEPTU power workers voted against supporting the miners. The TUC's fine words were being undermined.

By October, after 32 weeks of strike action, how many had gone back to work was still disputed. It wasn't many, relatively, considering the £557 million lost by miners at £200 a week. 55.5 million tonnes of coal lost including the effect of an overtime ban. The government loss was £1.8 to £2 billions by the end of the strike. Seven thousand five hundred miners faced criminal charges, of whom a miniscule number were found guilty.

Winter crept in and signs of desperation emerged. This was countered by an example of support for the miners. I reported: "There are few miners on strike at Coalville in Leicestershire. Yet thanks to the railway workers in the town, it has become the shining symbol of the solidarity in the coalfield dispute, for the 160 at the Coalville freight depot have stood solidly for the miners for thirty weeks.

Even though laid off, then threatened with the depot's closure, and having two men sacked, they had stood firm. "These members of the ASLEF union and the National Union of Railwaymen have refused to touch scab coal, despite being in the centre of coalfields surrounded by working miners. Coalville NUR's branch secretary, Roy Butlin, says defiantly "Hell will freeze over before we move scab coal".

Into November and a breakdown in talks allowed me the chance to label the Coal Board boss "Mr MacBlunder", after a chaotic press conference with ACAS ended without advances.

Under ever-darkening skies in the now bleak mornings, that stretched into the day, the cold took over from a benign summer. Despite the courage of the mining communities and the support of thousands, and although we did our best to paint a positive picture, there was real hardship with no end in sight.

Deaths in the struggle At Auchinleck, Ayrshire, a young man died when digging on an old railway embankment and the ground gave way. He was the fifth pit striker to die in similar circumstances. Two teenagers, whose parents were unemployed, died digging coal in Doncaster on that weekend.

Then on 30 November, I was on the desk when the news came of the death of Welsh taxi driver, David Wilkie, when two striking miners dropped a concrete block from a footbridge onto his taxi. Wilkie was driving a working miner from Rhymney to the Merthyr Vale mine, as he had done for ten days. With them were two police cars and a motorcycle outrider, and at the Rhymney Bridge roundabout, the two striking miners dropped a 46-pound (21 kg) concrete block from a bridge that went through the windscreen. Wilkie died at the scene from multiple injuries. His passenger survived.

Dean Hancock and Russell Shankland, were found guilty of murder by a majority verdict on 16 May 1985, by which time the strike had ended, and were sentenced to life imprisonment. The life sentences caused an outcry among the striking miners, who felt that the death of Wilkie was not a deliberate act. The strike had ended by the time the verdict was brought in, but seven hundred miners at Merthyr Vale walked out on hearing the news.

On appeal, their convictions were reduced to manslaughter, and their life sentences were replaced with eight-year prison terms, of which they would serve just over half, being released on 30 November 1989.

It was not an easy story to write from our position, the intro being "After a nine-months disciplined and solid struggle by the South Wales miners the news of the death of David Wilkie shocked the valleys yesterday. But there was always fear amongst miners that the Coal Board's attempts to break the strike, by bribes and cheap publicity could end with something like this happening".

I worked the rest through with Kim Howells, then the South Wales NUM area researcher, and later an MP and Labour minister, who said "We are not trying to excuse anything that happened. A man is dead and that's a tragedy". He believed that this death would set back the miners' cause greatly. But that "the Coal Board's attempt to persuade miners to work has raised the temperature in South Wales".

Just 170 Wales miners were then at work out of 22,000, eight months into the strike, and Howells said "the 'cheap publicity' the Board was using and the attempt to buy people back to work was 'clear incitement, which had played its part in the tragedy'. I think that was fair.

Prime minister, Margaret Thatcher in contrast, used the tragedy to tell the miners to give up the struggle and accept defeat; she being "horrified" and "utterly condemning the murderous attack". Gerald Kaufman MP, although also "horrified" said that violence could not be justified, adding that "It ill becomes Mrs Thatcher to preach to us about the need for conciliation when her confrontational policies had brought this about".

Councillor Peter Davies of Merthyr Vale, while deploring the incident, which would harm the miners' strike, believed that "this dispute has been escalated by the police tactics of preventing pickets travelling to the pit".

The lighter side to the strike These were difficult times, but there are occasions when a remark points up some absurdity of the situation and a smile could surface.

It seems that the opponents of the miners were devoid of a sense of humour.

his is accentuated by there being opponents devoid of humour altogether. The Coal Board's Ian MacGregor not only fell into this category, but at one point failed even to put two words together and needed a stand-in. The police may have had a sense of humour and would need one, when faced not only by angry miners, but the wit of picket lines.

There was even some wit shown in the case of the hated scabs, but it was hard to see the funny side of their actions. All was meat and drink to the *Star's* cartoonist Eccles, Frank Brown, whose cartoons ridiculed the antics of the miners opposition in scathing detail, They punctured the pomposity of the government, the Coal Board and its allies, and exposed the odds against the miners, through picturing the serried ranks of armed police facing determined but defenceless pickets.

Eccles produced the funniest cartoon I ever saw, when during a Fleet Street dispute at the same time, a prisoner in a US jail was to be put to death after thirty years of pleading for it to happen. With the prisoner strapped to the chair, a man entering proclaims: "Sorry, the electricians are on strike" ! The editor refused to run it.

Frank's twin, Sid Brown, newspaper designer and cartoonist, produced the *Morning Star's* ubiquitous "I didn't vote Tory" badge, and it took off, selling in tens of thousands and turning out to be the paper's most successful badge ever.

The badge production turned a sideline into a major production line during the miners' strike. The famous "Coal not Dole" badge sold in thousands, with young miners commissioning badges such as the Zulus, the Warriors, and Captain Kull's No1 Army, to express their active resistance to the brutal police occupations of mining areas.

Sid also produced posters, including "Government of the rich, by the rich, for the rich" superimposed on an image of Mrs Thatcher, and "If you think I'm green, you must be" to mock her pretensions to environmental concern.

Conditions at Easington In December I was in the thick of things with photographer Pat Mantle, joining the miners who were "Backing Monday's NUM decision to stand firm as they left their homes in Easington Colliery, County Durham's at 5 am." They were ready for picketing duty, continuing their defiance. In the glare of a police searchlight miners stood facing police in riot gear, as they have done for many months.

We had witnessed the miners of Easington gathering fuel on the cliff side and clifftop of the pit village in County Durham. which runs by the way of a 'clarty (dirty) path to the North Sea shore. The miners dug cheerfully away at a fifty-year-old slag heap on an icy December day. It was hard to hope for anything but victory for their courage.

On days when there is a large swell, lumps of coal are swept from the sea, from what is an opencast site just off shore. On days like this, a relatively calm one, the sea threw up only what were pebbles of coal, distinguished from the black stones only by the experienced eye of the miners. Even so, small stones would get into the grates of their homes, making for some very heavy dustbins from the heavier pieces, the miners said. The coal was loaded onto bikes, and here the cliff side diggers had it easier than the shore-line miners, who toiled up the narrow pathway past Easington colliery with their precious loads.

The best of the ashes were dug and sifted to provide heat for families deprived of warmth, as they struggled to preserve their communities from MacGregor's axe. Asked about this, one said "anything is better than nothing". From what they were collecting though it was hard to see that it would burn well.

On the picket line itself "Not a single miner on this bleak morning voiced any doubts at their pit delegates vote to refuse to pay the £200,000 fine, risking all their union's funds. As they stood in the cold air of the North Sea, police vans circled the town in increasing numbers. In what for the moment seemed a ritual, a bus carrying a few working miners raced into the pit. The tightly controlled police operation in Easington High Street allowed only the possibility of the strikers hurling abuse at the consciences of the scabs".

Among some pickets there was talk of the lack of support of the TUC. This was summed up by Sid Robinson of the Herrington pit, on the MacGregor hit list. "What they do today to us is what they'll do to them tomorrow" he warned the trade union movement.

"This was the stark and simple message from the frontline of working peoples' struggles. Then the miners of Easington joined the miners of other pits on buses to face yet more police and scabs at the Hawthorn and Murton collieries. Increasing numbers of miners are joining the picket lines in the area. Police have staggered the hours at which the few scabs are bussed into Durham's fourteen pits."

"The determination of the mining communities is being matched by the organisation built by them over the last ten months. At Murton Colliery large numbers of police are already in evidence with riot equipment as coaches arrive, and where the police will pen the miners in and around the 'Welfare', as nearly 1,000 pickets take tea in turns. It is often only the discipline and organisation of the miners which prevents such incidents. The police seem unconcerned about the risk of setting off violent scenes."

"Two young women, Alfreda Williamson, 17 and Margaret Morris, 22, had been there since before 6 a.m. to make and serve tea. They are canteen workers and proudly, NUM members from the Murton pit. They said as they poured the tea. 'We are here until we win'. At the entrance to the Hawthorne pit the picketing ended, after another few more scabs, some grotesquely masked in white balaclavas, swept by in darkened buses. On our coach, the driver said that he has taken Durham miners all over country. The only threats or aggression he met were from the police".

"At still only 9 a.m., the buses returned to the villages, where a busy day for the miners, their wives and supporters continued to sustain the strike. There was derision and some loathing for the Tory in Luxembourg seeking to plunder the miners money. But as miner's wife, Brenda Moorland, said while at the food kitchen 'We carry on regardless. We have to, don't we'".

While in Easington, I had the time to visit what was at the heart of all pit village communities over the 12 months, in a piece headlined "Cafe with magic on the menu". The intro being: "No matter how fierce the struggle of working people becomes, there are good times to be remembered. And it is through the struggles that working people learn their enormous powers of organisation.

"The Easington 'Top Club', where women talked of the ten months of the miners strike, both of these things could be seen. With the dinners and puddings ready to serve to 250 miners and children at lunch time, Margaret Foster, Joe Barnes and Marelyn Johnson told their story over a cup of tea. On 13 April, the 'cafeteria', – no question of soup kitchen – was set up with more than twenty women involved.

"Conditions were primitive, with just one oven and little knowledge of mass catering, but there was the will to win. Over the ten months things have improved. A second oven was added, and a solution was found for the problem that every time the two ovens were switched on, the lights fused! Now there are two ovens and five boilers. Even this was not ideal, particularly when the children's holidays mean that eight hundred meals have to be served.

"At the other end of the room, Brenda Moorland was busying herself in he shop, where she sells shoes and clothes five days a week. Cutting out the middle man by going to the wholesalers herself, she is able to provide shoes for as little as £3 a pair. She said "We had lots of clothing from jumble sales before, but it's nice to have new, isn't it".

"Brenda has two children of her own, and pointed put that "If you go to the shop, children's shoes can cost as much as £10 a pair. At the cafeteria it had been all hands to the till. Gardeners gave lettuce, cabbages, potatoes and beetroot. Harry at the chippy cooked the potatoes and baked the prepared pies. Anything that could be, was raffled, including a 20lb fish caught locally that raised £50 before being cut up and shared.

"Collections have been taken by trade unions, they said, and at the moment, Peter Hunt, the Easington lodge treasurer arrived with a bucket full of money collected at the Stockton, Darlington and Ormsby markets. Throughout the summer and autumn carnivals and events were organised for the children, making up for the lack of holidays away. Jean said 'we knew nothing when we started and have had to learn it all as we have gone along'.

"There have been regular meetings of the miners' support groups from all over Durham, at which to discuss common problems. 'All in all' Margaret said 'the bairns have had all that they had before and have not gone without'. Joan said that 'probably the greatest moment of the strike for her' was when she and other women of Northumberland and Durham went in convoy to the women's march in London on July 11. 'It was fantastic' she said 'when we were on the march, men unfurled a banner from a bridge ahead. You are magic it said' and so they are.

"If the spirits and determination of the NUM miners and their families showed them still up for the fight after nine months, there was equal determination backed by the full weight of the state and its media to do what it took to stamp out this courageous people's army".

A war of attrition was continuing, and on 15 December, the *Star* headline mirrored this. "Thatcher insists on fight to the finish – as Miners told 'surrender' then we will talk". The occasion was a meeting between the TUC leaders and Thatcher's energy secretary, Peter Walker, who demanded complete capitulation by the miners, which could bring peace to the coalfield. Take the redundancy money he said 'an offer which is as good as you will get'.

TUC general secretary, Willis, was "disappointed", adding that the flexibility of miners' leaders that was being demanded by Walker was not possible before negotiations were to resume. The TUC's request to the NCB to withdraw the original threat to 20,000, with twenty pits to close before talks began, was also turned down. Walker turned away any proposals, as he insisted again on the closure of all 'uneconomic pits', and made several personal attacks on Scargill.

Responding to a call from Mick McGahey, "MacGregor remained rooted in intransigence," was my version of events. In a statement, the NCB boss, who had been missing from the scene for three weeks, said there was "no way" talks could be reopened until the NUM changed its position", insisting that the NUM have to indicate "flexibility" from all-out opposition to the NCB's plan: to cut production of coal by four million tonnes, with the closure of twenty pits and 20,000 mining redundancies.

1 December 1984 – 39 weeks into the strike The trouble, that Thatcher and the NCB had gone to from the beginning of the strikes, was such that to accept anything less than total victory was unlikely. That this would have changed by the holding by an NUM strike ballot, even if won, has got to be living in cloud cuckoo land. This opinion where it was used was in fact a fig leaf for a lack of solidarity that at least, undermined, the miners cause.

By December the strategy was to drive a wedge between miner and miner, family and family by fair means or foul. As much as £1000 was being offered to return to work before Christmas, which some took up.

Down the line saw a Wigan NCB manager writing to a Lancashire miner to say his strike efforts were "futile", and to "join his mates who have already come back". "It is not too late to earn money, and Christmas holiday pay, and service bonus, to be paid before Christmas". At its worst this entailed working miners and police tapping their pockets full 'of cash' in front of the strikers.

In contrast, the striking miners, families and their supporters turned their attention to making as much of the festive season as they could. It was all hands to the pump to collect and distribute food, clothes, toys to the distressed coal-mining areas from within Britain, Scandinavia and the rest of Europe, and this despite the continuing pitched battles in pit towns and villages.

We spent Christmas at home, where at the local Labour Hall, there was a gathering from Ellesmere Port and North Wales in support of the North Wales striking miners. The Labour

Hall had been the centre of support of the miners involved in the 1926 miners' General Strike.

On 17 December, an IRA car bomb killed six people; three police officers and three members of the public, and injured ninety outside Harrods in London. On Christmas Day, a second IRA bomb exploded in Oxford Street, but this time nobody was injured.

A picture of miners and their families with the words of Derbyshire miner, John Dunn, were printed by the *Morning* Star at Christmas 2014.

A Striking Miner's Christmas: "Thirty years ago this Christmas, 2014, there was not a lot of festive cheer around. We had been on strike for nine long months, in the middle of a cold, cold winter with no heating and no money. Battered for nine months by Thatcher's paramilitary police, vilified as 'the enemy within' and abandoned by the TUC and Labour Party leadership, the NCB took the opportunity to break our resolve by tempting us back with an out-and-out bribe. The message was get back to work or starve".

Only a few took the thirty pieces of silver and climbed aboard armoured buses to scab on their fellow workmates, escorted into work by hundreds of riot police. The rest of us gritted our teeth, told the NCB where to put their 'incentive' and continued the fight. We might not have the money to buy our kids presents, we might be cold and hungry but we would never be tarnished with the indelible stain of scab".

While picketing and campaigning went on, efforts were intensified to make sure that, penniless or not, Christmas would be something never to be forgotten in our communities. Trees were cut down for logs, and surface coal seams were dug with a vengeance, despite the dangers. Three died when seams collapsed. I remember workers at a local furniture factory delivering lorry loads of off-cuts outside the miners welfare office for strikers' fires. We were determined to be warm if not festive. "Now I'm one of those bah-humbuggers that hate Christmas, but I have to admit that recalling that strike, Christmas brings a tear to my eye. It's impossible to explain adequately the sense of community solidarity that existed, showing the best of working-class versatility and strength at every level".

"At the Goldwell Rooms in Chesterfield, with the Women's Action Group, and seeing it crammed full of toys and gifts, with French lorries still being unloaded, I went outside to see fellow strikers overcome with emotion. We had braved the might of Thatcher's thugs only to be brought to tears by French teddy bears" !

Not only did I get a Christmas pud in my food parcel, I had two massive frozen turkeys, and me a vegetarian. So I staggered with one of the turkeys to my Dad, a retired miner, to be told: "I've got one, our Alan (my brother) gave it me from an Ireland pit". It showed the labour movement at its finest with solidarity, generosity and a fellowship never seen before or since. Add to that the local shopkeepers, our neighbours and friends who gave as much as they could to sustain us, we weren't just fighting for our jobs, but also our communities. "The scabs might have had the money, but we have the memories" John Dunn concluded.

Thus the year of 1984 ended for Britain's miners, their families, friends and neighbours in high spirits, after 41 weeks and three days of titanic struggle, that put Goliath's strength against David's courage in the shade.

Struggles of day-to-day existence The dawn of January 1985 arrived, and the miners' strike reached its tenth month. The longest I was ever on strike was six weeks, so my experiences have to be multiplied in this case (by January 1 1985) for the people here.

In time the money or gifts in kind will not be enough; there will be things to do without, small and great, a night out, then holidays. Then to missing out on some dearer food, from cakes to staple foodstuffs, dearer clothing, necessary for the winter. Debts that were afforded before a strike need settling. Weekly or monthly bills come payable. Rents and mortgage payments cannot be met in full. As the months go by the staunchest of hearts can buckle under pressure. In long-running disputes with strikers living in communities where others are working, comparisons are made. Friends and relations add to the pressures to return to work, as other families have what their family has not. Even the most closely-knit and determined families can question whether it is worth while.

In the case of the miners, they were all in the same boat, which lessened the pressures, but pressures there were, as the miners faced the New Year. These tensions were increasingly in play, as in some towns and villages miners started to return to work. Men fell out with men, woman with woman, and families with families. The pressure was piled on by the Government, the NCB and the media using thuggery at the pit heads, bribery to miners and propaganda directed at the mining and general public. Until, as South Wales NUM vice president, Terry Thomas, told a reporter: "We were picketing people who had stood on the picket lines with us for a whole year. Proud, strong miners crying, because they were going back to work. Even in situations nowhere near like this, I have seen men near to tears".

That the strike was still almost universally observed in South Wales, Yorkshire, Scotland, North-East England and Kent says much about the resilience of British miners resilience in the face of the greatest odds.

Splits in the Labour movement The TUC leadership was split between right and left. The right (the majority), the trade unions and the Labour Party and the Communist Party, all for their own reasons were in disarray. There was not the will to take a united stand on anything. It was left to the individual unions to do what they could in the absence of unity. The Labour Party was the more right wing under Neil Kinnock than after its defeat under Foot. It paid lip service to the miners' cause.

Kinnock blamed Arthur Scargill for all that was wrong, in the beginning, in the direction of the strike and at the end; most particularly for not holding a national ballot. To me this smacks of either guilt – methinks he doth protest too much – or ignorance of struggle. Even for the son of a miner, he after all never even, as they say "faced an angry chargehand".

The Communist Party supported the strike and opposed Thatcher's government, but some expressed reservations about Scargill's tactics. Industrial organiser, Peter Carter, said that Scargill: "had the idea that the miners could win the strike alone through a re-run of Saltley Gate". The 39th congress of the party, in November 1984, passed a motion that the strike could not succeed without sympathy from the wider public and other unions, and that the aggressive picketing was dividing the working class and alienating public support.

The divisions were not only over the miners' strike, but signified a fundamental difference over the way forward for Communists and the party in Britain, between the Eurocommunist tendency, by then a political majority on the party's divided executive and their opponents, including people around the *Morning Star*, whose views are reflected in most of what I have written in this book.

By January 1985, the strike was as much about the survival of the NUM in the face of Thatcher's attack on trade unionism, as saving the industry. This point was made by miners' MP Dennis Skinner, in a letter to energy secretary, Peter Walker, stating that given the cost of policing, extra oil burnt at power stations, increased nuclear power, compensation and the wages of scab workers, the cost of coal was by now £250 a tonne.

"What all this proves is that you are only interested in trying to destroy the miners' National Union of Mineworkers (though you will not succeed), at no matter what cost to the taxpayer".

The winter weather deepened to snow and ice gripping the country, and a consequent further increase in power stations' costs and the strike overall, was now costing an estimated £2.4 million.

The debate moved on to how many jobs would go when the pit closure programme was put into operation; the NCB saying it could not guarantee 'no compulsory redundancies' in the exercise.

Nevertheless the supporters kept collecting, while the communist-led Liaison Committee for the Defence of Trade unions LCDTU, arranged a meeting of the activists across the trade union movement's industrial base.

I wrote that: "An ever-growing list of delegates from all unions and areas of Britain is likely to make the conference at Friends Meeting House in Euston Road a tremendous occasion".

So it was, with delegates packing to the rafters, and promises of support ringing round the hall. Could it be though the "Last Hoorah?" Not for two Kent miners from Betteshanger Pit, who were sent to jail; Terry French for five years and Chris Pazey, for three years in youth detention.

On January 16, Tony Benn MP, one of the miners staunchest supporters and a member of the National Union of Journalists, told a meeting of Fleet Street workers that the case for coal was not being reported by the media, nor was "the hardship being suffered by mining communities, or of the solidarity being received. This was in a sustained campaign of distortion by Fleet street".

Solidarity action was planned, and carried out through January and into February. The London district of the Communist Party arranged a major rally, with McGahey and general secretary, Gordon McLennan. In Scotland, there was mobilisation for a massive demonstration and a call for "all kinds of action, including industrial action".

On 4 February a week of activities began, organised by the Yorkshire and Humberside TUC. The South East region TUC called for a Day of Action from the 4.5 million membership. On 24 February it was reported that in London there was to be a mass demonstration called by the LCDTU. These were all successes of various dimensions, proving that the rank and file, particularly the trade union activists were still up for the fight.

The rail workers, who had taken solidarity action with the miners and had been harried for their troubles by their bosses, also received support from their comrades. On 18 January, this was my intro to the *Star* splash: "Rail workers in the Midlands were joined by colleagues in London in a massive show of solidarity with those victimised by British Rail for refusing to handle scab coal. A great swathe was cut through services from Yorkshire and the Midlands, and hundreds of trains were cancelled at London's Waterloo station, as drivers and guards joined their colleagues in a twenty-four hour strike. British Rail warned that "wrongly-positioned rolling stock and expected blizzards could course further disruption to services today".

Reporting Jimmy Knapp I wrote: "There is a great deal of frustration and concern in the minds of our members, due to the intransigence and the failure of the government to settle this dispute". "On February 17 there were six hours of talks, at which the NUM accepted the agreement of the NCB with NACODS".

The meeting then producing nowt. Arthur accused the Tories of using the tactics of destabilisation, as the United States did in Vietnam, "by raising hopes of peace, and then dashing them down".

I want here to give readers the analysis of Frank Watters recorded in his book, *Being Frank*, Frank, long a mentor and confidante of Arthur's said. " A negotiated settlement was never in their (the government's) vocabulary". He said "They were looking for complete capitulation".

In January 1985, there surfaced the case for a return to work without the NUM's agreement with the Coal Board. The strike would end with the NUM's areas left to negotiate their ways of returning to work. My experience is that win, lose or draw, you go back to work in unity, maintaining the organisation you have. To do it any other way lies chaos.

Frank Watters, in dealing with this, said that "South Wales actually adopted this position early on"26 February 1984, a week before the SDC).

Arthur Scargill's view was that this was the very worst thing possible. Even in 1986, McGahey took the view that South Wales was wrong. The numbers game continued to the end, the NUM saying that by February 26 their were still 130,000 of 160,000 out, while the NCB say half the miners were back working. But in fact it was a phoney war, with only the miners knowing how many were returning.

The giant London demonstration, organised by the Liaison Committee for the Defence of Trade Unions, took place on February 24, with a march to the rally in Trafalgar Square. Miners came from every coalfield, and the Women Against Pit Closures were given a special place. Most trade unions and trades councils were there. It was like a victory rally, and we were not to know how near the end it was.

Meeting on return to work Five days later, on 3 March, I was outside the TUC's Congress House, as the NUM's supreme body, its coalfield Special Delegate Conference, was meeting to decide the fate of the year-long strong strike, at which we knew that an option to end the strike would be put. There was a less than the usual gathering of rank and file miners waiting anxiously and quietly to hear what the verdict would be. Among them was a number from the North Wales NUM, being the few from that coalfield who had gone and stayed on strike throughout the year. Eventually the meeting broke, and Arthur Scargill announced the end of the strike to the miners and the media.

I made my way back to the office with the news, and sat down to type the splash, which appeared with a strap: "Scargill pledge; the defence of jobs will go on. Headlined "Miners march back to pits tomorrow" the intro said: "Britain's magnificent miners' strike is over but the National Union of Mineworkers will continue to fight for the survival of the pits, Arthur Scargill said yesterday: "At pits all over Britain, miners will march back tomorrow morning with their banners flying and their heads held high".

"I regard the last twelve months as a tremendous achievement the NUM President, Arthur Scargill said. 'Not only has the threat to close five pits been withdrawn, but the Coal Board's programme for 1984/85 has not been implemented'.

The resolution to call off the strike, without agreement with the Coal Board, was accepted by the narrowest of margins of 98 to 91; remarkable after a year on strike!

The resolution moved by the South Wales miners' vice president, Terry Thomas, put aside a call from some areas only to go back to work with an amnesty for the 700 miners victimised and sacked during the strike. Instead "the national executive committee are called upon to negotiate with theNational Coal Board on a national basis on an amnesty for those dismissed during the strike".

The news of the return to work, without the sacked men, angered miners lobbying the talks. Boos and jeers and tears greeted the grim-faced delegates as they left the meeting.

The bulk of those voting to stay out were from Yorkshire, Scotland and Kent. The South Wales miners took the view, accepted by the conference in the vote. This was "because of the drift back to work in all areas", and because "it was clear that the Coal Board would have no discussions unless the NUM signed the TUC document which was rejected two weeks earlier.

"Mr Scargill said that the conference had decided 'that the dispute in this industry will continue until the aims are completely fulfilled, and there is an amnesty for those dismissed in the dispute'.That it was decided to set up a special fund in support of those miners sacked during the strike, was an indication of little faith in the outcome of the plea for amnesty. While Mr Scargill would have 'preferred more support from the trade union and labour movements', he said he 'did not underestimate the tremendous achievement. Men and women, through their wonderful support'groups, have fought a fight not been seen anywhere in the world" and paid "a special tribute to rail workers and seafarers".

The miners would "go back to work on Tuesday together, and fight on to retain pits, jobs and communities."

Given that at this moment Arthur Scargill was facing a bitter defeat, and the with little likelihood of any meaningful fight that could save the industry from the planned assault by Thatcher on not just the NUM, but the British trade union movement as a whole – her enemy within – he had praise for those who stood strong.

Kent NUM general secretary, Jack Collins: "saw the decision not to stick out for an amnesty as a decision we will live to regret" and leaving miners on the sidelines as "an act of treachery". In the circumstances, the return to work was pretty orderly, with most back within three days; Kent being the last, on March 10.

Why the return to work? The decision to end the strike was questioned at the time and since. The claim of those advocating a return among the NUM leadership was that miners were returning to work in increasing numbers, so better to return in some order. To sanction a return to work was, as per Jack Collins, the Kent Area NUM secretary said was "abandoning principle" by "leaving your mates on the cobbles".

The NUM decision to go back without an agreement was also debated

It seemed to me to be a question not, as attributed to Aneurin Bevan in relation to negotiating nuclear disarmament, "going naked into the negotiating chamber" but rather not entering the chamber at all!

Traditionally at the end of many a strike (won or lost), in the negotiations on a return to work, the time-honoured trade union pledge would be a return only with those victimised being granted an amnesty. It wasn't always won, but it was tried and it could be successful. It is pretty certain though that a plea for amnesty to the NCB and Thatcher's government would have been refused, knowing that the NUM could not threaten any further action. Solving these riddles required the wisdom of Solomon, and not even Arthur had that. So it seemed that without a decision, disorder was increasingly setting in, and the return to work would restore some order.

South Wales NUM, with 97% of the area's miners out at the beginning, and still at its end, moved the motion. The intensity of dilemma was reflected in the vote for a return to work, of 98 to 93 of the delegate meeting. Whatever; the deed was done!

The new review procedure, promised to supervisors' union, NACODS, as an inducement not to go on strike in October 1984, was not enacted.

The towns and villages left behind The decision to go back to work without an agreement nationally meant the NUM coalfield areas having to find a local accommodation. The NCB area chairmen's attitude was varied. In South Wales, where the miners were 99% on strike and 93% at the end of it, the return to work was relatively peaceful.

In contrast, in Scotland, NCB chairman, Albert Wheeler was vicious. In the strike five hundred Scottish miners were arrested and were heavily fined. Hundreds of them were subsequently sacked; both before and after the strike ended.

The Kent miners stayed on strike and continued to picket other coalfields to demand amnesty for sacked miners, returning to work on 8 March, only to stop work again on 11 March, when they were warned of a cut in allowances, conditions eroded and were warned about future conduct.

At the collieries there was trouble where the majority in a pit were striking miners, and also in pits where the majority were working miners. At Hem Heath, North Staffordshire, Jim Saunders was told by its NUM branch secretary Jim McMillan of the "great difficulties" faced by returning strikers.

"The area board are treating those of us who went on strike as a disruptive element to those who worked during the strike. Skilled men have been given pick and shovel jobs and placed on menial jobs, on jobs away from the rest of the miners at the pit". "At sixty years of age I've been forced to go back down the pit to do pick and shovel work. Eight lads who were dismissed have not been reinstated. We're getting the boot put in on us".

The Notts coalfield communities, as with all coalfields, were devastated and left to rot, with unemployment reaching over 11% in the UK throughout the second half of the 1980s, and reaching about 50% in mining communities by the late 80s.

The plight of the sacked miners During the strike, 11,291 people were arrested, mostly for breach of the peace or obstructing roads whilst picketing, of whom 8,392 were charged and between 150–200 were imprisoned. At least 9,000 mineworkers were dismissed after being arrested whilst picketing, even where no charges were brought.

In another aspect of the strike's aftermath, a striking Nottinghamshire miner, Norman Lynch, was ruled by an industrial tribunal to have been unfairly dismissed when he was sacked by the Coal Board for a civil offence, and given a conditional discharge for assault. Mr Lynch didn't get his job back and could have sought compensation. But this cut across the NUM's insistence that the Coal Board should not be allowed to victimise miners because they took part in the strike.

The Justice for Mineworkers, established in 1986 took up the cudgels and campaigned for the alleviation of all victimised miners problems, pointing to Scotland, Kent and the North-East areas as facing the most difficulty in getting the NCB even to review cases Few got their jobs back. Many were blacklisted for work outside the coal industry.

A national campaign in 1986 helped to fulfil the promise that those victimised would not suffer hardship. This it did by alleviating the hardships with support of Labour MPs, the solidarity and women's support groups. To this end the Miners Solidarity Fund was a tremendous assistance to those worst affected, inasmuch as it helped the sacked men, and indeed the families of those incarcerated in jail, to live to a reasonable standard.

Aftermath Arthur Scargill was still president of the NUM, and from 1992 its general secretary as well, until retirement in 2002, and honorary president from 2002. Disillusioned by Labour, Arthur formed his own party, the Socialist Labour Party, and recruited a number of others disillusioned across the Left.

I was offered such a chance at the 2003 TUC in Blackpool. I was walking across the conference floor when Arthur came over to me. In all the time I had known him he had always treated me as member of the industrial correspondents grouping although, at times, I had helped him with helpful questions. He was never unfriendly, and sometimes called me 'comrade', but was never quite 'hail fellow well met'. This time he greeted me in friendly fashion. Twigging what I was going to be asked I quickly said: "Arthur, I'm not joining your party".

Some prominent Communist Party members had done but I was sticking with ' the party', so we parted with a grin. I met him once more, when we were 'comrades' still.

In this account have tried to show that – more than anything else about the miners' strike of 1984/85 – the most important thing was the ability of ordinary working people to organise and manage their own lives, supporting each other under the most difficult of circumstances and managing without the bosses or politicians to guide them. They showed how working together that the most difficult tasks can be accomplished. It raises the question: what more could we do in better circumstances to defend and advance our society in unity rather than in competition or division?

There followed the ritual slaughter of the industry, with twenty-five pits closed in the eight months of 1985, seventeen in 1986, eighteen in 1987/88, sixteen in 1989 and thirty in 1990/91.

It was one hundred and six closures in six years, and was soon to be none left, except for privatised super pits and a few small ones. Now there are none.

None on of them were classed as 'uneconomic', but it didn't matter. The three centuries of King Coal were dead. As Arthur Scargill said, it was cheaper to buy the coal from South Africa or Chile, where pit boys and girls cost nothing but their blood.

The best evidence of the inexact science in defining an uneconomical pit, or not, was Tower Colliery, in South Wales' Cynnon Valley, which British Coal closed on 22 April 1994, on the grounds as being uneconomic.

Tower was the last mine of its kind to remain in the South Wales Valleys. the oldest, continuously-working, deep-coal mine in the world. Its 239 miners joined Tower Employees Buy-Out, TEBO, and pledged £8,000 from their redundancy payouts covering the price of £2 million that was eventually agreed. An uneconomic pit in April 1994, was mined happily until 2008. How many scores of Britain's other collieries could have done the same, given the opportunity?

Many of the pit villages and towns have been left to fend for themselves, and with their communities continuing to pay the price for decades of poor diets, poor housing, disease and illness. Their industry was dead, with little put in its place, bringing poverty and deprivation.

Wakefield, in Yorkshire was also classed in an EU report of being one of the most deprived areas of Europe, along with Grimethorpe in South Yorkshire and Knowsley in Merseyside; all ex-mining communities.

In 2007, the Justice for Miners was still demanding a full amnesty "for all those involved, and stated that thirty-seven men are still being supported by the NUM and Justice Campaign, through the Miners' Solidarity Fund, a registered charity".

When an industry becomes unfit for purpose there should be an orderly retreat with arrangements made for other work made available, with work sharing, reduced working hours, investment in new technology and training. It seems impossible for a capitalist society to even attempt.

The last colliery closed on 19 December 2015 at Kellingley in North Yorkshire.

GCHQ – January 1984 to June 1997 In January 1984, on a black winter's night, I added to my curriculum vitae of visits to famous establishments: Parliament, Buckingham Palace and military, naval and air force bases and entered Number 10 Downing Street.

Margaret Thatcher had decided for "national security reasons", to ban staff working in the Government Communications HQ (GCHQ), from membership of a trade union. This was enforced through an Order of Council, an exercise of the Royal prerogative. It was a move challenged by the Council of Civil Service Unions (CCSU), first to the High Court, which ruled the Order was invalid, then the Court of Appeal proclaimed it valid, judging it a national security issue. An appeal to the International Labour Organisation, that ruled the government's actions as a violation of Freedom of Association and Protection of the Right to Organise Convention, was ignored.

The civil service union leaders were inside challenging Thatcher's action face to face. It did no good. Thatcher said the ban would continue. The union leaders filed past a press queue, ashenfaced, making no comment. About twenty of us from the press, crammed into the Number Ten press office to hear the bluff and bulky Yorkshire figure of Bernard Ingham, Thatcher's press secretary. He told us was that the decision was made, and would stand. I did manage to get a row going between Bernard and myself, which if short, was sweet. The end result was about the same as when I was carried out of parliament by the police.

The GCHQ union members refusing to give up their union membership were suspended from work. The government offered each employee the choice of £1,000 to give up union membership or the sack! The deal was accepted by all but fourteen trade union members. There the matter rested, until the first four sackings, in November 1988, were followed by ten more during December and into the spring of 1989. The fourteen employees were thirteen men and one woman. To give personality to this, the first was Mandarin-Chinese linguist, Mike Grindley, executive officer Graham Hughes, telecommunications technician Brian Johnson and radio officer Alan Rowland; dismissed on 18 November 1988.

The civil services trade unions and their GCHQ members never gave up marching and demonstrating on every occasion, from January 1984 to June 1997, including a march and rally every year at Cheltenham on the date of the ban being imposed.

They were led by Michael Grindley. His diminutive five foot two inches figure with his sandwiches and leaflets in a plastic bag appeared with other comrades on every mass protest, conference and meeting, voicing his and their defiance at the ban. This was the second-longest, continuously fought dispute in British trade union history.

A non-TUC GCHQ Staff Federation was set up in the place of the banned unions.

The ban was lifted by the incoming 1997 Labour government. The fourteen former dismissed GCHQ employees were offered re-employment, of which three accepted. Mike Grindley said "We always knew in our heart of hearts that we would win our rights back, but if we had been told it would take 13 years, the prospect would have been daunting indeed" insisting that "essential services have always been maintained during industrial action".

In February 2000, the Labour government announced that the sacked GCHQ employees shared a compensation payout up to £550,000 after tax, to compensate for lost earnings and pension rights. After this announcement, Grindley said: "We are relieved that at long last our pension rights have been sorted. We have not got everything back we were owed, but we have written that off. It has been a long, hard struggle".

The struggle was recorded and celebrated with an excellent book *A Conflict of Loyalties* by Hugh Lanning and Richard Norton Taylor, now available as an e book republished at www.manifestopress.coop.

Shipbuilding Who was it living on an island for six centuries, with its big rivers, raw materials of wood, iron ore and copper, and the skills acquired to build great ships, could be so blind not to see there were still opportunities for a properly-managed, successful shipbuilding industry in the 1980s? Thatcher and the Tories, that's who! Aided and abetted by the greed and the ineptitude of Britain's ship owners, builders and managers, any such vision failed them. Then they put the blame on 'the workers'. Who else?

It was a time when the great shipbuilding facilities in great cities fell silent; on the Clyde, Tyne, Wear, Mersey and elsewhere. On 2 September 1983, I forecast a "bleak future for the shipyards" under a new boss, Canadian Graham Day; "the £80,000 a year chairman" bringing "little joy for the shipyard workers".

At a press conference, where again I had words with the company chairman, to little affect, "Day made it brutally clear that if British yards had a future, it would have to be off the backs of the workers". Jobs would go if the shipyard staff failed to compete in the "market place". As it turned out, there wasn't much that we could take to market.

On February 1 1984, a face to face meeting between Thatcher and shipyard workers – seeking to save the jobs of hundreds of staff at Clydeside's Scott Lithgow – provided a cameo of the outcome at most of Britain's shipyards as the workers themselves attempted to save their shipbuilding yards.

After a post-war boom, Scott Lithgow was one of Britain's shipbuilding yards being brought to its knees by failing to modernise with the new world of super tankers and bulk carriers being filled by European and Japanese yards and later in Taiwan and South Korea.

The Callaghan government in 1977 had founded British Shipbuilders; initially nationalising thirty-two shipyards, six marine engine works and six general engineering plants. British Shipbuilders accounted for 97% of the UK's merchant shipbuilding capacity, 100% of its warship-building capacity, and 50% of ship-repair capacity.

By the end of 1982 British Shipbuilders' "main achievement" had been to have cut its "over capacity", and with the aid of the 1979 Thatcher government, had closed half of Britain's shipyards. The British Shipbuilders Act 1983 required British Shipbuilders to begin privatising its remaining assets. The result; the end of Britain's 'big' ship building industry.

Scotts of Greenock and Lithgows of Port Glasgow were twin yards on the lower Clyde, but a 1969 merger never really worked. Scott Lithgows did modernise and diversified, but the work won was never enough.

On February 1 1984, a twelve-man delegation from Scott Lithgows met Margaret Thatcher in Downing Street, in a fight to save the Greenock yard, threatened after an order from Brit Oil vessels was cancelled, after new technology difficulties.

Thatcher, "turned aside the logical arguments of the twelve-man delegation for a resumption of the work on the advanced oil rig". The delegation added that: "It became clear during a meeting Mrs Thatcher was hell bent on the jettisoning of millions of pounds of taxpayers' money, and giving away the shipyard to her Tory friends".

Duncan Mac said "If there was to be a new start, why not with the present workforce and as a nationalised industry". Accusing Thatcher of "sticking to the dogma of privatisation" he warned that "the threat is real and still dangerous and no different than it had been for weeks. The campaign against the closure goes on".

The Tory's preference was to sell Scott Lithgows off; this time to the Trafalgar House Group. Offering the site, not the staff employed, meant writing off £160 million of losses and estimated redundancy pay, and sacking the then management. No further shipbuilding was undertaken, and the 270-year-old Scott shipbuilding company ceased trading in 1993. Four years later it was demolished, and today is a shopping centre.

This brush with workers fighting for their jobs was always was a joy, amongst people I knew work-wise to be the best, workers with a deep knowledge of their trade and their industry.

On January 11 1984, I wrote a piece on shipbuilding talks by experts: "Media pundits will blame alleged out-moded, time-wasting practices for the rundown of the British shipbuilding industry. Most won't know a plumb bob from a door knob, a fabricator from a ventilator or a welding arc from Noah's Ark."

Dan Milmo, writing in 2014 in the *Guardian* by Dan Milmo on the closure of the Portsmouth Dock yard said the decline of the UK shipbuilding industry was not inevitable. "It was an industry that at its peak built great ships, such as the Queen Mary, constructed in Glasgow in the early 20th century. The boom lasted well beyond the Second World War. There were 134 vessels – 1.47m gross tonnes of shipping produced in the UK in 1976."

By 2020 this had been reduced to three shipyards; two being BAE's Upper Clyde Govan and Scotstoun sites, the only UK shipyards used to design, build and commission sophisticated naval warships, and at BAE Systems Maritime, submarines were built in Barrow-in-Furness, Cumbria responsible for the development and production of submarines.

Sir John Parker, the former chief executive of Harland and Wolff, the Belfast shipbuilder, said the industry missed an opportunity in the Thatcher era.

"One of my big industrial disappointments, or even failures, is that I failed to persuade the government of the day that there was a big future in building cruise ships. Thatcher was not into listening".

In early 1985, Isolda McNeil, a teacher from Dublin, joined the industrial department at the *Morning Star*. She is a larger than life personality with a commanding physical presence and was the first woman to hold an industrial reporter's post on any national newspaper.

She was always an interesting read and I thought her forte was reporting the human dimension, the intricacies and inner workings of the trade union movement. As a rank and file communist and a party branch officer in Hackney she voicing her political disquiet at the path sought by the *Marxism Today* crew in relation to both the party and the paper and added a great deal to our industrial reporting.

Continued in-fighting on the Left There was plenty to do in the 1980s in our attempts to win back the trade union and Labour movement from political and circulation losses brought about by *Marxism Today* faction. In the intense political atmosphere this meant, or the *Morning* Star this meant standing room only at the paper's fringe meetings at the TUC, union and Labour conferences.

Newswise the paper hardly missed a dispute with the team making contact with leaders at local and national level and particularly from the shop floor. At union conferences we recorded the battles won and aims achieved by trade unions. The paper's feature pages were developed around the main themes of conferences with union specialists analysing the problems of every sector and group of workers and key pieces from union leaders.

The sense that the *Morning Star* was the paper of the trade union and labour movement meant that the columns were open to every legitimate trend. We started at the top by getting figures like general secretaries, in the case of the TUC Len Murray or Norman Willis to write a piece for the first day of the TUC Congress followed by union leaders writing about their own union or industry,

We did this with the Scottish and Wales TUC conferences and with individual conferences making the *Star* the paper of record for the labour movement. This was hard work and with the emergence of new and younger – joining people like Arthur Scargill, Rodney Bickerstaffe, John Edmonds and Ron Todd – the paper's appeal broadened.

On one occasion I sought articles from the group of entertainments unions; the film, television radio and theatre s union, BECTU, the Musicians Union and from the Writers Guild This was submitted from Alan Plater, the renowned playwright. Only the actor's union, Equity, refused.

I took the view that even right-wingers who were sound on their subject should be commissioned. When there were elections for middle and top union posts, we would commission or interview the leading candidates in that election.

At most conferences a *Morning Star* collection is usually facilitated by a supportive official, including those from the top table. Big envelopes are circulated to regional delegations at union conferences and for each union at the TUC, Scottish and Wales TUCs. My most memorable collection was at the GMB conference, when my retirement was announced, to a standing ovation and £600 collected!

At conferences *Morning* Star sales are organised by supporters, although I occasionally had to do it myself. Our conference coverage and contacts led to an increase in trade union advertising in the paper, most especially on May Day. Turning conference buyers into regular readers was then the work of the late Ivan Beavis, formerly a leading Unison activist and now Bernadette Keaveney. Today every major Labour movement event such as the Tolpuddle Martyrs festival attracts advertisers.

New technology at the *Star* – January 1984 to August 1984 In January 1984, the *Star* management committee, the prime mover being Mary Rosser, decided on a new printing facility. This was because the *Star's* printing press; circa 1947, then the last hot-metal printing press in British newspapers, had in the previous summer suffered a major breakdown.

The management committee further decided on a British machine, the "Urbanite". produced by Goss of Preston. This was able to print a thirty-two page tabloid newspaper, with about 30,000 copies an hour capacity, and a spot colour for commercial printing in full colour.

"The Urbanite would give us the best of two worlds" a *Star* feature proclaimed. It did not mention its cost of £1 million. The old press was removed from the basement of William Rust House for the building work, in order to accommodate the new press and one tonne reels needed. A *Star* feature concluded that: "The management committee does not expect that project to be easy but is prepared to work for its success!" The *Star's* printing was contracted out to the *Socialist Worker* facility, while to the accompaniment of considerable noise and dust, the building work was completed and the Urbanite installed.

This was followed by six months of in-house, and out-of-house technicians hard at it trying to get the thing to work, which they never quite managed, although coming near! This was before it was sold on; but for how much, I don't know. From that time in 1985 the *Star* has always been contract printed by an outside printer.

Marxism Today, Eurocommunism and the Star   While the work of promoting the *Star* and renewing its trade union and Labour movement reputation was underway new troubles emerged from the machinations of the *Marxism Today* group.

During the 1970s a euro-communist trend emerged emphasising the role of 'new social forces' – sections oppressed by gender and race – with a tendency to downgrade the central significance of class in exploitation and oppression and thus the role of the organised working class in the revolutionary process. This tendency was influential in both the Italian Communist Party (PCI) and the French Communist Party (PCF) and was taken up by the 'Euros' in the British party.

Some European parties began to distance themselves from the rest of the international communist movement. The two European parties' post-war advances had stalled since the 1960s, so they sought support on a broader basis. It was not a problem-free process. In Britain, the *British Road to Socialism* (BRS), the long standing party programme had 'the organised working class' as the central force for revolutionary change.

There were Communist Party members, not exclusively amongst the younger comrades influenced by the student movement, arguing for the recognition of social movements as critical forces for revolutionary change alongside the 'organised working class'. Indeed some argued that the social movements should be substituted for organised working class.

Of course this is a shorthand account of the controversy but at the 1977 Congress, the text of the party programme included a reference to "other social forces".

Party traditionalists, young and old, opposing this diminution of the working class role, were assured by the draft committee chair, Bert Ramelson, that things would be sorted in the work of the Broad Alliance.

The reasons for this are too complex to define here! So this formulation was accepted.

The tendency around *Marxism Today* was advanced helped further when Martin Jacques, a leading eurocommunist, was appointed editor of *Marxism Today*. Under Jacques' editorship the significance of various social movements was promoted, but the role of the organised working class diminished, while trade union weaknesses and shortcomings were emphasised.

The eurocommunist tendency gained ground when the party's general secretary, Gordon McLennan, threw in his lot with the *Marxism Today tendency*. Its members seem to have dazzled some of their older executive comrades. Both Gordon McLennan and Mick McGahey told me of these "wonderful young comrades" with great ideas were our future.

Through the 1980s, the *Marxism Today* people gained greater control over the party's executive committee with its views prevailing even when at odds with decisions of successive congresses. The *Marxism Today* journal was successful in its own terms, but was enormously subsidised from party funds.

So it was that Tony and Mary decided to fight for its readership in the ways detailed above. There was a minority, or very possibly a majority, of the party's membership, which saw the trade unions as the main organising force in their understanding of the *British Road*. There was too, a substantial residual loyalty to the international communist movement, the Soviet Union and the socialist countries. *Marxism Today* thus had power in the party apparatus, but was somewhat short on hearts and mind.

When faced with opposition to its line, ironically the executive committee tried to overcome them with "administrative means". This approach, condemned by the eurocommunists when supposedly used in the Soviet Union against dissenters from the party line was used to drive out opposition, expel members and shut down branches and district organisations.

It eventually included leading members such as Bert Ramelson and many others with years of service to the party and working class. The strengthened position of the *Marxism Today* group in the party leadership then moved to fight for control of the *Morning Star*.

The *Daily Worker* was launched on 1 January 1930 as the daily newspaper of the Communist Party of Great Britain. It retained this status until 1946, when it was relaunched as a paper owned by its shareholders grouped in the Peoples' Press Printing Society (PPPS). According to cooperative principles a reader with a £1 share exercised the same one vote as a reader with 2,000 shares. The shareholders elected a management committee at an annual general meeting, in a secret ballot, and this committee ran the paper including appointing the editor. It became the *Morning Star* in 1966.

Formally the Communist Party stood outside the process. In practice, before the rupture in relations, the editor had always been a member of the Communist Party's political committee, and shareholders had regularly re-affirmed that the paper's editorial line should be guided by the principles and strategy embodied in the *British Road to Socialism*, i.e. the Communist Party line.

During 1982 and 1983 the strained relationships between the party's executive committee and the *Morning* Star's management committee deepened. These tensions were heightened by an September 1982 article by university lecturer Tony Lane, in *Marxism Today*. He portrayed the shop stewards' movement as the "creation of a new working class elite, sharing the perks of the expense accounts syndrome and fostering shabby deals".

Star editor Tony Chater got the party's industrial organiser, Mick Costello, to condemn the piece in a front page article. This precipitated a labour movement-wide debate the significance of which seemed great at the time.

Mick left his party job and joined the *Star's* Industrial desk. Mike Pentelow left early in 1983 to join the TGWU publishing department, which produced both the T&G's union journal *Review* and the recently merged Agricultural Workers' *Landworker*. Mick took on the Industrial Correspondent's title and Jo Stanley left soon after, leaving just Mick and me.

The most significant confrontation between the party leadership now, under its majority euro communist leadership, and the dissenters came in November 1984, when Gordon McLennan peremptorily closed the party's London district congress, when it looked like electing a leadership with an oppositional majority.

The delegates divided with a large number leaving. This challenge to the party leadership led to a raft of subsequent expulsions and branch closures. This in turn left a sizeable grouping of London-based comrades organising in opposition. Similar processes took place around the country and this then led to the formation of a 'Communist Campaign Group' and later, in 1988, the formation of a parallel Communist Party of Britain on the basis of the existing version of the *British Road to Socialism* and party rules.

In January 1985, the CPGB executive voted to expel editor Tony Chater and deputy David Whitfield from the party. With seventeen others, they were expelled by a 2-1 majority. There then took place a thorough going witch hunt entailing the expulsion of life-long members.

By then I had been working for the paper in nearly four years of inner strife on two fronts. One was in the office, where most of the staff, editorial, printers and admin staff were party members, with a *Morning* Star party branch. There were perhaps three factions; for the *Star*, for the party leadership and those against Tony Chater.

Peter Pink was the branch secretary and would receive instructions from the party general secretary, Gordon McLennan, and the EC, instructing him to call a meeting in order to engineer a vote to sack Chater and Whitfield and to install diplomatic editor Chris Myant and Frank Chalmers.

Of course staffing was a matter for the management committee and the editor and the business before the party branch was simply intrigue and manouvering.

The Marxism Today group made the case for the removal of the two editors for no longer following the party line, and earnestly for the promotion of the other two, as if it were just an administrative matter, and nothing personal!

This proposal was lost three times. After the heated debate and the deep differences expressed between those working at the *Star* at the end of each meeting we would all return to producing the paper for the day.

The dispute took place in party branches branches throughout the country. I was a member of the Camden borough organisation, which generally sided with the Star, although it got personal.

I was often on the road at the height of the dispute in places where it did get personal, especially in Scotland. The Scottish TUC usually met at Easter. An edge was put on things by thgose whose sympathies towards the *Marxism Today* faction which were also fueled by their affection for fellow Scot, Gordon McLennan. The Scots had always shown the greatest of comradeship and help to me, but by 1985 some let it be known that they regarded me as one of those out to steal the *Star* from the Communist Party. It was a difficult time.

I was helped at the STUC by my colleague, Scottish reporter Martin Gostwick and others, like the *Star's* Scottish circulation manager, Andrew Clarke, who was sympathetic to what we were trying to do at the *Star*. People in the broader trade union and Labour movement, who saw the great value of the *Star* in their struggles, were a source of support.

Marxism Today renewed the attack, accusing the *Star* grouping "of being disloyal to party policy. When PPPS AGM held its special conference at Wembley in June 1985 hundreds of communists and non-party movement activists rallied or in support of the *Morning* Star. Leading party officials called on members to sack Chater and Whitfield and vote their nominees onto the *Star's* management committee.

This failed badly. The call for the sacking was heavily defeated and *Star* supporters won the majority of seats on the Management Committee. The victory, if that's what it was, was sealed and soon the party leadership majority gave up on what was an impossible fight. Both groups then went their own way.

In March 1988, the Communist Party leadership produced *A Manifesto for New Times* to replace the *British Road to Socialism*. This led to further membership losses and the abandonment of the main features of communist ideas and organisational principles and in 1991, when the Soviet Union was dismantled, the much reduced party, now led by Nina Temple decided to replace it with a Democratic Left, a left-leaning political think tank rather than a political party. I left and joined the Communist Party Britain..

In 1984, *Star* supporters had set about founding a network of *Morning* Star readers' groups.

In 1988 and largely from these groupings and from the Communist Campaign Group – and with disaffected and expelled party members – the parallel Communist Party of Britain was formed in with print worker Michael Hicks as its general secretary, and Tony Chater and Mary Rosser in its leading group.

I did not leave the Communist Party of Great Britain until it finally abandoned its name and the *British Road to Socialism* in 1991. I didn't think that the *Marxism Today* group should have been able to get away with its takeover of the Party, and that the 1985 walk out by delegates to the dissolved London district congress of 1985, was tactically wrong.

It gave the *Marxism Today* clique full reign to purge those forces it opposed. I could have been wrong. It was when the CPGB was disbanded that I joined the Communist Party of Britain, which fitted my belief that the *Morning Star* had to be kept going.

The British car industry: A strike on November 6 1984
In November 1985 the TGWU was the latest union to be fined for contempt in the amount of £200,000, after refusing to instruct its members to return to work, and to hold a strike ballot after two weeks strike action by 28,000 workers at the Austin-Rover car plants.

The postwar history of the British motor car industry where I had worked as a pipe fitter and then covered as a hack fascinated me.

William Morris, born in 1877 aged of fifteen was apprenticed to a bike repairer, and then moved into cars. At Cowley he pioneered Henry Ford's mass-production methods, and between 1919 and 1925, built factories in Abingdon, Birmingham and Swindon, increasing production from 400 cars a year to 56,000.

Herbert Austin built three-wheeled cars, setting up in 1905 at Longbridge to become one of the greatest car manufacturers in the world. In 1922 his Baby Austin sold for £225, making it affordable to working people. From 1907 Henry Spurrier of Leyland Motors, Lancashire, made steam-powered commercial vehicles It soon became a manufacturer of petrol-driven lorries and buses. The Rootes group were dealers, and became car makers with plants in Coventry, Birmingham, Acton, Luton, Dunstable and Linwood in Scotland. It made Hillman, Humber, Singer and Sunbeam vehicles.

In 1947, with limited competition from Europe and with demand for new vehicles in America and in Australia, British car exports reached record levels, and the UK became the world's largest vehicle exporter. The home vehicles' market lived just for the day, with the minimum of modernisation and investment and by the mid-1950s the American industry production had caught up with American demand while continental European production was recovering.

The new(ish), US-based and now modernised Ford and General Motors Vauxhall plants shared 29% of the British market, exceeding the share of either of the UK's two home-owned manufacturers, Austin and Morris. This situation was further accelerated by the introduction later of cars from Japanese and other far-eastern companies.

In 1952, the two British giant car builders, Morris at Cowley, Oxford, with MG, Riley and Wolsey, and Austin at Longbridge, Birmingham merged to be the British Motor Corporation (BMC). This was the first of mergers, buy-outs and nationalisations (and later re-privatisations).

By 1960, the UK had dropped from being the world's second largest motor vehicle producer into third place. In the 1960s, Ford opened the plant in Halewood, Liverpool to add to the one at Dagenham, and General Motors, Vauxhall, opened a plant in Ellesmere Port, with 12,000 workers.

Of the two most revered brands in British car-making history – Austin had been killed off and Morris lingered on. The MG Rover Group was the last domestically-owned mass-production car manufacturer in the British motor industry.

Today Germany's BMW, Volkswagen AG, India's Tata Motors, PSA France, Vauxhall and China own Britain's car-making industry. Japanese-owned Honda, Nissan and Toyot manufacture here.

In May 2000, Ford's passenger car assembly at its Dagenham plant ceased, ending ninety years of Ford passenger car assembly in the UK.

Working in the Vauxhall and Ford car plants in the 1970s, what struck me was the sheer monotony of car building. A pathetic measure to lessen the boredom was the broadcast of music by loudspeaker. I wonder if this accounted for the number of strikes for which the industry was renowned. A half day out on strike on a Friday was surely driven by this.

Who to blame for the end of British car making? A *Guardian* piece blamed Britain's obsession with putting our national assets up for sale while the reason for France and Italy retaining major indigenous car industries is that the French and Italian governments would never countenance the sale of Renault and Fiat to foreigners.

One analysis came from one Roy from Southend. His view was that anybody who lived through the industrial relations disasters of the 60s and 70s will know what happened.

"The car industry, and many others, were destroyed by union sabotage, weak and spineless management, and don't-give-a-damn attitude to quality by the workers."

Or it was all down to Derek Robinson, the communist union convenor at British Leyland's car plant at Longbridge in Birmingham.

I reported that when I first met him and again after he was sacked in November 1979 he was a soft-spoken Brummie who, in his speech, was courteous and who reasoned with vigour but without bombast.

Graham Stevenson, who became president of the European Transport Workers Federation, wrote in his appreciation of Derek Robinson that the events which led to Robinson's sacking was a pamphlet exposing mismanagement and Robinson's advocacy that British Leyland's future lay in capital investment, modernisation workers participation.

Anyone thus proposing British Leyland's modernisation, worker participation and claiming mismanagement was bound to get in trouble. Derek was a revolutionary, and paid the price for principle. Following his dismissal and within fifteen months over 18,000 jobs were lost with car plants closed. There followed another 25,000 job losses and thirteen further factories closed.

In the midst of media hysteria a mass meeting of Longbridge workers voted against striking in support of his reinstatement. Derek told his fellow stewards "You must go back into the factory, elect a new convenor and give him the support you gave me. Thanks, comrades".

This is hardly the attitude of a person pursuing the destruction of the car industry, or one without feeling for the future of the people he had worked with since a youth.

Institute of Directors – February 1985 On 27 February 1985, the Albert Hall hosted a meeting of the 4,000 representing the highest echelon of Britain's bosses. The Institute of Directors was renowned for their luxury luncheon boxes and no much else. Far from the miners' picket lines this allowed me a chance to make mock of these far from figures of fun.

It went like this: "Britain's bosses in the late, late Christmas show were given a taste of American razzmatazz yesterday by John Imlay, from Management Science American Inc. He gave a lecture on new technology, accompanied by a video show, the waving of a Samurai sword and a violinist playing the *Impossible Dream. Impossible Dream* is from the musical *The Man from Mancha* based on Don Quixote, which in itself says something about the Institute, on which "the survival of industry depends".

The Institute is still playing the old tunes but then the appearance of industry secretary, Norman Tebbit, at the convention helped them on their way. Tebbit, an ex pilot, was at the time rubbishing trade unions and help plot their downfall.

In its fixation with the trappings of technology the IOD had auto-cues and two screens tripli-

cated. With the speakers' images showing three Norman Tebbits, I thought it to much.

Tebbit's message was the need to create an "enterprise culture. He pointed to J R Ewing's and Alexis Colby's unscrupulous bosses in the US soap, *Dallas*, not as villains, but "the honest caring people which you really are".

Present were Prince Charles and Coal Board chairman, Ian MacGregor. Mr MacGregor gave a clear warning in his speech that wages would be his next target. He looked to the "lean" steel industry, which had no pay rise for three years, as the way forward for British industry.

Ford's sewing machinists The path to equal pay began in earnest with a three-week strike that started on 7 June 1968 at the Ford Dagenham plant. It was led by Rose Boland, Eileen Pullen, Vera Sime, Gwen Davis, and Sheila Douglass, and their trade unionist sisters walked out, followed later by those at Ford, Halewood. The women made car seat covers, and as stock ran out the strike halted all car production.

The June 1968 protest action came when the women's jobs were graded in Category B (less skilled production jobs), instead of Category C (more skilled production jobs), and they would be paid 15% less than that received by men. This triggered the three weeks' strike.

On 26 April 1985, the saga ended and I got the front page with a genuine piece of trade union history. "A 17-year struggle, which flared up in a six week strike last year (1984), culminated in a major victory for women's rights in their battle for equal pay with men for work of equal value. An Independent Arbitration Panel's decision yesterday that the 270 machinists, 263 of them women, should be regraded to skilled status, was hailed as a tribute to the Ford women."

A representative at the T&G's Transport House in London, where the arbitration decision was announced, was Teresa Taylor. "This is the day for women" she said. "When we heard the news this morning we lifted the roof off, as some cheered and some cried with joy". The women from Ford Dagenham works were "feeling great" when they heard of the decision at the plant yesterday and there were kisses and hugging all around.

They heard that they had been upgraded from B to near the top of C, in the five-grade Ford pay structure, meaning a £7 a week increase. Above all they were pleased to have achieved recognition along with male cutters as skilled operators. Rita Sharpe, a Dagenham shop steward said "it was not the money it was the principle that we were concerned with".

Labour's Barbara Castle the employment secretary promised the same rate the following year. This was a promise never kept.

The strike was the precursor to a women's trade union movement aimed at ending the inequality of treatment between men and women in Britain. This led to the Equal Pay Act of 1970 that recognised equal pay for work of equal value. All that was to come, but it was only when the Ford sewing machinists took to the cobbles that victory was achieved.

Amalgamations and Wages Councils In May 1985, Thatcher's attacks on the poorest in favour of the rich continued with the proposed abolition of the Wages Councils, "meaning increased poverty and hardship for the worst off in our society" said the TUC.

Wages Councils covered retailing, hotel and catering, and farming. I reported: "The workers are mainly women, ethnic minorities and young people, and also part-time workers and home workers whose pay is already low".

A Tory "consultative" document argued for the abolition or lessening in the scope of Councils, which were set up early in the 20th century to protect workers in poorly-organised occupations and industries". I wrote that: "The document is based on the Tory philosophy that taking away protection of wages pay rates will find a lower level, and employers will take on more labour". Those pigs are flying once more."

The TUC said that lower pay would mean workers not having enough to live on, and being reliant on benefits, thus transferring their support from the employers to the state. It pointed out that the bulk of monies paid out in benefits from taxation were paid by working people. The poor were again paying for the relief of the poor, made poor by the actions of Tory governments. Nevertheless, the Wages Councils were abolished.

At the return to the TGWU conference in June 1985, the banner headline on our front page said: "Biggest union says 'No' to Tory laws". Ron Todd, by then the general secretary-elect of the TGWU, was for standing firm and "brought the 900 delegates to their feet, as he told them that the union's boast and its proud record 'wasn't given to us by the employing class, we had to fight for it".

"By a huge majority the TGWU conference gave a resounding 'Yes' to the call by Mr Todd to 'stand and fight for what we believe in'. It reaffirmed total opposition to the anti-trade union laws and condemned the Tory government's expressed support for the Wembley conference, while it maximised solidarity against attacks on trade unions."

The problem was that some trade unions were already in retreat, as was shown by the AUEW in the case of Austin Rover,with some unions submitting to the law as, one after the other. they came across the penalties for disobeying those laws.

Polling for Political Fund In August 1985 trade unions were forced into of ballots for setting up a political fund, dedicated, for example, on producing material in support of a political party or anything depicted as political.

It was imposed, but proved to be a triumph of trade union organisation as the TUC took on board Bill Keys, the ex general secretary of SOGAT union, and Graham Allen later an effective Labour MP. They helped organise the ballots, which were won by thumping majorities by union after union announcing to the world and Thatcher that trade unions were still strong.

In August 1985 the long battle by the rail unions against the de-staffing of trains began, and goes on to this day. British Rail introduced driver-only trains on some routes, leading to walk-outs in Scotland and London in protest at the refusal of British Rail to negotiate.

In September of 1985, I reviewed an excellent history of the 350 years of the Post Office union entitled *The Post Office Workers, a Trade Union and Social History*, by Alan Clinton. It was commissioned by the Union of Communication Workers (UCW), and gives a glimpse of where trade unions started in the struggle for their members.

In its introduction Clinton wrote: "In 1832, a 24-year-old letter carrier called John Barret was the last postal worker to be executed for letter stealing. The history of postal workers mirrored the history of all the working classes in their trials and tribulations, and the gallants efforts to overcome them in unity, as shown as vividly as could be, in John Barret's execution.

" . . . from its early days to the present, their high-profile work in the community had given them problems. Special dress was proposed by Postmaster General Walsingham and Chesterfield in these terms, 'Security would be deprived to public correspondence if all our letter carriers were to have a uniform which would draw public attention to the persons. It would occasion their ebbing observed, either loitering in the ale houses when they ought to be delivering letters, or if they were frequently seen in pawnbrokers shops'.

The book describes how ". . . all the iniquities borne by postal workers were fought by them, and trades unions established the cost of hundreds of the victimised over three hundred years and more, all are chronicled in this book. There is nothing like the 'riot' on Christmas Day in 1886, as men who had worked 24 hours non stop, made a bolt for the door when asked to do another two hours. Nor do postman walk 28 to 41 miles a day, as did the rural messengers in the 1840s."

Truly a great history.

Becoming an NUJ activist and lay officer – 1984/85

In my first years at the *Star* I was an inactive member of NUJ's London Farringdon Branch, but I must have attended regularly, for one day in 1984 at its AGM, I was elected its chairman. It must have been something I said.

The branch members were of the *Times, Sunday Times, Guardian*, the *Observer*, the *Times Educational Supplement* and the shipping paper *Lloyd's List*. There were over 1,000 members, but the branch was poorly attended. The regular attendees were a group of activists of which I was one. There were among its ranks ultra left(ish), but no organised political base; simply, the group thought it could run the union better than whoever the leadership was.

I had come from industrial unions where rules backed discipline procedures, designed for unity of purpose in a struggle. Democracy was all to the NUJ, and its rule book, though comprehensive, lacked rigour, and in practice was open to challenge and interpretation; and always was.

This was so in all NUJ forums. Delegates had lots of differing views and the ability to debate to exhaustion, the conclusions not always being clear. Tony Dubbins, general secretary of the print union the NGA, summed it up thus after talks with the NUJ over amalgamation. "We have spent many hours talking about democracy, but once democracy inhibits the ability to make decisions and act resolutely it, becomes a handicap".

NEC for me I moved higher when I became London's representative on the National Newspapers and Agencies Industrial Council, and just after being elevated, I acted in a job share with John Richards of the *Daily Telegraph* to the NEC seat for National Newspapers. This was the highest position I ever achieved in seventy years in the trade union movement. As usual, my elevation, other than to shop steward, was only attained with little or no competition.

I was thus a concerned trade union 'leader' when, on 24 January 1985, the print union members at Rupert Murdoch's News International, employed at the T*imes, Sunday Times, Sun* and *News of the World*, went on strike over the introduction of new technology.

Newspaper production was served by craftsmen; compositors, type setters, and machine minders of the National Graphical Association (NGA).

The off press operations, including delivering the papers to wholesalers by van, train and air at home and abroad were carried out by Society of Graphical and Allied Trades (SOGAT 82) members. All of these, who were all men, were steeped in the history of print. Very few journalists entered the print floor and were not encouraged to do so. SOGAT covered administrative staff. The Amalgamated Union of Engineering workers AEU and the electricians union the EEPTU were the maintenance staff, and were all in closed shops. The NUJ was recognised as the union of the editorial staff, but without a closed shop agreement.

The historic place of printing in Britain and its language remains in words and phrases, typically: against the grain, stereotype, broadside, dog-eared, flush, catchword, dummy, baseline, gutter, headline, deadline, hairline, imposition, landscape, ligature and to justify.

The trade unions' strength, and it was great, arose because any dispute leading to a possible stoppage meant the loss of an edition or a whole day's paper. Once lost it could never be made up.

There was a period when Murdoch was shaping all his papers in his own image and to his own right-wing politics and, of course, to make money. His titles included the *Sun*, with the *News of the World* a right-wing Sunday paper for the general populace, the *Times*, right-wing for the educated classes and the *Sunday Times* for maintaining a reputation for "proper" journalism.

Murdoch's decision to introduce the new technology for his four titles meant that journalists could write, subedit, and fit the stories and the headlines on the page without the intervention of the traditional crafts. Complete papers could be sent down the line readied for the printing thus causing the loss of 5.500 print workers' jobs.

Murdoch also announced plans for sites at Canary Wharf in Wapping, and Kinnerton Park, Glasgow to be built and equipped for the use of new technology. Wapping was specifically for the production of a London Evening News paper.

Negotiations on the agreements needed to bring in this new way of working were exhaustive. In 1984 stalemate was reached. Murdoch's negotiators proposed an agreement "legally binding, with a no-strike deal, a ban on closed shops and the management's right to manage".

It laid out also a string of reasons for which the employer could dismiss a staff member. One of the *Times* staff remarked that the only thing missing was a tied cottage.

Murdoch's men knew that legally if a moment came when it was necessary to dispense with the present workforce at Times Newspapers Ltd, and at News Group Newspapers, the cheapest way of doing so would be to dismiss employees while they were taking part in a strike or other industrial action.

Murdoch anticipated that the print trade unions were certain to reject this, and so announced the go ahead with plans to launch without the agreement of unions.

On 30 December, Murdoch said he had, "given instructions for his new printing plant in Wapping to be brought into a state of operational readiness". The Glasgow plant would be commissioned at once.

By design or accident the plants could be used to produce one or all of his News International newspapers; *The Sun, News of the World, Times* and *Sunday Times*. This was with the collaboration of the electricians union, the EEPTU, which recruited labour from South Coast unemployment black spots. The new staff were trained to publish the papers with the new technology. When eventually the Fleet Street workforce was sacked, 250 existing members of the EEPTU were among those sacked.

My colleague, Isolda McNeil, went on an assignment where she was shown electricians from the South Coast being trafficked into Wapping, during which mission she ended up by witnessing the events whilst hiding in a ditch!

The negotiations dead locked and with Wapping and Glasgow readied for Murdoch to make his next move, a last minute offer was made of redundancy payments of £2,000 to £30,000 to each printer to quit their old jobs, and this was rejected by the trade unions. On Friday 24 January the 5,500 staff went on strike and were sacked. This action included printers and the administrative staff who had never taken strike action, some with years of loyalty to their papers. They were summarily escorted off the Fleet Street premises and thrown on the scrapheap.

Within hours there were thousands of union pickets at the 'Fortress Wapping' gates, well prepared, as shown in the *Star* story with a picture of "a plant defended from trade union organisation" behind 10 foot high concrete wall.

The barbed-wire fences were protected by helmeted, shielded, and baton wielding police who lay readied to protect the plant and its scabs from a jeering crowd of sacked print trade union members and their supporters. This was to remain so for a year. Any time as police were battering away at pickets, they faced the satirising chants by strikers of "Only doing me job, Sir!"

I reported on 28 January that: "The TUC general council meeting is to investigate allegations by the print unions that the electricians union, the EEPTU, acted in a manner detrimental to the trade union movement at Wapping and Glasgow."

Journalists of the NUJ The relations between the journalists and the printers, "the Inkies", in newspapers played a part, but not a decisive one in the Wapping dispute. This was because at times, after slaving over a hot story all day, a printers' dispute would mean it was never printed. Even at the *Morning Star* this happened to me.

Here are the words of an NUJ member who refused to go to Wapping, a 'Refusenik': "When the printers were sacked, there was little sympathy for their plight among the journalists."

If print workers were dispensable at Murdoch's newspapers, journalists were not, so it was important to get them to go to Wapping and Glasgow. An obstacle was immediately put in the way when NUJ's general secretary, Harry Conroy, elected in July 1985, put to his National Executive in emergency session, "an instruction not to cross the print workers picket lines" and got its approval.

This instruction to the journalists was matched by Murdoch, they being crucial to his plan, with an offer of £2,000 apiece to those going in. An added incentive was the threat that not to go in would result in the same fate as that of the striking print workers; the sack.

By then I was on the NUJ's Newspaper Industrial Council, (NAIC) and one of two NEC delegates for National Newspapers. Being on the industrial beat I often met for a drink with colleagues at the *Times*. Thus I was close to many fellow hacks working for Murdoch.

My chosen politics and trade unionism had threatened my ability to make a living, but here were people in the same boat likely to lose their jobs by simply being in this particular place and time. Within moments of the dispute beginning, the NUJ members were forced to take sides; their jobs, their family's futures, their union principles and organisation were all at issue.

The dilemma was spelt out by their editors. On Friday night, 23 January, it was move to Wapping and work the new technology that would help replace the printers, in exchange for a £2,000 pay rise and free health insurance.

Somewhere there was a promise of a swimming pool on site, but that never happened.

Refuse, and they would be regarded as having 'dismissed themselves'. The *Sun* and the *News of the World* chapels voted by large majorities to bow to the ultimatum. At the *Sun*, relations between the journalists and the printers were strained after printers had produced the paper during an earlier NUJ strike.

In the first of two long and tense meetings on the day after the strike was called, Saturday 25 January, the Times chapel's 'father', Greg Neale the courteous but unwavering champion of the NUJ's official position, called on his members not to go to Wapping.

A Refusenik, Ian Griffiths, business reporter at the *Times* told of being "fed the line that the printers were denying us access to the new technology that would change our working lives irrevocably for the better". In the *Guardian* in January 2006, he recalled these meetings 20 years on. "At the time it seemed like a simple decision. The free and independent press I cherished was incompatible with Rupert Murdoch's view that *Times* journalists should go to work in an armoured bus and report on the world's affairs from a ghetto ringed with barbed wire and security guards".

Ian also exposed as fallacies the benefits to journalists and journalism by the releasing from the bonds that bound them by the 'Spanish customs' of the Inkies. Such clarity of thought as to what was at stake was shared by a few.

The *Times* editor, Charlie Wilson, did however "stand shaking on a table before his staff at Holborn's Conway Hall on the Friday night, explaining the company's case".

"In fact, technology made newspaper production cheaper, not better. It was an error to believe that technology represented the dawn of a golden age", Griffiths concluded.

One journalist present reported: "The journalists in meetings over the next two days were eloquent and articulate. But for all the posturing, the bluster, the brow-beating and the rhetoric, there was no hiding from the ultimate reality. Murdoch was asking the journalists to take him on. "Through Wapping he set the tone for a compliant and non-confrontational press. He dealt a body blow to journalism, from which we have not yet fully recovered".

This, written in 2016 seemed harsh at the time, but Griffiths was entitled as a Refusenik, to take this stance and he was right. Where Murdoch led, others followed, not so dramatically, but as effectively. The influence of journalists over what they could write diminished, as the newspaper tycoons, Murdoch at the *Times*, Robert Maxwell at the *Daily Mirror* and Conrad Black at the *Telegraph* took an increasing hand in what went into 'their' newspapers.

On the Saturday of the *Times* Chapel meetings I met up with Harry Conroy and Mike Smith, the NUJ official for national newspapers, and we waited throughout the day for the talking to end and the decisions to be taken.

By then I had talked to some of those I knew from the *Sun*, who told me that they were going in to work on the Monday, and roughly why.

It was to do simply with their families and the uncertainty of a decision to break with a career that paid for their present and futures. Nobody I met was gung-ho about going into Wapping and the trauma that would bring.

I could only sympathise with their plight, with no thought of chastisement, but I told them that I thought they might regret it.

By early evening Harry, Mike and I had retired to the Royal Scot Hotel bar in Kings Cross Road, to await results, and late in the evening they arrived. It was bad news as described to us. At a later time the three industrial corespondents, Don MacIntyre, Dave Felton and Barrie Clement of the *Times* turned up and asked for a word with Harry in private.

Mike and I watched from across the room as a discussion took place. We learned later that there had been a vote between the three about going in or not, and I took it that it had gone two to one to go to Wapping. I further learned that Harry had explained the perils they would face, not only from the union but as 'industrials' plying their trade that involved meetings with other trade unions. He also assured them he personally would make that more difficult.

The three then discussed it further and decided not to go and we all got a drink in, and they took their places beside the other Refuseniks. I shared a car with Dave Felton on the way home, where he expressed himself worried about the future, to which I offered the opinion that he and his two colleagues' proven talents would ensure a bright future. And so it proved.

On the Sunday, the *Sunday Times* voted by 68 to 60 to go to work. and so it was Wapping for them. To return was against the advice of its NUJ father of the Chapel, Kim Fletcher, who later was to become the editor of the *Observer*).

The aftermath of Wapping Besides Ian Griffiths there were twenty-two Wapping Refuseniks. Paul Routledge, ex *Times* labour editor. In Singapore the Far East correspondent adopted an electronic picket line by refusing to telephone copy.

A NUJ official, Peta Van den Berg, was given the task of helping the Refusniks to supplement their strike pay by finding work, mostly with trade unions and publications sympathetic to the cause, through shifts and work on journals etc. The three industrials and others started in October 1986 with the new *Independent* daily newspaper

Along with Harry Conroy and other officials and Refuseniks, I went on the picket line and talked to our members going in. We were delighted then one day, to meet up with Peter Wilby, then of the *Times*, who told us he was going in to resign. He had seen the light! Err, he had another job.

The options of what to do about those now working at Wapping, despite heavy picketing, ranged from hanging and quartering to constructing stocks with attendant rotten fruit stalls at Headland House, the NUJ's HQ in Gray's Inn Road.

As the NEC member for national newspapers for both the Refuseniks and the 'scabs', my position was that the NUJ should keep those NUJ members in Wapping as an organised/recognised NUJ presence, as long as possible, while basically, waiting for something to turn up.

The members working at the *Times* and *Sunday Times* came up with their own tactic. A number of them turned up at the Farringdon Road NUJ branch, of which they were the members, and led by Peter Wilby demanded that action against them should be dropped. They argued that they had not been balloted for strike action and were not guilty of breaking any NUJ rules. To be "instructed by the NEC not to go into work was in fact illegal". We heard what they said!

Things came to a head at the NUJ's Sheffield Annual Delegate Meeting in May 1986. A motion instructing the union executive to discipline those members still working in Wapping found a number of the Refuseniks speaking against. A narrow majority voted for disciplinary action.

In what became a chaotic and shambolic attempt to carry out the ADM demand a disciplinary panel was set up and eventually "charged and convicted" ninety-seven of the many hundreds that went into Wapping. If any disciplinary measure was imposed, it was never carried out and was later dropped.

The defeat of the trade unions involved in the Fleet Street national newspapers dispute, despite its drama, was a small corner of a vast industry of regional and local newspapers, magazines and books. Here the owners and managers were able through technology to displace people with machines. Here also, instead of the predicted shorter hours, better pay and longer holidays there came mostly increased unemployment.

Nor would journalists escape the ravages of ill-considered automation. When added to computerised paperwork, came on-line publishing, rendering in many cases its own sweat-shop conditions. For the National Union of Journalists, as with all industries, there was an avalanche of trade union de-recognition throughout the industry, starting with News International enterprises.

At Wapping the riot and mounted police pursued their war on the Wapping pickets with many arbitrary arrests on trumped-up charges. Such was the police overwhelming presence that the Wapping area became a mini-police state.

Communist Party general secretary, Mick Hicks, was jailed for 16 months for pushing a megaphone into the face of a police inspector. I covered the trial, which was peculiar in that the defence argued a possible case of mistaken identity, possibly an error, as Mike had a commanding presence that was unmistakable, even in a crowd. In the canteen after the case had been dealt with, Mike did admit that it was him with the megaphone.

Death at Wapping – January 11 1987 The forecast of tragedy at Fortress Wapping came true on 11 Januay 1987 when "death ended the nineteenth birthday celebrations of Mike Delaney, after the TNT Juggernaut had just left Murdoch's plant".

The TNT heavy lorry delivery company was set up by Murdoch to deliver his papers throughout Britain. This was done at speed aided by the police, who "ignored the safety of citizens in order to ensure the safe delivery of the scab newspapers produced at Wapping and in Glasgow".

"Dan Jones, the chairman of the Tower Hamlets Trade Council, said yesterday 'it was a disaster waiting to happen'. Mr Delaney was talking to three companions at the corner of Butchers Row and Commercial Road at 11.45 p.m., when he was struck by the lorry. He was taken to London Hospital, but he died from the injuries."

A trip to Strasbourg I was with the NGA members when they took their case to the European Union Parliament in Strasbourg, which was less exotic than it sounds. They started by boarding their bus at Kings Cross at 4 a.m. one black Monday morning embarking on what was to be the longest ever day trip.

The company was good as we travelled to the Dover Ferry and on to Calais for the trip across northern France to the border with Germany. The 500 miles trip to the Palais de l'Europe took ten hours. The printers aboard the coach were excited by the trip, as Johannes Gutenberg, born in Germany, had made his first experiments printing with movable type when in Strasbourg. The last remnants of his pioneering work were now about to perish.

After a sparse meal in a cafe adjacent the Roman Catholic Strasbourg cathedral with its Gothic architecture I took a look. At 142 metres (466 feet), it is the highest extant structure built entirely in the middle ages and was magnificently lit against the blackest of black nights.

Gladys saw it for itself when we stayed in Strasbourg on a trip to Austria. After ten hours and home at Kings Cross by 6 o'clock I had no real story to tell. Let it not be said that a journalist's trips abroad can be always be described as a jolly,however entertaining your companions.

Womens' part in the struggle "A pregnant Mary Turner, with husband Denis and one-year-old Denise were squatting on the top floor of a dwelling in Kilburn. A suspect roof was leaking rainwater when one night it became worse than usual. At this Denis climbed into the attic to investigate. As soon as he entered, there was a crash as the roof caved in and below Mary and her child were covered with rubble. In the dark Mary sought frantically for her child and found her".

I wrote this in October 1985 as a feature for the Labour Party conference in Bournemouth. It was about Mary Turner, a school dinner lady, and a member of the GMB, whose election to the GMB executive council was announced. She was later to serve for many years as the GMB's lay president. As a member of the Labour Party she was a GMB delegate to its conference.

This short eulogy is to be taken as a tribute to all those women of the trade union movement, who gave it a campaigning edge. They were working class women, who combined a warm, womanly glow of courage and fortitude that carried them along, with in Mary's case, with many a joke at the expense of the Tories and the bosses, born of experience of both.

Mary used this interview to say that women in the past had been "put down, but they wouldn't be put down any more. That in our union there has never been a better spirit, with women taking to the union and the union taking to the women. We have been held back, but never any more".

At the heart of the problems for women at work was then, and remains, pay. At that time, and until 2018 when she died, Mary was at the forefront of women fighting their corner through the trade unions and in politics.Women at work and their communities have been short-changed, and still are low paid. They are the unskilled majority of the workforce, and are denied their rightful places.

The same 1985 Labour Party Conference was where Labour's then leader Neil Kinnock delivered the final insult and end of the Militant Tendency's reign as leaders of Liverpool's Labour council. This signalled the end of its presence in the Labour Party, after an heroic but failed attempt to resist Thatcher's on local government.

Kinnock told delegates: "I'll tell you what happens with impossible promises. You start with far-fetched resolutions and you go through the years sticking to that, out-dated, misplaced, irrelevant to the real needs, and you end in the grotesque chaos".

In comparison Kinnock's problem was that he failed dismally to meet with his promises and deliver what was "relevant to the people's needs", failing by some margin to win their votes to govern in two general elections. Then he went off to a European Commissioner's job and a peerage, still never short of advice to others.

To Kinnock's themes of change and adaptation Blairism, a decade later would elaborate. Kinnock developed a theory of contemporary social democracy in which government should intervene in social and economic life, but as an 'opportunity' or 'servant' state, whereas Blair argued for the withdrawal of government from each of the vital arenas.

The nuclear industry The Chernobyl nuclear power plant disaster in northern Ukraine in April 1986 was a catastrophe that led to the abandonment of the town of Pripyat, north of Kiev, and concentrated minds on the dangers of nuclear power.

In November 1986, the conclusion of a fact-finding delegation to the Soviet Union by the GMB, nuclear power's biggest union, was that it would be "unwise to build more stations now, and called for a freeze until the industry had learned all the lessons of the Chernobyl disaster.

For the Communist Party and within the *Morning* Star generally, the policy was opposition to nuclear power as an answer to Britain's energy needs. The editor, Tony Chater, whose profession was as a physicist, I think supported it, but didn't argue the case.

There were problems of supply, as in mid-January 1987 Britain was struck by extreme winter weather. I reported that "electricity supplies to large industrial consumers were heavily cut between 4:30 and 6 p.m. last night as demand overtook supply. General voltage reductions were also expected throughout Britain last night, and electricity chiefs warned that power cuts could not be ruled out. Board officials said that the freeze indicated that two coal-fired stations were needed quickly. I wrote "But ominously Board Chairman, Lord Marshall, a nuclear power advocate used the crisis to push the case for a new nuclear power station at Sizewell".

The working class way to politics through trade unions The shop-floor route to the top in politics starts by dealing with the day-to-day problems that arise for individuals and groups. Dealing with the workplace problems and accepting the outcomes good or bad provides a unique training ground.

There's little theory; its all practice, which puts a bit of iron in the soul. My Auntie Kate's view was that indulging in union affairs and politics was a waste, when ". . . a big man like you could have been a foreman".

There is no doubt that many more trade union activists could have made it in other trades, professions and politics. Some did; some going into business management, personnel management and labour relations, (a favourite), and politics at local and national level with some becoming ministers of state.

Auntie Kate may have seen me as a councillor. If I had said yes to the many times Labour Party members pleaded with me to join them, I could have become the mayor of Ellesmere Port, as at least five of my comrades on the trades council did. It was not beyond the bounds of possibility that I could have made it to MP. But I didn't.

A trade union activist who did make it was James Callaghan. Leaving school at fourteen and becoming a senior tax inspector and the Kent branch secretary of the Association of the Officers of Taxes (AOT) he was, on being transferred to London on a merger of unions in 1936 was appointed assistant secretary of the Inland Revenue Staff Federation (IRSF).

He entered the Royal Navy Volunteer Reserve as an Ordinary Seaman in 1942. On leave from the navy, Callaghan was selected as a Parliamentary candidate for Cardiff South. He was encouraged to put his name forward by an IRSF colleague, a friend of the local Labour Party secretary. The only person ever to hold the four highest offices of state, Callaghan was just one of an army of trade unionists from every shop floor, and they were by no means all of the left.

In 1979 the Labour Party was still filled with working class members particularly in local government, and as MPs through the influence in the party of trade unions. The main areas of union influence were Scotland, Wales, the North-East, the North-West, the Midlands, London, Bristol in the south west, and bits of the South (at ship yards and docks).

In Scotland's industrial belt there were 'miners seats' where the NUM was decisive, in steel-making with the Iron and Steel Trade Confederation (ISTC) and in shipbuilding the Confederation's engineering unions, the AUEW and the Boilermakers unions. In Wales it was the NUM and the

ISTC. The Transport and General Workers and the AUEW predominated in the car industry areas such as in Birmingham, the Midlands and Essex. The AUEW and metal trade unions were powerful in Manchester's engineering industries. The Agricultural Workers Union – eventually joining the T&G – had a hand in sending progressive MPs to parliament over the years.

Unions donate huge sums to Labour sustaining the party and funding campaigning at local and national government elections. Traditionally this influence meant that a place could be found in constituency Labour Party shortlists for working class candidates. It also provided opportunitys for the left as when Michael Foot who he lost his Portsmouth seat and was selected for Merthyr Tydfil.

However, declining union membership brought shrinking political influence throughout the late 1980s and 90s. Among Labour MPs the numbers of miners, bank clerks, steel, dock and car workers, seamen, draughtsman and farmers declined and were replaced by young and ambitious career politicians, with university degrees in economics and politics and careers as spin doctors and political advisors. These changes were writ large by Tony Blair with his launch of New Labour and a draft manifesto, *New Labour, New Life for Britain*. It was presented as the Third Way brand of a newly-reformed party that had abandoned the socialist Clause Four of the Labour Party constitution and endorsed market economics.

The New Labour brand attempted to widen its electoral appeal, and by the 1997 general election it had made significant gains in the upper and middle-classes, which together with the still loyal working class gave the party a landslide victory. Labour maintained this wider support at the 2001 general election and won a third consecutive victory in 2005 for the first time ever in the history of the Labour Party.

It maintained high unemployment, wages and conditions deteriorated, as trade union powers remained shackled by Tory anti- trade union law.

Blair's vainglorious decision – in the worst imperial tradition – to join with US president George H Bush, led to the disastrous war in Iraq.

The most damning aspect of the New Labour years was Labour's continuation of Thatcher's celebration of market forces and a failure to reverse the damage to Britain's production and manufacturing industries. The reliance on banking and finance industries led catastrophically to the 2008 banking crisis.

The roots of the banking collapse lay in the deregulation that swept away many of the regulatory controls, led to an unsustainable speculative boom along with exposure to the US sub prime speculative bubble.

Aftermath of the strike In February 1987, I described how "Nearly two years after the end of the miners' strike ended, one of its last dramas was played out in the icy atmosphere outside a Sussex jail yesterday.

"At 8.15 a.m. through the gates of the Northeye prison Kent miner, Terry French strolled out from his two years and one month of incarceration in four jails. There to greet him was his wife Liz and still-sacked, fellow, now ex-miners, with the Kent Area NUM's banner still held high. It was some sentence, handed out to a person who had thrown punches at the height of hostilities in that epic battle". There was not one word of complaint from Terry, but only a vow to carry on the fight. A misty day on the Sussex Marshes turned to bright sunshine, and "there were shouts of here he is now" a hug and kiss from Liz followed by the Miners Anthem of "Here we Go".

We travelled in cars and vans to the Miners' Welfare at Deal, where celebrations continued, with a commitment made for support for five miners still in jail and for all sacked miners of Britain. "Another day in the history of the Kent coalfield was written today, a day to remember and as Terry French told his supporters "the fight starts from here" as he appealed for unity in the Kent coalfield".

The dockers and the Docks Labour Scheme Dockers are famous for looking after their own. But among dockers and their families and in their communities there are strong traditions of solidarity. In 1936, dockers joined in the battle of Cable Street in London's East End, and fought the police trying to clear a way for fascists to march into the Jewish quarter.

In Britain's ports grand buildings bear testimony to the wealth of merchants and shipping owners and the shipping owner. There is little to be seen today in tribute to the generations of dockland communities that lived and laboured, or of the families deported since to green fields and vast housing estates.

Gone are the cargoes of spices, fruits imported and coals exported. All loaded and unloaded manually in dirty, physically demanding and dangerous conditions. The maiming and deaths of dockers were routine. The irregularity of shipping arrivals and departures meant that differing numbers and skills needed. In any port, even in good days, there were always a pool of unemployed dockers. Jobs were handed down through the family. The workers were hired twice a day; in the morning and at midday, and often sacked twice a day or hired for half a day at a time, as needed.

The foremen would stand on waste ground, with tallies to give out to those hired, and so the family and favourites came first. Any tallies left could be thrown in the air and the men left at the gates would scrabble after them in the dirt. Those still without work tried again.

The war changed things with the Dock Labour Scheme (DLS), introduced in 1941, when port employers and the employed (through their trade unions), stood together to improve efficiency, which was vital for victory.

In 1947, the Labour government introduced the Dock Workers' (Regulation of Employment) Scheme to sixty-three larger (DLS) ports. These were administered by the National Dock Labour Board, and by local boards, with equal numbers of employers and dockers. In 1967 permanent status as registered dockers was attained. Local dock boards kept a register of employers and workers. This provided job security and removed the ability to favour the hire of one individual over another thus consigning the tally system and scrabbling in the dirt to the dustbin of history. A basic, minimum, fallback wage was paid by the employer rather than the dole being paid by the state, when there was no work. At some of the bigger ports half of a gang working a ship would work the first four hours of a shift while the other half did the second part of the shift. Dockers had workplace power and the power to shut down the country.

During the 1960/70s things were changing. Cargoes were packed into giant containers in factories and depots. These were rolled on and off ships. The first move to deal with this ended as told earlier the Pentonville Five incident, when dockers demanded to follow the work into container depots.

Unable to find a way to resolve this peacefully – if losing thousands of jobs could ever be solved thus – the matter was solved by a fight to the end for most dockers and their families in a battle instigated by the bosses. The mechanism to sack thousands of workers was by way of abolishing the National Docks Labour Scheme; the jobs for life guarantee. In the centuries-old trade of dockers, there ended this brief period of being treated with the dignity that their labour deserved.

By 1987, a powerful propaganda campaign was put in train, making the case for the abolition of the DLS, mounted by the government and the private owners. The ports outside the national scheme and privately owned, located especially on the east coast, were thriving and the privateers wanted some of that action.

This was undertaken by the Association of Port Employers' (APE), and chairman, Nicholas Finney, aided Iain Dale, a right-wing, Tory journalist who was appointed as the public affairs manager in 1987. Dale, later a Tory radio and TV pundit, revealed later that: "My task was to launch a campaign to persuade Margaret Thatcher to do the necessary and get rid of this piece of iniquitous employment legislation". It was said that Thatcher was afraid to take on the dock workers!

The APE launched 'a hearts and minds' campaign aimed at politicians and the media. Barely a week went by without someone writing an op-ed calling for the scheme to go, or for a tabloid news report to appear about 'Spanish practices' in the industry.

An Early Day Motion in parliament attracted more than 400 signatures, and kept up the parliamentary pressure, with debates, questions and meetings.

A Tory think-tank, the Centre for Policy Studies, said in a report that up to 48,000 new jobs would be created. How this was possible with containerisation, and automation on board and ashore, was not explained.

The cherry on the cake for the sixty-three DLS ports, which included all the major ones, would be a law allowing any non port-related activity within their boundaries. If the Scheme didn't exist, they could utilise their land however they wished. So they sold priceless prime property in increasing amounts.

At 3.30 p.m. on 6 April 1989, Norman Fowler, the employment secretary, told the Commons, to roars of approval from the Conservative backbenchers, that the scheme would be abolished. The next day there was unofficial strike action at London, Bristol, Glasgow, and at other ports. Several trade unions had been heavily fined, the TGWU being one, or worse, had their funds grabbed for taking industrial action under the anti-trade-union laws.

A meeting of the TGWU's executive council on 14 April, lobbied by reps from most of Britain's dockyards, gave 'overwhelming support' to general secretary Ron Todd's proposal to use 'all lawful means' to oppose the government plan to abolish the NDL. It also sanctioned his wish to meet with the port employers to negotiate an agreement 'to establish national conditions that are no less favourable than the current provisions.' *(Western Daily Press* 15 April 1989).

The chances of this happening was pretty well nil and the dockers knew it. The militant dockers had no real alternative to the reorganisation except defence of a *status quo* increasingly made impossible by technological change. After some initial anger by the lobbyists, the proposal was accepted. Talks with employers over an agreement to replace the NDLS collapsed, and the docks' committee delegates sanctioned the holding of a national ballot on 20 April (*Bristol Evening* Post 21 April 1989).

While all this was going, on the Dock Labour Scheme (Abolition) Bill slowly made its way through Parliament and eventually received Royal Assent on 6 July. Fowler said there would be generous compensation of up to £35,000 for men laid off as a result of the scrapping of the scheme.

When the ballot went ahead the result went in a three to one vote for strike action. The Port Employers challenged this in the High Court only to lose, but when they took their case to the Court of Appeal it granted the employers an injunction to prevent strike action. The appeal was successful, but as 28 days had elapsed the TGWU was obliged to hold a fresh ballot. In the meantime, on 3 July, the NDLS was formally abolished. In this case, state intervention was not only decisive in curtailing the ability of trade unions to take strike action, but also delivered to the port employers the power to dismiss registered dock workers, and hire casual workers as replacements. The dreams of the bosses of privatising the seventy ports was realised.

Confederation's 37-Hour-Week Campaign The working week in post-war Britain went from forty-eight to thirty-nine hours, then stalling in August 1987, with no cuts for fifteen years. In 1979 there was a series of one-day and two-day national strikes. One million workers took part in the strikes, and sixteen million working days were lost. Nothing was gained. At the CSEU Annual Conference in June 1983 a motion called for "a 35-hour week without loss of earnings," and "without changes in working practices".

There was nowt then till April 23 1988, at the AEU's rank and file National Committee conference, when the "Shorter Hours call" was made to clear the decks for the next attack. This was put to the CSEU's conference on September 14 1988, where the unions leadership promised that "Over one million engineers will form the vanguard of the workers' battle to bring the 35-hour-week to Britain".

The campaign slogan was "Unite for 35", and for the first time white- collar and blue-collar workers are shoulder to shoulder". In February 1988, the "Confed" proclaimed that "To achieve our aims means a basic programme of rallies, booklets, car stickers and the like, and this would cost £75,000. Meetings of activists, regional rallies, press conferences and numerous meetings raised the money for two booklets and four million leaflets putting the case.

In February 1989, the CSEU tabled a draft national agreement, proposing two one-hour reductions in November 1989 and 1990. A levy asked for £4 for craft workers, technicians and supervisors, and £2 for all others.

A strategy council announced strikes at six factories; Smiths Industries, Cheltenham, Rolls Royce, Coventry and Hillingdon, Glasgow and BAe at Preston and Chester. All held mass meetings and voted to ballot for strike action, by then compulsory. At all sites the manual workers voted in favour; white collars not. On 30 October 1989 British Aerospace factories in Preston and Chester, and the Rolls Royce factory in Hillingdon, Glasgow were called out. At the announcement of a strike Smiths Industries' and NEI Parsons' bosses settled for thirty-seven hours. This was quickly followed by Rolls Royce bosses at Hillingdon and Coventry. Four down. The strikes at the British Aerospace factories at Preston, and Chester and Kingston continued into 1990, then settled for thirty-seven hours. At all sites there were promises to cooperate with improving productivity.

This meant that gone were the times when women like Gladys as a tea lady at Vauxhall's night shift pushed her tea-trolley from plant to plant with hot tea and sandwiches to serve the queues at 'team break'. She was replaced by a tea machines.

The CSEU was able to claim over five hundred agreements, and the campaign clearly achieved a major reduction in working hours, but it was the trade unions' last significant achievement of its sort.

Struggles of seamen and in the car industry In 1988, the *Star's* industrial desk experienced the two years of hectic work, with disputes abounding and many continuing when there came a victory to report. Ford UK's plant of 32,00 workers went on strike over pay successfully, or so the unions said.

A favourite phrase for the industrial reporter came into play as I and Jimmy Arnison reported the call for industrial action over pay by Ford's EuropV1 plants. This caused closures and cuts in production in Belgium and West Germany.

The six unions were in united in rejecting a 7% increase in the first year, and a 2.5% increase in the next two. Eleven days of strikes saw the Ford bosses drop the demand for a three year deal, and settle for the two-year at 7% and 2.5% over the second.

In March 1987, the P&O Ferries ferry *Herald of Free Enterprise* overturned in the Belgium port of Zeebrugge with the loss of 191 passengers and crew members. The owners expressed regret but pushed on with trying to maximise their profits by cutting jobs, lengthening the remaining workers hours and cutting their pay.

At the port of Dover, the National Union of Seamen was in a fight with P&O Ferries over the company's intention to reduce the annual wage bill of £35 million by £6 million, by cutting 500 out of 2,300 jobs, and reducing earnings by an average of £25 a week. This was in anticipation of the Channel Tunnel opening in 1993!

The strike lasted 16 months, with the now familiar pattern of a militant workforce willing to put up a fight for pay, conditions and jobs, hampered by the threat to their union of fines or sequestration should they fall foul of the anti-trade union laws. This happened to the P&O strikers.

The seafarers refused to accept the ultimatums, voted to strike, and stopped work on 6 February 1988. Many felt betrayed by a company to which some family members and friends had literally given their working lives. Mass picketing by the seafarers and supporters, (mainly ex-miners led by ex Kent miner Terry French), had some success, and a number of lorries booked on rival ferry operator, Sealink, were turned back.

The deployment of very large numbers of police soon assisted the scab lorry and bus drivers to break the lines. The picketing did stop people going to work, and for almost two months P&O ferries lay idle.

There were two key moments. The first was when a proposed ballot of the NUS's 21,000 members was cancelled in the wake of a court injunction threatening sequestration of the union's funds, thus signalling to the NUS leadership general secretary, Sam McCluskie, to remain within the law.

At Easter 1988 P&O de-recognised the NUS, and was pulling out of the industry's National Maritime Board agreements. Sealink's NUS members in Dover, recognising that this was an attack on the rights of seafarers to defend themselves, decided not to cross the P&O picket lines.

Sealink then took NUS to court for secondary picketing by Sealink members, now country-wide. The courts ordered the sequestration of the NUS assets, its offices were seized, staff pay was stopped and investment funds frozen. McCluskie threatened defiance, but after just nine days, and only three days after a 2,000 strong supporters' march in Dover, the union purged its contempt and ordered Sealink workers back to work. The Sealink injunction was lifted, only to be replaced by one from P&O itself, so that the union did not get its assets and funds back.

Nevertheless, a threat to all ferry operators in Britain was replaced by a dispute between an increasingly isolated workforce and an international employer, supported by the government, police, media and the courts. Strikers continued picketing, money continued to be raised for families and to maintain the support kitchens operating in the Dover area, and speakers continued to raise the issues at meetings and demonstrations.

Rob Cathcart on the industrial desk did most, if not all of the heavy lifting work. Reporting on this dispute was his first taste of reporting a major dispute and he did it brilliantly.

This was appreciated by the P&O Dover seafarers concerned more than anyone else, and they took him in over the long months as one of there own. So much so that Rob was asked to, and did speak from a Dover NUS seafarers' platform in their support. I suppose you could say this revealed a lack of objective reporting, but hey, where ever any *Star* reporter went to a site where the workers were in struggle, their was no doubt as to whose side we were on. On this occasion though, we were not able to help, as the dispute dragged on until it was formally abandoned by the NUS after 16 months in May 1989.

Ron Todd and Big Jim When I once tried assisting the PA reporter in his work, it didn't turn out well. It was when Ron Todd stood for T&G general secretary, he won, but the result was challenged with an accusation of ballot rigging. To avoid court proceedings Todd was asked to accept a re-run. This he would answer at a T&G executive meeting, and then at a press conference. On decision day we gathered to await the verdict. Just before it was due I took advantage to go for a wee and meeting with a 'reliable contact' on the Executive Council who told me "Ron will not stand again but will seek a vote of confidence".

This I relayed to Big Jim Foulkes, the Press Association industrial, who via the PA passed it on to the world. On the way back from making the call, Jim, six feet five inches tall, met the T&G deputy general secretary, who told him that Ron would be standing again. Jim corrected the copy and took me to lunch, but never (quite) forgave me.

In 1990 I was elected chairman of the Labour and Industrial Correspondents Group.

The Employment Secretary held a 'do' for the Group at Christmas time, as did most other employers organisations, both public and private, including the Coal Board, the Post Office and Telecoms (in the Telecom Tower), the Electricity Council, the Engineering and Buildings Federations, the Electricity Generating Board and ACAS.

Such was the reputation of this grouping, that our invitations to then government ministers, and opposition shadows, and trade union leaders were usually accepted, with meetings either at a Fleet Street pub, or one particular favourite, *The Red Tape* in Whitehall.

As chair, and with Kevin Maguire, the secretary but mostly because of him, we managed a goodly number of meetings during my year, with the opposition Labour Party, including shadow chancellor Gordon Brown and trade union leaders.

Tony Blair, then shadow employment secretary was invited for an audience with the group. Unfortunately, on the day the meeting was arranged, Arthur Scargill, who could still a draw crowd, called a press conference in Sheffield, to which most of the group attended.

When Tony, as I addressed him, arrived, the attendance had diminished to about eight, but it was no problem. Tony gave us a talk, we asked questions, and he answered over a couple of pints. We couldn't get rid of him.

Once, at the TUC in Blackpool, at one of the trade union receptions, where we industrials always went after filing the day's news, Tony turns up and joins our company and chats away. As we were soon off to a Blackpool back-street pub in search of 'real ale', Tony asked someone where we were going and said he might pop along.

We were settling into the first round when Tony enters. Not all of the group knowing him or he them, he introduced himself first to the *Daily Mail's* Dave Norris, a bluff Mancunian, who mistakes Blair for a free-lancer to whom he had once lent a fiver, and demanded it be repaid.

A startled Blair turns quickly to acquaint himself with Mick Costello, who tells him to "Fuck Off". How much of this story is embellished in the retelling I dont know. The story spread and accepted and people laughed over a lot at Blair's expense. Whether it was sensible to act this way to a prominent politician is a moot point.

Blair certainly remembered the incident, for when in future he spoke of the Industrial and Labour Correspondence Group it was with a curled lip. In hindsight it was possibly a mistake for journalists to get on the wrong side of a future prime minister.

Making speeches When I was angling for the group chairmanship it was partially to get the publicity for the *Morning Star*. One honour or task entailed giving the vote of thanks th the end of Congress and the same at the Labour Party Conference. Naturally, in my work and life I had made hundreds of speeches of varying quality. Tony McClellan, the Communist Party Liverpool area secretary on one occasion advised me: "best stick to writing".

At school, when I was twelve, Miss Jones, the English teacher accused congratulated (or perhaps accused me of having the "gift of the gab" but that must have been about chattering.

I was competent at mass meetings on sites, when I knew to the nth degree what I was talking about, OK at committee meetings dealing with interjections. At conferences and from the rostrum it was bit more hit and miss. Sometimes it worked and sometimes not. The fact was I wasn't always very good at speech making.

It was noticeable that when I was on hand at a group where the erudite Kevin McGuire was present my colleagues – subtly they thought – discouraged me from making formal speeches.

At the TUC in Blackpool I faced the serried ranks of trade unionist delegates with a prepared script of 2,000 words of the smallest print possible. It was to be delivered from a rostrum with a dodgy microphone. It didn't go well.

I was announced by the chair, Ada Maddox, as Roy Jones of the *Morning Star* who was blacklisted when he had previously worked in the construction industry. This was greeted with loud applause but it was all down-hill from there!

An offer from Terry Patterson from the *Daily Mirror* of some lines to help me on my way, and the advice from Jimmie Airlie of the AEU to keep it short, I had loftily set aside. I wasn't very far into the script before I knew it wasn't going well and it got worse. As I went on I had difficulty keeping to the script to which I added some ad libs, making for some confusion.

It was the last morning at the end of the Congress's week of speeches, and following a night on the ale the audience had thinned and everyone wanted to get home. The faces of Jimmy Airlie and others told me things weren't going well. I knew it was time to give up, but this was easier said than done. I frantically went through my papers to find a finishing place and made a dignified exit. Or so I thought.

The delegates and my colleagues were kind but were without praise. One mentioned my accent and another the microphone. Mary Rosser simply swept by me.

When I mentioned getting a video of my speech, Pete Fuzzy, a T&G London taxi driver and communist dismissed it as "That fucking rubbish". For long afterwards – when the incident was raised in company – the impression was given that I had been the worse for drink.

A week later I was at the very same rostrum for the Labour Party conference to deliver the thanks from the press. A lesser person would have ducked out of this, but that I'm made of sterner stuff, or with a thicker skin.

The Winter Gardens was packed to the rafters and no one had gone home. Behind me on the platform were Neil Kinnock and the Labour Party Leadership. I had learnt lessons by then. The speech was about half the length, four paragraphs to a page, in large print and with obvious pauses marked. I started on the script and never left it.

"You will excuse me for bringing politics into the conference at this late stage" I started.

This was when Labour was trying to duck its left-wing associations. I asked the delegates had seen John Cleese the previous week on the conference platform of the Liberal Democratic Party. "This is the man who in his Monty Python days used to know a dead parrot when he saw one". (Laughter and applause!).

A week later in her speech to the Conservative Party Conference, Margaret Thatcher told the conference my joke, word for word. Hers was broadcast mine stayed the walls of the Blackpool Winter Gardens although a *Financial Times* diary piece reported Thatcher's joke and pointed out that it was Roy Jones of the *Morning Star* who had first told it at the TUC.

The speech did go down well, and I treasured for some time a wink of approval by the *Guardian* politico, Ian Aitkin. The result was that the adrenalin flowed, and the bottle of whiskey consumed on the way home didn't help. I didn't come down from the heights for about a week. Unfortunately, few who witnessed my shame at the TUC Congress were there.

The Poll Tax A Thatcher-inspired proposal to change the rating system of taxing the owners and tenants of houses by their value to a new Community Charge became a big political issue. Swiftly designated as a Poll Tax it passed through parliament, and was first introduced in Scotland from April 1989, and England and Wales from April 1990.

It was unfair and discriminatory. The more people in a house, poor or rich, the more was due. It was open to fraud by simply not telling the council the number of people per dwelling. It lead to Thatcher's downfall.

The decision to introduce it first in Scotland was met with immediate and enduring hostility. A Scotland Anti-Poll Tax Federation was set up, with Militant the driving force with Tommy Sheridan as chair. This was one of the fare times a ultra left organisation was effective in leading a mass struggle and they deserve credit. The campaign brought the still-existing Communist Party, the

Socialist Workers Party, Left Labour people, including a number of MPs and the *Morning Star*. An all Britain Anti-Poll Tax Federation was set up at a conference at Manchester Free Trade Hall attracting around two thousand delegates. A steering committee organised twenty regional federations. The campaign organised a mass campaign of non-payment of the poll tax, which resulted in up to 18 million people refusing to pay the tax. The demonstrations on 31 March 1990, included the 200,000 strong one in London, parts of which turned into the famous Poll Tax riots alongside a 50,000-strong demonstration in Glasgow.

The 'Three Ds' slogan – Don't Register, Don't Pay, Don't Collect – was taken up by hundreds of local Anti-Poll Tax Unions. In Scotland, where the tax was implemented first, the APTUs called for mass non-payment and as the tax neared its implementation in England protests began to increase. With large numbers refusing to register or to pay, local councils responded with enforcement measures but they were ineffective given the huge numbers of non-payers.

Mike Ambrose, amongst others at the *Star* refused to pay the Poll Tax. I chickened out. Non payers contested efforts to get them into court, which anyway were unable to cope. In November 1990, South Yorkshire police said it was "physically impossible for the police to enforce the laws because of the large number of defaulters".

The situation was so grave that the Tory's chances of winning the next election looked doomed, with Michael Heseltine challenging Thatcher for the Conservative leadership in November 1990. Thatcher scraped home by 50 votes, thus triggering a second vote, and on 22 November 1990 she announced her resignation after a decade in office.

Changes in Labour Policy and at the *Star* The successful candidate for Tory leadership, John Major, appointed Heseltine to the post of Environment Secretary, responsible for replacing the poll tax. It's abolition was announced on 21 March 1991.

In 1989 the Labour Party gave notice of the shape of things to come when it abandoned its policy on trade union closed shops in line with European legislation. According to the BBC it was "A move away from the party's old-style socialism towards a more European-wide agenda". Labour sources said the new policy would counter Tory accusations that the party was dominated by trade unions.

Enter Labour's shadow employment secretary, one Tony Blair, who said the move was crucial for a sustainable approach by the party to employment. "We have got to bring our law into line with the rest of Europe" and the move was "a key thing for rebuilding our industrial base".

This never happened. The move was denounced as a 'sell-out' of socialist principles and "met with anger from MPs on the left of the party" and was a further move away from traditional Labour policies.

It was also the first of Blair's plans for a Labour Party bereft of working class influence through the trade union movement and socialism embodied in Clause Four of the party's constitution.

George Anthony, a North London AEU official told me of workers being locked out at an Essex engineering company. On arrival I was confronted by fifteen workers at the workshop gates. I was told a story of ill-treatment by a boss who had taken over. It was a tale of injustice and ill treatment, with no redress for a number of months, with a refusal by the boss to meet with either the workers' trade union rep or George, the AEU regional officer.

Their case was clear cut, well-told by the workers and easy to write.Page lead; job done!

Three days later I was called in to Tony Chater's office, where he was with Mary Rosser, to be told of a letter from the solicitor of the boss of the East End engineering company claiming my story as untrue and detrimental to the employer's good name. What's more the workers quoted had denied it all.

I told Tony and Mary that what I had written was true as told to me by more than one of these workers. I told the *Star's* solicitors, Seifert and Sedley the same thing. I was told to make sure I had my notebook of the day of the interviews. Back at the office I searched for the note book, which I could not find and never did. In the end there was no way out of that, and £2000 damages had to be paid. To my surprise, Tony and Mary never broached the subject again or complained to me.

In 1986, 75 Farringdon Road itself was sold.

The building had been designed by the famous Hungarian communist architect Erno Goldfinger and sited in London EC1, was a prime property ripe for development. Mary Rosser I presume did the deal for £1.2 or £2.1 million as reported and it was bought by pornography millionaire, David Sullivan, who sold it for £2.1 (or £3.1 million it was rumoured.)

Many plumb central London properties were sold off by trade unions and other organisations. The Communist Party of Great Britain sold off its offices in King Street, Covent Garden. The palatial NUM and the NUR sites in Marylebone Road were sold off either for profit or because of falling on hard times. The *Star* moved to rented offices in 74 Luke Street, London EC4, a short walk from Old Street Station. In 1988 it moved again to purpose designed newspaper offices at Ardleigh Road in Islington.

From its founding and with little money and limited resources the *Daily Worker* was produced to high standards of journalism. It was designed by Allen Hutt, a renowned typographer, journalist and a communist. The *Daily Worker* won three annual awards for newspaper design.

The several changes in the paper, from the hot metal presses to those of contract printers presented an opportunity to keep up with changing newspaper fashions. The major change was from broadsheet to tabloid. The original and major changes were made by the deputy editor, David Whitfield in 1987. This entailed a some changes in writing copy. Tabloid journalism is shorter and more to the point. An ideal for a splash was about 300 words and 200 words for a page lead.

At Ardleigh Road, Islington, thousands of pounds donated by readers and supporters allowed the much needed newsroom technology to be installed. Larry Braithwaite, a Fleet Street electrician and comrade set up the system, and David Whitfield the lay-outs.

Those of us 'on the road', Isolda, Rob and I and Mike (Ambrose) and Tony Clarke in parliament, or anyone reporting at conferences were supplied with the first of the new laptops, the ubiquitous Tandy. The paper was written, subbed and set, online. This was before autumn 1991.

Once, in the Blackpool Winter Gardens at a CPSA conference, l left the Tandy on a shelf about five yards from the phone I was on. A man snatched it and headed for the door, only to be chased by two women delegates, who frightened him that much that he dropped it.

The *Star* kept up with, and matched any other national newspaper. On distribution, as with other small circulation papers, the paper had to overcome Rupert Murdoch's decision to switch from rail to road, making it difficult to get the paper to the wholesalers, and in Scotland it was unavailable for a time. Ivan Beavis, who became the *Star's* circulation manager, worked wonders, notably breaking WH Smith's refusal to include the *Star* with other papers on sale or return.

The paper also became available at independent newsagents and shops, such as Martin McColl and the Co-op, local supermarkets such as Budgens, at railway stations and on motorway service areas. There were also deals with other outlets. All of this led to an increase in sales and visibility throughout Britain.

The Star's Ads Department In making up somewhat for the lack of commercial adverts, the Ads department became experts in marking, as described, any day of significance for the advancement of Labour, peace and progressive movements, nationally and internationally. May Days were always good for greetings to be added, and on Tolpuddle, Labour festivals and other anniversaries several pages of greetings are always found.

All of this was helped and improved by a genuine regard by workers for the Star's support for their struggles. This was especially so when they were subjected to abuse and bias by other newspapers and what they saw being said about them on television.

In analysing the Industrial and Labour Correspondents group, one *Financial Times* journalist reckoned that had the group developed an expertise and experience in the way in which men and women were choosing, or were constrained to work, journalists could have greatly enriched the narratives of globalisation, privatisation and immigration. "Rather than posing as being on the side of the workers, we could have been describing their work".

The *Morning Star* and its staff were on the side of the workers and greatly enrich the narratives of globalisation, privatisation and immigration from the standpoint of the working class.

For example, in June 1991 we recorded on our front page, a landmark moment of trade union history. Jamaican born Bill Morris, born 1947, became the general secretary of the Transport and General Workers union; the first black person in the UK yet to be so elected. He had lived with his father, a policeman, but joined his mother, who was a science teacher living in Handsworth, Birmingham in 1954.

Bill's trade union life began in 1958 when he joined the TGWU. He was then elected a shop steward at Hardy Spicers in 1963, where he was involved in a major dispute for union recognition. In 1982, when I met him, he had been made national secretary for the Passenger Services Trade Group, responsible for leading national negotiations in the bus and coach industries.

I always got on well with him; some didn't. He endeared himself to me when I first met him as he had the *Morning* Star clearly showing in his back pocket. Bill insisted though that he was not a black trade union leader, but a trade unionist who was black. On retirement he became Lord Morris.

On Wednesday 1 Jan 1992, Tony Chater's New Year message was optimistic in seeing "ingredients coming together for a situation which could see the relaunch of a socialist offensive".

Two months later, Tony was launching a £60,000 financial appeal, the day after robbers broke into the offices and stole all of the computer equipment. This was accomplished with the aid of our intrepid *Morning Star* supporters groups, through the trade union and labour movement raising the funds to replace the stolen equipment.

In February that year the European Union Maastricht Treaty – opposed by communists and the left and campaigned against in the *Star* was endorsed by Thatcher's government.

In March 1992, parliament passed the Further and Higher Education Act. This allowed polytechnics to become new universities. Legislation passed under the Act on 4 June, allowed them to award degrees of their own, and they thus reopened in September for the new academic year with the status of universities.

Today Britain is lacking many of the skills needed in civil and engineering industry. Rather than funding well trained specialists and skilled workers successive governments have relied on attracting foreign workers to make up skills shortages or fill low paid low skilled jobs.

Under Thatcher's reign, unemployment, which for most years ran at three million, in 1989 was down to 2.2 million, but under John Major grew to 2.95 million by 1992. Despite this, Neil Kinnock managed to lose the June 1992 election; the Tories winning a fourth-term general election victory.

IRA Bombings On 10 April 1992 at 9:20 p.m., we were startled by an explosion, when a huge bomb was detonated in front of the Baltic Exchange building in the City of London, two miles from where Gladys and I lived. A year later on 24 April 1993, we heard the frightening noise of a bomb exploding in the city at 10:27 in Bishopsgate. The blast shook our building and raised a mushroom cloud that could be seen across much of London.

On 31 August 1994, the IRA called a unilateral ceasefire. Sinn Féin agreed to a political process that eventually resulted, in 1998, in the Good Friday agreement in. The ensuing peace in the island of Ireland was matched by peace of mind in London.

The effects of Russian reforms on the *Star* The year 1992 proved taxing for the *Morning Star*, its staff and its supporters, if a battle for survival can be called that. In 1985 Mikhail Gorbachev was elected as general secretary of the Communist Party of the Soviet Union, with his stated aim being "to revive a stagnating Soviet economy", to which end he announced a programme of reforms.

In February – March 1986, the CPSU proposed a change by "creating a dependable and effective mechanism for accelerating economic and social progress" characterised as 'perestroika' or, in English 'restructuring'. Then in February 1986 with a policy of greater transparency or 'glasnost'. Gorbachev expanded on this, claiming "a new era of transparency and openness. This involved more freedom for the press, the ability to criticise the Russian leadership and elections to parliament".

Perestroika did not bring 'economic and social progress. A new class of business oligarchs throughout the former Soviet republics rapidly accumulated wealth during the 1990s orgy of privatization and asset stripping of Soviet collective property.

Tony Chater, in particular, looked favourably on perestroika and glasnost and promoted it. Although I have never fully discussed it with him I sensed that Mick Costello – who grew up in the Soviet Union and spoke fluent Russian – saw dangers to socialism and said so to Tony.

During this time Tony and Mary made two visits to Moscow, where they met and talked to Gorbachev, with Mary certainly enamoured with the Soviet president. On 25 December 1991, the Soviet hammer and sickle flag was lowered for the last time over the Kremlin, and was replaced by the Russian tricolour, and Germany became united and fully capitalist, as the wall came down.

With the need to replace Mick Costello who had left the paper and appoint a successor to the post of the industrial correspondent and head of department which, frankly, I thought I would get. It turned out to be Isolda McNeil, about which you could say I was unhappy and sulked a bit.

Rob Cathcart, he of the Dover Ferries dispute previously mentioned, was a Cambridge graduate, and from Cambridgeshire. His Fen burr hid a sharp mind and a very clever writer. We three just got on in a pretty collegiate and affable manner doing what we had to do, of which there was plenty.

The Soviet's bulk order cancelled The depressing chronicle of events in the Soviet Union led to a great challenge to the *Star's* survival when, in two tranches, the Russian administration cancelled its bulk order, with only a week's notice, causing a "huge financial disruption" and threatening the *Star's* very existence. Its enemies hoped and expected it would perish.

The number of copies bought and the amount this put into the *Star's* coffers is not clear. A reported 6,000 a day (it might have been more) seems to be the most reliable number of the bulk copies the Soviets bought. If, as was the case at the time the retail price was thirty pence, and wholesale twenty pence, this would generate £300,000 a year; a third of our income.

A staff member at the time told me they recollected seeing a letter from Tony Chater to Gorbachev – that may be in the archive – with an appeal for support. If so it fell on stony ground.

On both occasions concerning the successive losses of the Soviet order, the whole staff was brought together in the newsroom, where Mary, with Tony at her side, put starkly before us the situation confronting the paper and ourselves, and laid out what was to be done to try to save the paper. It was drastic.

Both meetings yielded news of cuts in pagination, an increase in the paper's price – a second an 25% increase from thirty to forty pence. There were to be staff cuts in all departments, together with the need to raise cash from increases in the fighting fund targets, Save the Paper appeals, and share drives.

I was sent on a money-raising tour of Scotland's industrial organisations. The only one which I clearly remember was the AEU Glasgow district committee, a fearsome bunch but they promised help. I was escorted by and stayed at the home of Andrew Clarke, the *Star's* Scottish circulation agent, where on the last night we put away a bottle of whisky and a half-bottle of brandy.

Rather than crying in our drink we were drinking to the *Star's* survival!

The London *Evening Standard* sent a couple of reporters to our office to interview staff on what the *Standard* surmised from the news of the Soviet order, would be the demise of the paper. I was one of those interviewed, and when asked what I would do if the worse happened, I answered with something that I thought would make the story. I said I would cry! and so it duly appeared.

To the surprise of our critics and disappointment of our enemies the *Morning Star* survived. The response to our appeal was astounding, again, starting with individual *Star* readers and supporters. Lots of older readers who could little afford it sent impressive amounts. Hundred of trade unionists responded to the appeal.

In a 2005 interview John Haylett, who became editor, identified the 1980's victorious struggle with the *Marxism Today's* tendency as laying the political and organisational basis for the *Star's* survival when the Communist Party of Great Britain was eventually to dissolve.

The renewed appeal to the trade union and labour movement and the paper'srecord of clear service to the movement as the way forward for the had proved to be correct.

What happened to the staff? Those going to work for the *Star* earned little money but a solid grounding in journalistic skills and wider range of experience than they might get in a bigger paper, Many go on to work in the trade union movement, on newspapers, magazines and in PR.

Natural led to a number of posts lost. There were redundancies because of the loss of the Soviet order adding to the paper's always precarious financial position. Staff redundancies started before the Soviets stopped the order.

Some resulted from the introduction of new technology in the moves from Farringdon Road to Luke Street and then to Ardleigh Street. With the shift to contract printing printers, maintenance and administrative jobs disappeared. Opponents of the paper's direction still working after the struggle moved on. Chris Myant and deputy editor, Frank Chalmers left.

Some accepted with equanimity and some not. Made redundant were those in sport, including Stan Levenson the long time sports reporter. The three provincials correspondent posts went; Jim Saunders in the Midlands and Wales, Jimmy Arnison in the North West, and Martin Gostwick in Scotland, all long time members of the Communist Party. Jim was bitter and contested his sacking. The picture department including the once NUJ FOC Ernie Greenwood were all replaced by the Press Association picture service. The industrial desk was reduced to two, parliament to one. Features, reporters and subs posts were lost.

After this, when Roger Bagley left to do social work Paul Corey became news editor, supplemented when necessary by Mike Ambrose and me! I then joined the important editor's daily conference helping to shape the paper and I admit I was a bit chuffed with myself.

We had more than our fair share of problems such as when the C88 Nazi outfit tried to set fire to the offices. A night shift was mounted to guard the place.

Wages were £8,500 in 1982, rising to £10,500 in 1987 with no rise over eleven years. Some were not totally dependent on the *Star* wages, mostly, like me, because we had partners working. We were asked to take less than our wages when money was tight. This was paid when the paper's financial problems eased. It was tough and by the time I retired I was owed £2,000 and agreed to have it paid to me £500 at a time.

In a 2005 interview with the *Guardian* John Haylett said that the journalists went on strike and since then we've insisted on a rise every year.

By then a staff of fifteen journalists and ten administrative staff – running a six-day operation– were on salaries ranging from £15,000 to £18,000 a year.

The *Guardian* interviewer referred to "understaffing and low pay leading to lots of mistakes in the left-wing press" to which John handed over that day's paper and said: "Well, look at that. I think you'll see that's a national paper, produced on a budget sure, but still a professional job". The interviewer concluded "I left the interview saying, and he's right. The *Morning* Star is an informative read for anyone on the left, and in the confines of its twelve pages it does what a daily paper should do".

Winding down New Labour When, in July 1992, John Smith was elected leader of the Labour Party it was thought at last it had a 'solid performer' ; an intelligent Scot, free from bombast, with the promise of at last winning a Labour government.

I met him once, and was struck by his clear approach and the twinkle in his eye. He carried through Kinnock's election promise to abolish the trade unions' block vote and introduced one person one vote. Smith's sudden death in May 1994 saw Blair elected leader and New Labour was begin..

In January 1993, Isolda McNeil and Rob Cathcart had left for pastures new and we ploughed on. By 21 January 1993 I reported that unemployment had increased for the 31 months running, and had reached three million, and at a rate of 10.6%.

Business as usual In July, I was celebrating – with the officials of the new public sector union Unison – the merger of the National and Local Government Officers Association (NALGO), the National Union of Public Employees (NUPE) and the Confederation of Health Service Employees COHSE). This was a merger that made sense for a change, and was not exclusively about money, but also about being better able to fight for their members. Alan Jinkinson became general secretary, and Rodney Bickerstaffe a deputy.

On 31 May 1994 Tony Blair and Gordon Brown had dinner at the Granita restaurant in Islington, and reportedly made a deal on who was to become the leader of the Labour Party, and ultimately, the next prime minister. The rumour was that Brown was the agreed candidate, but on 21 July Tony Blair ran for and won the Labour Party leadership with John Prescott as deputy.

On 29 April 29, there was some good news when the number of unemployed fell to just over 2.5 million. In February 1995, I wrote of the manufacturing sector reporting the biggest rise in employment since the Conservatives first came to power sixteen years earlier, though still in excess 2.5 million.

It had not been below this mark since late1991. I was reporting on unemployment for the last time. I had done so for thirteen years and it was always a difficult task. I knew a bit more than most about unemployment and I felt for everyone of them not knowing how they were going to manage.

In capitalist Britain, along with death and taxes unemployment is always with us. This was true even with the profits of the industrial revolution and empire accumulated at the cost of slavery and the exploitation of at the expense of colonial people.

A system that finds it impossible to find productive work and sustainable life for all is obviously not fit for purpose and should be thrown into the bin of history and the socialist alternative tried.

Retirement and reflections on my personal life Marrying Gladys I put down to perception on my part as to whom it would be good to spend 65 years with. But chance interceded decisively on my behalf on a couple of occasions, taking me on uncharted new paths. Colin Clarke's gift of a car, my job at the *Star* and Gladys' job at the *Grower* magazine. which earned us enough for the travels before and after retirement, were a gift.

We toured England, Scotland, Wales and the Irish Republic, France and Austria with trips also to Spain, Cyprus, Crete and Canada, and the retirement itself was a pretty satisfying and lengthy time. Maybe this was made up for the earlier occasions when being denied the right to earn a living made for difficult times.

I am glad for the opportunity to serve the working class directly in their struggles afforded me by the *Morning Star* and the Communist Party. It had been another chance meeting on a picket line in 1969 and a conversation with Jim Arnison, the *Star's* north-west correspondent, who told me that the paper was looking for someone to report the Everton matches, which I did for 13 years. That event led to thirteen years full-time work.

We moved into retirement in Colwyn Bay, North Wales, and I got my seat back at Everton for another fourteen plus seasons. In 1996 I started a Wales Diary in the *Star*, which ran monthly for fourteen years and I was a frequent letter writer.

I also worked on locals, covering sport in North Wales. In April 1995 I covered my last conference for the *Star* where I had started at the Scottish TUC Congress at Perth. This was just one of hundreds of gatherings of trade unions attended, reporting the lives and activity of thousands of trade union members. By then, the majority of Scottish communists comrades had accepted that the *Morning Star* had been right in challenging *Marxism Today* group over the direction of the paper's future and were welcoming comrades and friends. There was not I'm afraid a trip to a whisky distillery with the comrades of the GMB Union, but there was no shortage of a dram or four in a few hours of goodbyes.

That was not the end of reporting trade union conferences as covered a number of them for a reporting for the trade ubions concerned. Roy Rogers, bless him, got me the job alongside him reporting the TUC Congresses for the *Glasgow Herald* and I was paid handsomely.

The joy, and sometimes the agony, of working at the *Morning Star* – with all those many comrades who gave of their all for the paper and are responsible for its survival is an abiding memory. I hope I helped a bit. A fellow journalist of another newspaper ended a 2005 interview with John Haylett with the lines: "It's ironic that *Marxism Today* and *City Limits*, another left-wing collective, and even the Communist Party of Great Britain have gone the way of all things mortal, whereas the *Morning Star* is still there at the barricades flying the red flag high".

John Haylett pointed out: "The Communist Party has fewer than 1,000 members, so less than 10% of the paper's readers are members of that particular communist grouping.

"Our political relationship is still with the Communist Party of Britain," he said, "but we represent a broad movement dedicated to peace and socialism".

I will end with Tony Chater, *Star* editor for 21 years and not known for hyperbole. Emerging from one of the *Star's* perennial financial crises he said: "The paper is not called 'the miracle of Fleet Street' for nothing. The *Morning Star* has only very meagre resources at its disposal, yet despite this, its staff produce a daily newspaper of high quality". Tony Chater is here revealing a pride of which he never boasted and a good place to end this memoir.

That's all, folks, except for the following. Together with John Traynor, I reopened the North Wales Coast branch of the NUJ, and stayed as an officer. I retained my seat on the NUJ Newspaper and Agencies Council, for twenty plus years, was a member of the NUJ's Pensioners Committee, and a founder, and member of the NUJ 60 plus Council for twenty years. For services to the union this was recognised by a life membership in 1995, and a Member of Honour in 2012.

Roy aged 12

In RAF uniform, with Aunty Betty and Les 1948

Glady and Roy 1954

Wedding Day 1955

third grandson Paul, Ellesmere Port 1980

With Gladys and great grandson Dion

www.ingramcontent.com/pod-product-compliance
Ingram Content Group UK Ltd.
Pitfield, Milton Keynes, MK11 3LW, UK
UKHW021909080125
453309UK00008B/217